Pope on the Dole

David E. Miller & Michelle Miller

Copyright © 2013 David E. Miller & Michelle Miller
All rights reserved.
ISBN: **1490324593**
ISBN-13: **978-1490324593**

CONTENTS

1	The Pope Vanishes	1
2	The Pope Goes Down	6
3	The Pope in Paris	9
4	The Pope's Flight	19
5	The Pope Hits a Dead End	29
6	The Pope and the Pot of Gold	44
7	The Pope and Two Ladies	58
8	The Pope Goes Camping	71
9	The Pope and the Prophet Tree	81
10	The Pope on Palm Sunday	92
11	The Pope and the Kiss of Life	106
12	The Pope Celebrates Easter	115
13	The Pope's Slippers	130
14	The Pope Looks to the Skies	147
15	The Pope Performs Miracles	165
16	The Pope at the Auberge Ginette	178
17	The Pope Goes to Hollywood	189
18	The Pope's Folly	197
19	The Pope and The Fishing Hole	209
20	The Pope Says a Prayer	226
21	The Pope Goes Up	237
22	The Pope in Memoriam	251
23	The Pope Returns	258

1 THE POPE VANISHES

On the parvis of Notre-Dame de Paris, a man in his early 60s with graying hair, a silver Van Dyke, and piercing green eyes seats himself on a bench near an imposing equestrian statue of Charlemagne.

"My dear Carolus Magnus," he sighs, unrolling an e-paper, which immediately goes online. "You were the Pater Europae; the Imperator Romanorum. You defended the Church, and protected the Pope. If only you could spring back to life, I would pray for the success of your army, just as Papa Leo did."

After a moment's reflection, the stranger continues, with a pinch of bitterness in his voice. "You know? Papa Leo didn't have it so bad, really. At least he was a worthy protégé–an accomplished pope, as it turns out, and one destined for sainthood.... As for the Church, it was merely in *peril* at the time. But now? Well, now things are different. Times have changed. There is nothing left to defend. And nobody left worth protecting. Not only that, but I doubt God would even bother to listen to my–to the prayers of a rambling idiot.... I don't think you're listening, either."

2 Pope on the Dole

The man on the bench abandons his pointless soliloquy and turns his attention to the English language headline that appears on the e-paper, which, once unrolled, flattens itself and becomes rigid. This gives the man a free hand, and he uses it to rub the back of his neck as he reads the headline aloud: *Catholic Apocalypse: First Anniversary.*

The reader then mumbles something to himself in Italian, and continues silently. His lips do not move; only his eyes.

> *The House That Peter Built.* What the Vatican Hotel & Casino development company calls a "conversion" is seen by many former Catholics as a "perversion." According to the manager of the Pitchfork Palace–

The inner voice suddenly halts. An insolent pigeon has just landed on the head of Olivier de Vienne, one of the two vassals accompanying Charlemagne.

"Not on *Olivier*! Raise your sword, Roland!"

The sword, Durendal, does not budge, but the pigeon nonetheless flees.

"Humph!" No harm done. A slight gesture of the hand advances the article a bit.

> *Banished Pope Appears to Have Vanished.* Theories abound as to the whereabouts of Pope Ignatius I, sometimes referred to by the popular press as "Papa Ultimo." As recently as last month, it was reported that a Mafia insider, who goes under the alias "Signor Aponti," could not deny rumors circulating among members of the Calecchio family that rival godfather Umberto Maldiavos had ceded authority to a *papa nostro* who goes by the name Bruno Gratiano, and that said Gratiano is none other than the pope, formerly a Jesuit priest from Burano, Italy, whose actual name is Niccolò di Montachiesa.

"Good job, Signor Aponti. How much did Bruno pay you for that little red herring, eh?" The man chuckles quietly, and then scrolls down to the next subheading.

Band of Rebels Discovered in Venice. Despite efforts to convert the Last Catholic, a handful of rebels keep the faith alive in a small church in California. The exact location of the church has not been disclosed publicly, but speculation has it that the congregation, whose numbers are apparently growing, meets secretly every other Sunday somewhere in Venice.

The reader is stupefied. He raises his eyes towards Charlemagne, and whispers, incredulously, "Venetia!"

He shifts his position nervously on the bench, and then scrolls down to the last subheading of the article.

Mormons Abandon Bid to Take Montmartre. A bitter dispute between the LDS Church and the Church of Scientology has been settled out of court, according to an official spokesperson for the Church of Scientology. The LDS Church has abandoned its plans to buy and convert Sacré-Cœur, which has been shuttered for six months, into a Mormon temple. Instead, the basilica will be renamed Church of St. Elronde in honor of the late Elronde Hatheborne, a former Catholic missionary who famously went undercover in a French brothel, saving a hundred souls one convert at a time, and who later refused to pursue the path of papal beatification in favor of accepting the newly created, and highly paid, position of Immortal Minister with the Church of Scientology, a decision which led ultimately to martyrdom and sainthood thanks to a well-executed Mafia contract allegedly backed by the Vatican.

"Nobody likes a whistleblower, right Umberto?"

4 Pope on the Dole

A teenager approaches the bench. He has wheatish skin and disheveled raven hair, and clutches an ornate leather bound book in his left hand. In his other hand is what remains of a submarine sandwich. Without hesitation, the teenager seats himself beside the sexagenarian engrossed in the news, slowly turns to him, and, with a friendly smile, says, "As-salam alaykum."

"Walaykum asalam." The greeting is returned in a flat, unenthusiastic voice.

The teenager pays no mind, though. Nor does he show any real interest in what the old man is reading. He carefully sets the Quran down upon his knees. In this way, the sacred book will escape the falling of crumbs and the dripping of mayonnaise which is likely to occur as he continues to peel back the sandwich wrapping.

No one can claim sole ownership of a public bench, but neither is one forced to share it. His thoughts in disarray, the frustrated reader slowly rolls up his e-paper, slips it under his armpit, rises to his feet, nods coldly–but politely–to his momentary bench companion, and begins to walk away.

His mouth full, the teenager sputters proudly, "Allahu Akbar!"

Rather than ignore the provocation, the departing infidel stops abruptly, turns about, and fixes the teenager with green eyes that can penetrate the darkest of human souls. Then he makes the sign of the cross, and replies, in a calm but firm voice, "Dominus vobiscum."

The teenager swallows. A look of puzzlement crosses his face. "Dominus Pizza?"

To avoid showing his indignation, the Latinist turns away. Then, regaining his composure, he offers a farewell gesture to Charlemagne. "Videbo te mox. See you soon."

After taking a few steps, he spots another pigeon flying towards the statue. The pigeon lands in a nearby tree, its red eyes pondering the various perches a good bronze can offer.

Charlemagne's would-be defender, rattled by an unpleasant vision of what is to come, cannot refrain himself from having a go at the pigeon. "Hey, you over there! Creature of God. Can't you show some respect?"

Somewhat surprisingly, the pigeon turns its red eyes towards the green-eyed human. And then it poops on the parvis.

Annoyed, but perhaps also encouraged, by this response to his plea, the man waves the pigeon away…. The pigeon hesitates, but then takes flight. It makes an arc over his head, and settles on the ground near the teenager. Folding its wings, it disappears beneath the bench, where it begins feeding on the bread crumbs scattered about. The meek shall inherit….

With an air of vague satisfaction, the pigeon master crosses the parvis towards the Left Bank. In so doing, he glances back at the cathedral that towers above the Ile de la Cité. It is now undergoing a complete transformation under its new Mormon proprietors.

"Might as well turn it back over to the Goddess of Reason."

He accelerates his pace, and soon crosses the Petit Pont. He appears oblivious to passersby, and they do not notice him. In fact, other than his emerald eyes, which are now turned inward, there is nothing particularly unusual about this man. He is of average stature, and he wears everyman's clothes. There is a certain weariness in his stride, but also a certain elegance.

Later in the day, after a long walk along the Seine, he will reread the article, this time in its entirety. But it really doesn't matter. He dreams already of a new headline. A headline in which the Church is depicted as the new phoenix. But this dream demands a real world decision that will change the course of his life–and the lives of countless others–forever.

2 THE POPE GOES DOWN

"Our culture has aged, our churches are big and empty and the church bureaucracy rises up, our rituals and our cassocks are pompous. The Church must admit its mistakes and begin a radical change, starting from the Pope and the bishops.' –Carlo Maria Martini

As the 21st Century rolled along, the world became more secular, and Church scandals escalated. Many Catholic priests became taxi drivers or blackjack dealers, though a few joined the Orthodox Church in hopes that this branch of Christianity would endure a bit longer.

However, adherents of both the Catholic and Orthodox Churches were diminishing in number at an alarming rate. Self-proclaimed agnostics were encouraged to drop their veil and openly declare themselves active members of the worldwide community of atheists. Those who remained devoted to God began shopping their faith around. The LDS Church moved into Europe in an attempt to market the American brand of Christianity. This campaign was largely successful. However, the LDS Church found a major rival in the Church of Scientology, whose brainwashing tactics found easy prey among disenfranchised churchgoers willing to give secularism serious consideration.

The Pope Goes Down

As secularism flourished, more and more Catholic churches closed. In short order, the Vatican found itself in dire straits. The Pope, a philosophical disciple of Cardinal Martini, made efforts to liberalize the Church, but this only angered conservative Catholics (especially the Hispanics in South and Central America) and encouraged liberal Catholics (especially the Europeans) to demand more concessions. Priests went on strike; entire congregations defected. When the Pope fell ill, there was talk of a 30-something pope, a woman pope ("Mama Jeanne!"), and even a gay pope to appease the liberals. There was also talk of another Hispanic pope to appease the conservatives. This was fueled by speculation that the Pope was convalescing in a villa in Peru, but various disclosures by one Cardinal or another, perhaps intended to balance the public debate, or, more likely, to mock it, allowed the arguments of liberal proponents to gain traction. When the Pope finally recovered, many were disappointed. Meanwhile, the Church fell deeper into financial disarray.

The Church engaged in television fundraisers. The bishops sold gold and silver on the shopping network, and some of the Vatican's collections were auctioned off, but to no avail. Media accounts of the Vatican's troubles only exacerbated the downward trajectory of the Vatican's lot.

Pundits often referred to the Catholic Church as a sinking ship, and cartoonists had a field day illustrating this rather obvious metaphor. One of the first cartoons to do so depicted the Pope as the ship's captain, pinching his nose, and riding an anchor cross to the bottom of the sea.

The Pope, however, was not quite ready to give up the ship. In an effort to delay the inevitable, he ordered a Fire Sale. Everything had to go, with more and more heavily discounted items sold on world markets and on site. Next, the Pope directed the Vatican Museums to sell their collections to other museums.

But they could only absorb so much, and soon private collectors were buying up priceless works of art at bargain basement prices. Once the Vatican Museums had been emptied of their treasure, the complex was sold. It became a pie factory. But Pious Desserts went bankrupt, and the factory was purchased by a sex toy company, St. Peter's Toys. Sales skyrocketed.

By now, the Pope readily admitted that the Church was doomed beyond all hope. The Vatican itself eventually hit the real estate market and was purchased by a hotel/resort company. St. Peter's Toys would not sell, so the resort decided to create an adult atmosphere. The Vatican Hotel & Casino opened its doors, complete with indoor swimming pool, adult theatres, cancan room, restaurant, and strip club (the Pitchfork Palace). The Sistine Chapel was converted to a lounge for private dances: the Laptop Chapel.

The Cardinals were already offered a job at St. Peter's Toys, but the Pope was laid off, though he claimed he was "Fired!"

3 THE POPE IN PARIS

Flashback.

The Church confiscates the Ring of the Fisherman (the *annulus piscatoris*), the signet ring which is to be destroyed upon the Pope's death. The Pope does have an official emerald ring, and he fears he will have to turn it over, too. He summons an old biker buddy, Bruno Gratiano, who he hasn't met since he was a Jesuit priest in Burano. When Bruno enters the papal chambers, the Pope rushes to embrace him.

"Bruno, it's good to see you."

"Wait till you see this," replies Bruno, setting a black glossy gift bag down on an inlaid pedestal table. He reaches down into the bag and produces a golden box of Ferrero Rocher hazelnut chocolates.

"A sinful pleasure," smiles the Pope. "You shouldn't have."

"You haven't lost your fondness for chocolates, have you?"

"No, I haven't." Noticing that an envelope has been slipped beneath the box's golden bow, the Pope asks, "What's in the envelope? A card?"

Bruno winks. "Actually, there are a few hundred euros in there. I didn't spend *all* the money on chocolates."

"Thanks, Bruno. I knew I could count on you."

The Pope bids Bruno have a seat. Then, he narrows his eyes, drops his smile, and gets down to business.

"Here, take this ring. Sell it. Buy me a bike. A *good* bike."

"Sure, Nic. Anything you say. But this won't pay for a good bike. I could lend you 'Jotabacco'–"

"You still have the old smoker?"

Bruno nods. "Riders may bite the dust. But an old Laverda never dies. And, yes, it still smokes. But you can still *squeeze* that orange. It'll run 230 if you push it."

"I'm sure it will. But I don't want to turn heads. Not on this trip."

Bruno shrugs.

"Now, one more thing. Before you sell the ring, show it to Umberto Maldiavos."

"That's a pretty big name."

"Tell him the Pope is unhappy. Tell him you're the new *papa nostro*."

Bruno is dumbfounded. He is no stranger to the Mafia, but neither is he an insider.

"But if I sell the ring, there's nothing in it for him."

"Umberto and I go back a few years. I know a few things. I can bring him down. He'll be happy to know I'm asking him to retire. Step aside." The Pope makes a sweeping gesture to emphasize his point.

"What about Alec? Does he know about this?"

"You're the first to know. But I'm willing to bet that before everything is in place, you'll get one of Alec's famous *Calecchio Communiqués*. He'll want to know where things stand between the families."

"They'll stand where they've always stood," asserts Bruno.

"I wish I could say the same thing for the Church."

The Pope reveals that the Church is about to collapse. The Cardinals have plotted against him, the Vatican has been sold, and his position has been terminated.

"Now go, my good friend. And deliver the bike to this address."

The Pope hands Bruno his tailor's card.

"But where are you going?"

The Pope opens a Bible. He takes out a postcard. "Paris. I had to take a rain check on a trip. Many years ago. But now I'm ready to go."

"What's the cash for?"

"Traveling expenses. Thank you."

After Bruno leaves, the Pope goes to a private closet. He takes out an old leather suitcase, crosses the room, and sets it on a desk by the window. He opens the suitcase, and the light falls on some old biker clothes. The Pope ponders the contents, and then looks out the window. "Arrivederci, Città del Vaticano. Arrivederci, Roma. Arrivederci, Italia." Then he reaches over to his laptop and gently closes it. "Goobye Facebook. Goodbye Twitter. Goodbye Tumblr." Finally, he looks up, somewhat imploringly, somewhat bitterly. "As for you, Lord–" He shakes his head slowly, sighs with resignation, and whispers, "Non è importante."

A few days later, the Pope is riding a used bike–a bright red Ducati. He is headed for Paris, where he is to meet Olivier, who has offered to put him up for a while. He needs to stay out of the public eye in order to plan his future as a religious refugee.

Niccolò met Olivier Casali when the latter came to Rome on an English language teaching assignment in an Italian liceo. When Olivier purchased a Horex VR6, Niccolò invited him to accompany him on some of his motorcycle gang escapades. Niccolò was a medical student at the time, but spent more time biking than studying. His courses did not particularly interest him, although he did have a certain gift for Latin.

Eventually, Olivier was introduced to Giulia Vanetti, an Italian girl with whom Niccolò had a tempestuous on-and-off relationship. Olivier knew full well that Niccolò often bedded girls on his bike outings, but was surprised to learn that Giulia was not totally in the dark. She had convinced herself that Niccolò's transgressions were due solely to the occasional lover's clash. But the truth was that it didn't really matter whether they had fought. Niccolò was simply unfaithful, probably because Giulia was so damn possessive, overbearing, and unpredictably moody.

When Olivier left Rome, he returned to Nice and taught for a number of years at the Université de Nice. During this time, he often took a train to Burano, then Rome, to visit his friend, who was rising up in the Catholic hierarchy. Olivier eventually married a graduating student from Paris, with whom he had a daughter. His wife did not like Nice, and when Olivier was offered a teaching position in Paris some years later, he took it. Olivier's wife eventually divorced him, and his teenage daughter moved to England shortly thereafter.

Niccolò arrives in Paris. Olivier, who has been called unexpectedly to London by his daughter, has left him a keycard along with a note saying he'll be back in a day or two. Niccolò therefore finds himself alone in Paris—and for longer than anticipated, as Olivier does not return until a full *week* later.

The first thing Olivier notices is that Niccolò has a new hairstyle, and is beginning to grow a mustache and goatee. Niccolò explains that he has changed his appearance because he does not want to be in the media spotlight right now. He wishes to remain incognito while he formulates a plan.

Olivier also notices that his friend hasn't changed out of his old biker outfit, and that he is looking a bit haggard. Niccolò explains that he'd hoped to go shopping for some new clothes, but his pockets were empty. The last few days, he's been living on the dole–hitting the streets in search of ways to make a few coins. He approached tourists with an open hand, but they hastened their pace. He hit the Métro with a sign begging for mercy, but his cup remained empty–the competition was too great. He even filled plastic bottles with water from the Seine, and, with the help of Ezekiel, blessed them. But his bottles of Holy Water were taken with a grain of salt. For his daily bread, Niccolò turned to the Restos du Coeur, a charitable organization that feeds the homeless. That's where he learned to avoid saying "God bless!" whenever someone sneezes, as the expression was always met with scornful eyes. In short, Niccolò could use a good meal, and some money to spend.

The next day, Niccolò and Olivier go shopping. Niccolò buys some cheap contemporary casual clothes, and Olivier fancies a shirt. As he sheds his old shirt, Niccolò takes note of Olivier's tattoo–"La dolce vita" written in an arc across the chest of Anita Ekberg–which is on his upper arm.

"It's held up," remarks Niccolò.

"Yeah? Let's see yours," prompts Olivier.

Back at the apartment, Niccolò showers and changes, looking fairly spiffy. He and Olivier set out to find the address on the back of the postcard. Olivier asks who lives there.

"An old flame. I was supposed to meet her at this address 40 years ago."

They find the address, but are disappointed to discover that it belongs to a Laundromat with both French and Chinese wording inside and out.

Olivier wants to know what's behind the postcard.

"I've never explained to you how I ended up a theology student."

"You had a knack for Latin?"

"Yes, but there's a lot more to it."

During his biking days, but after Olivier had returned to Nice, Niccolò met a French girl named Francine. For a week, they romanced. When Francine returned to Paris, and, as requested, called Niccolò to say she'd made it home safely, it was Giulia who answered the call. Giula blasted Francine over the phone, informing her that she and Nic had been engaged for years, and that Francine was just another of his dalliances. Whenever she and Nic had a spat, Nic became a sexual predator, albeit a charming one. He would go for whatever girl he could grab off the street–usually a foreigner, because it was easier to terminate the relationship–but he always came back to his love nest a few days later.

The conversation ended abruptly, and Niccolò, who was subsequently grilled by Giulia, fled the apartment in great haste. He took his bike to the nearest bar, drank a few beers, and decided that he was going to ride his bike straight to Paris and tell Francine that he loved her and wanted to marry her.

The main road out of Rome was a bit wet, because it had rained previously. The dark clouds were quite ominous, but it wasn't a second downpour that threatened…. Niccolò was weaving in his lane–and speeding, as well–because he was rather intoxicated. He flew through Santa Marinella en route to Civitavecchia. He abandoned the Via Aurelia for the Viale Della Vittoria, in order to closely follow the coastline. He had a clear view ahead. But he fell behind a shuttle bus from the Hotel Isio d'Oro, which was transporting a few passengers to the port, where they were to take a cruise ship to Sardinia, Sicily, or some other destination. Without even considering the risks, he passed the shuttle bus, zigzagging, and nearly bounced off the side of the bus. As he whipped by the bus driver's window, he let go the handlebars for a moment and treated the driver to an Italian *bras d'honneur*. He then cut back in front of the shuttle bus, and looked back over his shoulder to see the driver's reaction. When he turned his head back around forward, he was blinded by a divine shaft of light, which shone down miraculously through the rainclouds, as if burning a hole through them. He lost control of his Moto Guzzi, hit the top of the seawall, which separated him from his bike, sailed over the seawall, and fell to the beach, where he bounced off a few lounge chairs and rolled into a badminton net–which flung him to the ground without serious injury. He opened his mouth in awe, remembering the shaft of light, and a flying shuttlecock landed right between his teeth. Meanwhile, the shuttle bus driver had hit the brakes. A major earthquake had struck, and pieces of cracked building façade had begun raining down mercilessly on the bus. There was a fissure in the pavement ahead, and the bus skidded on the wet asphalt until its front tires fell into it. Chunks of brick and mortar littered the roadway. The road was completely impassable. Niccolò clambered back up to the roadway, pondered the disaster, and praised God for delivering him from certain death. The shuttle bus driver was dead, but Niccolò helped evacuate the few surviving passengers on board. Then he returned to Rome, finished his studies, parted with Giulia forever, and enrolled in a seminary.

"Of course, the day I entered the seminary, I left my past behind. Until now."

"Did you expect to find Francine here after all these years?"

Niccolò shrugs.

16   Pope on the Dole

Niccolò becomes quite comfortable living in Paris, though he still searches for a "sign" that will lead him on the correct path into the next stage of his life. He doesn't get out too much because he is writing his version of the Catholic Apocalypse story. He is also keeping a journal.

One day, he is riding his motorcycle in heavy traffic. He pulls forward alongside a taxi, then falls behind, and then pulls forward again. The taxi driver, meanwhile, is frustrated, as he wants to be in Niccolò's lane. Niccolò is preventing him from accomplishing this. The taxi driver begins to shout obscene threats at Niccolò, who can't hear the words, but who gets the gist of the message. The taxi driver cuts short his tirade, though, when he suddenly recognizes the Pope, even though he is wearing a helmet and already sports a stubby Van Dyke. The taxi driver is a former priest forced into a new profession, and he feels totally humiliated. He makes a humble, apologetic gesture. Niccolò squeezes the brakes, and then makes a sharp turn into a side street where a sign reads "Sans Issue."

Another day, Niccolò and Olivier are walking towards a Métro station, and they encounter an old beggar. Niccolò asks Olivier for a few euros, and is handed a bill. Niccolò takes the beggar's hands in his, slips in the bill, presses them together, and kisses the top hand. The beggar looks deeply into Niccolò's green eyes. "Are you the Pope?" Niccolò answers, "Haven't you heard? There's no more Pope." The beggar is astonished, and watches Niccolò as he regains the company of Olivier. The beggar then looks down at the bill. He can't believe his eyes.

Then, there is the day when Olivier takes Niccolò to the Montmartre cemetery to put flowers on his father's grave. Olivier's father, Vittorio Casali, has been dead for a couple of years now, but his mother is presumably still alive somewhere. Niccolò kneels in front of the stone marker. He folds his hands in prayer, and recites a psalm in Latin. A couple happens by. Not only is the image perfectly papal, the voice is undeniably the Pope's. They approach for a closer look, and agree it must be the Pope. "Your Holiness...?" Niccolò rises, and shrugs off such a preposterous notion. He replies with his best German accent. "No, please! Not again! I get this all the time. It is very annoying. I assure you that I am definitely *not* the Pope." The couple stands firm in its conviction. "Your Holiness, come on now. You can't fool us!" Olivier comes to the rescue. "Werner, show them your tattoo." Olivier winks at the couple. Niccolò begins to unbutton his shirt, mumbling something in German. The man and woman look at each other confused, and then depart quickly. However, as they walk away, they engage in argumentative whispers. The woman looks over her shoulder suspiciously. "Werner" is rebuttoning his shirt.

One night, the Pope takes his motorcycle to the Latin Quarter. He parks his bike, then takes one of the narrow alleys to a CinéClub, where there is a late night showing of *The Godfather*. He's never seen the film, and the ticket price is a steal. It's not a 3D conversion, but Niccolò is indifferent. After the film is over, he exits into the alleyway, where two low speaking couples, a cheerful group of teenagers, and a handful of quiet loners are either standing or strolling. Niccolò desperately needs to relieve himself. He grumbles, walks to the wall, and unzips. At that moment, the street becomes deserted. Some have taken a side alley. Others have entered a nightclub or regained the boulevard. Behind a garbage can, though, a drunk with a nearly empty bottle of wine peers through the crack between the can and the wall. He watches quietly as Niccolò makes the sign of the cross, then does his business. As Niccolò turns about in order to walk towards his motorcycle parked on the boulevard, the drunk staggers into view. "You, sir, are the Pope!" Niccolò is stunned, speechless. The drunk continues, as the alley once again becomes peopled. "I saw everything." He makes the sign of the cross. "And everyone disappeared. Like that!" The drunk is having trouble snapping his fingers to emphasize his point. Niccolò replies. "Everyone except you, that is." The drunk is perplexed by this. "Why do you suppose that is?" Niccolò smiles, then taps the man on the chest gently. "Because you, sir, are a drunk!" Niccolò leaves, triumphantly. But the drunk follows him. "I may be a drunk. But I know the Pope when I see one!" Niccolò replies over his shoulder, as he walks a little more briskly, "But you've never seen one, have you?" The drunk catches up from behind. "I've seen one tonight!" Niccolò hurries his pace, as the drunk shouts, "It's the Pope! Look there! It's the Pope!" To escape the scrutiny of onlookers, Niccolò begins to run. He flies around the corner, jumps on his red Ducati, which recognizes him, and takes off into the night. "There he goes!" shouts the drunk. "There goes the Pope!" The drunk tries to give chase on foot, but falls to his knees on the sidewalk. A passerby helps him to his feet. "Did you see him?" asks the drunk. The man frowns, "See who?" The drunk points his wine bottle in the direction taken by the motorcycle. "The Pope, you idiot! The Pope!" The man replies, "You've had one too many, old man. Go home."

Niccolò has spent nearly a year in Paris. He is still waiting for a sign. He decides to walk to Notre-Dame. He borrows Olivier's e-paper, rolls it under his arm, and sets out towards the Ile de la Cité. Upon his arrival, he relaxes on a bench near an equestrian statue of Charlemagne, and, after uttering a few words of despair, unrolls the e-paper. Headline: *Catholic Apocalypse: First Anniversary*. Niccolò rubs the back of his neck, and begins to read.

4 THE POPE'S FLIGHT

Niccolò is having dinner with Olivier. He puts down the e-paper, which he has now thoroughly read.

"I've made up my mind, Olivier. Read this." He points to the section of the article entitled, "Band of Rebels Discovered in Venice."

Olivier reads it. "You're leaving?"

Niccolò nods. "It's the American Dream, Olivier! And I'm going to *live* it."

Having made up his mind to fly to the States, Niccolò "sells" his bike to Olivier, buys a nonstop ticket to L.A., and pockets the rest. At the airport, Oliver bids his friend farewell.

"I'll be tracking your flight," promises Olivier, momentarily distracted by a 3-D poster heralding Boeing's new fleet of blended wing aircraft. Although the Dreamliners have been plagued with a few technical problems of late, they remain the company's workhorse on international flights, and have many years of service left in them. Niccolò, however, has booked a seat aboard an Airbus A350.

"And I'll be expecting your call. Greenland, right?" Niccolò glances at the departure gate, noting the time. He is oblivious to the gentle rain that is falling from a gray sky.

"If you see any golden spikes lying around, drive them in, will you?"

Olivier, who suffers from aerophobia, is referring to a proposed vacuum train tunnel connecting London and New York by way of Nuuk, which is considered the midpoint of the so-called "Godthaab Staar" project.

"There's always the Muskox Express." Niccolò is thinking about a film, based on a true story, in which an escaped convict travels the Arctic by every means possible over land and sea.

"I'll keep that in mind. But, of course, if you get into some kind of emergency situation, you can count on me to face the sky demons."

An hour or two later, Niccolò is admiring the clouds from his window seat. The sun is setting in the west, and the clouds are ablaze.

"They look kind of like red cauliflowers." The voice is that of a young lady seated directly behind him.

Niccolò twists in his seat, props himself up a bit, and peers over the headrest at his fellow cloud gazer.

"Or maybe red *demons*. If you're afraid of *flying*, that is."

The young lady, who is returning from a trip to Paris with her parents, snorts with laughter. "Yeah, you have a point there!" She glances at her parents, who are listening quietly to music.

"I'm Camille."

"Niccolò." His back in a bit of a bind, Niccolò adjusts his position. In so doing, he notices that Camille has slipped her hand between the seat and the cabin wall, and that she is wiggling her fingers. He is astonished that a young lady would beckon an old man with a handshake.

Niccolò studies his own hand for a second. It's not nearly as steady–or as sacred–as it once was. He extends it, taking care not to show any sign of reluctance. He feels the warmth and vigor of Camille's hand, which shakes his in a way that is firm, yet undeniably feminine, and notes the reaction on her face when the hand is withdrawn. Camille is beaming with pride.

"So, do you live in L.A.?"

"I'm relocating."

"It's sunny mostly. The weather in Paris was dreadful." She shakes her head, heaves a sigh, and shrugs–all at once. "But I didn't mind. I'll dry out when I get home."

"Were you on vacation?"

"Sort of, yeah. But while I was there, I checked out AGS. I'm thinking of enrolling."

Niccolò's eyes lose their edge.

"The American Graduate School in Paris," explains Camille. "I'm going to major in international relations. Diplomacy. You know, that sort of thing."

"I see." Niccolò glances at Camille's hand. Now he understands the handshake.

"There are plenty of programs in the States, of course. But I want to get away for a while. You know what I mean?"

"I know exactly what you mean," replies Niccolò approvingly.

"Cami?"

"It's okay, Mom. This is Niccolò. He's from Paris."

Camille's mother removes her wireless headset. She is in her early forties; her husband, who is annoyed by the interference, bites his tongue. He is at least five years older.

"Actually, I was just passing through," corrects Niccolò. "I'm from Burano, Italy."

"He's moving to L.A.," adds Camille.

"Oh? What part?"

"I don't know yet. Somewhere near the beach, I think."

"If you can afford it…. We live in Apple Valley."

Camille glances at her father resentfully. "We're known by everyone in town as the *Crabapples*."

Niccolò can't help but look puzzled.

Mom raises her eyebrows apologetically, and rolls her eyeballs accusingly towards her husband. "You can thank Mr. Crabbes for that."

"And his real estate agent. Who just *happens* to be his brother," complains Camille.

"That would be her Uncle Clay."

"Barclay Crabbes, realtor extraordinaire," mumbles Camille under her breath.

"At least we don't live near the beach, Cami. I mean, can you imagine what they'd call us then?"

"Thank God for small favors," she concedes.

"You have to stop saying the G-word, Cami. You know your father doesn't like it." She shifts her attention back to Niccolò, who doesn't flinch. "My name is Libby."

"Olivia," whispers Camille.

Libby ignores her. She taps on her husband's head. "And this is Blaine."

This time, Camille is more cautious. Her lips silently pronounce "Chamberlain."

Blaine acknowledges the head tapping with a twitch of the eyelids, and then turns up the volume on his headset. He is immersed in his music, and does not wish to be annoyed any further.

"Cami has a brother–"

"Half-brother," interjects Camille.

"–named Abe," finishes Libby.

"Abraham?" Niccolò is not sure to whom he should address his query.

"Abelard," huffs Camille.

"Cami doesn't care for nicknames. What about you, Nic?"

"It's *Niccolò*, Mom! Am I right?"

Niccolò closes his eyes and nods.

"Olivier!" Niccolò adjusts the Bluetooth, which is packaged by the airline and distributed to passengers who wish to avail themselves of the airline's own discounted in-flight phone service.

"Please. Call me Libby." It's the voice of Camille's mother.

Niccolò pops his head up. "I'm speaking to a friend of mine. His name is Olivier." He takes care to pronounce it with a genuine French accent.

"Oh! I'm so sorry!"

"No, I'm talking to a lady on the plane," explains Niccolò. He offers Libby a reassuring gesture, and then slumps back into his seat.

"It's totally dark out there. I can't see a thing. Are we over Greenland?–No, he didn't announce it.–Most of the passengers are sleeping already.–Are you watching something? I mean besides the flight tracker.–Oh, what are you writing?–Yes, I remember. That's a good anecdote.–Yes, I can use that in my book.–Don't worry. I'll send you an e-mail.–I'll find a way, don't worry.–Absolutely not! Don't change a thing.–Which part?–I'd prefer you leave that out, but…you *must* leave in the zucchetto. Just–"

"Your friend lives in a ghetto?" It's Libby again. She's been arguing in a hushed voice with Blaine, and apparently has only begun to eavesdrop.

"I'm talking about a…*calotte*." Niccolò knows full well the English equivalent, but is loath to use it, because he dislikes the sound of it. But Olivier is talking in his ear, so he spits it out. "A skullcap."

Unconvinced, Libby snaps back, "If you say so!"

"What's that? No, I never fished it out of the river.–It was an accident.–That's silly. It wasn't your fault. You can't…you can't…blame…"

There is a tap on Niccolò's shoulder. He can hear the vertebrae in his neck pop as he strains to look at the fingers. They are a man's.

"Blaine, can't you see he's on the phone?"

"Just a second, Olivier." Niccolò once again props himself up. "Yes?"

"Libby says you're Italian," begins Blaine.

Niccolò holds up his index finger. "One moment, please." He suddenly realizes that he is not sure whether it is Blaine who should yield to Olivier, or the other way around.

Niccolò blinks heavily, and makes a snap decision. "Sorry, Olivier. You know the lady I mentioned a moment ago? It's her husband now. Listen, can you call me back in about an hour?–Okay, Canada it is!"

Niccolò massages his neck. "Thanks, Olivier. Talk to you then. Bye!"

No sooner has he removed the Bluetooth than someone taps him on the head. Niccolò is pretty sure the head tapper is Libby. He stretches, turns about slowly, hoists himself up against the back of his seat, and comes face to face with the Crabbes. They are still arguing, but cut themselves off in mid-sentence, turn their heads towards Niccolò, and fix their eyes upon him. Niccolò, embarrassed, realizes that it was his own imagination– not Libby–that tapped him on the head. But the shoulder tap was real. The culprit starts to say something, but instead turns his attention swiftly back to his wife, who has just jabbed him in the ribs with her elbow. Blaine and Libby resume their argument without the benefit of an impartial opinion from an Italian perspective–if that is what the husband was after, as Niccolò suspects.

Niccolò taps his Bluetooth indecisively.

"No, I'm tapped out," he mutters to himself.

Niccolò yawns, closes his eyes, and settles in for a long nap.

Somewhere over North America, Libby and Blaine engage in a conversation that catches Niccolò's attention. They have just watched a news broadcast that floats a new theory–namely, that the Pope may be living in Peru. After all, the papal villa, located high in the Andes, was never sold. Instead, it was donated to the Archdiocese of Cusco, which abandoned it after the Catholic dissolution.

"They pulled that one out of thin air," quips Blaine.

"Not really," counters Libby, quite seriously. "That's where the Pope went after his nervous breakdown."

"Nobody knows that for sure."

"So how do you explain Shepherd One?"

"Anyone can charter a flight to Cusco."

"Yes, but–"

"If I were the Pope, that's the last place I'd go. He's probably under the protection of the Knights of Columbus."

"They've disbanded. And so has the CDA."

"The Catholic Daughters of the Americas," mumbles Niccolò, happy to have deciphered an acronym, albeit an obvious one.

"Don't believe everything you hear, Libby. The fact is that they merely dropped their association with the Church, kept a low profile, and reinvented themselves under a different philanthropic banner. In other words, their mission continues. But you can be sure they'd welcome the Pope if he came knocking at their door."

"So, if he's not in Peru, where do you think he is?"

"Who cares? Maybe he's dead already."

Niccolò can't help but intervene.

"I think people still care about the Pope. Otherwise, he wouldn't be so prominent in the news. And by the way, he didn't have a nervous breakdown. He was fending off the Cardinals, who were plotting against him. It was a very stressful time for him, and he lost a lot of sleep. Then he came down with the flu. He took this as a sign of God's mercy—"

Predictably, Blaine winces in spite of himself.

"—and spent a few weeks in bed, during which time he consulted with, shall we say, a 'circle of sympathizers' in an effort to trump the Cardinals."

"I guess the Italians are better informed," concludes Blaine, who finds the explanation plausible.

Libby is skeptical, though. "What about Peru?"

"The Pope was too sick to fly anywhere. But he was also advised against Castel Gandolfo. That was deemed a bit perilous. So he accepted an invitation to stay at a private residence. He had an entire staff at his disposal, plus the services of a personal physician. His privacy was guaranteed. And whenever he summoned friends and advisors, they were provided with a discreet shuttle service. As a result, the public never learned the truth. As for the Peru story, that was a bit of disinformation. The media jumped on it."

Libby is flabbergasted. "Then how do you know about all this?"

Niccolò anticipated the question. "The Cardinals eventually caught on to the Pope's whereabouts, but only after he returned to the Vatican. It just so happens that Cardinal Vassi Milanuovis is an old acquaintance of mine. He filled me in."

"So you have connections at the Vatican." Libby is impressed, though only momentarily. After all, the Vatican no longer exists. "At the time, I mean. So, where's the Cardinal now?"

"It's hard to say. He turned down the toy factory job. It was just too humiliating. Oddly, most of the Cardinals were only too happy to avoid going underground."

"Abe and Cami went to a Catholic high school in San Bernardino." Libby glances at Camille, who is sleeping soundly. "And after the school shut down, the teachers scattered to the four winds. I guess they were afraid of being persecuted."

"Someone up there doesn't give a damn," Blaine complains sullenly.

"What about the Mormons and the Protestants—and all the rest? They're doing fine, aren't they?"

Blaine shakes his head. "It's just a bubble. Christianity is on the way out. Am I right?"

Niccolò sighs. "It's hitting the exits. And I agree that the Catholics are the first ones out—and that others will follow. But a world without faith cannot endure for long. Non-Christian religions will certainly find some takers, but they are seriously flawed, and will, in the end, be soundly rejected. At least I hope so…. As for Scientology, which masquerades as a church, it would seem to hold the most promise in a world given to increasing secularism. But I would submit that its teachings ultimately fail to nourish the soul. It simply cannot fill the spiritual void that we, as God's children—"

This time, Blaine is unable to suppress a physical reaction to the G-word. His entire body convulses—if only for a second. And a terrible expression—fleeting but remarkable—usurps a face that, by force of will, is typically calm. Blaine tries to laugh it off.

"I'm a bit cold. Libby, have you seen my blanket?"

"I'm so sorry, Nic. My husband is allergic to the Lord."

Blaine glances at her disapprovingly.

"I used to be solid in my faith," he explains. "But I feel like the rug's been pulled out from under my feet."

"He blames the Pope for that," adds Libby. "And now he's turned his back on–" She points upward with her thumb.

"I can assure you both. Christianity will survive. And Catholicism will make a new entrance."

Blaine shakes his head. "Not if the Order of Diocleti succeeds in its mission to eradicate religion from the face of the planet. I assume you know about that."

Niccolò nods vaguely. He is aware of similar religious vigilantes.

"Nobody knows exactly who's behind it," says Libby, "but there's a porn star–Mianu Haubs–who puts a nice face on it. And she's a Scientologist."

"So they say," interjects Blaine. "But–"

"Right now, their focus is on the Catholics," continues Libby. "That's why they're running scared. But soon all Christians will be targeted."

"Trust me. Their mission will fail."

"I think you've been in Italy too long," sneers Blaine. "How can you be so optimistic?"

Niccolò is unfazed by the question. "I have some inside information."

5 THE POPE HITS A DEAD END

It's a sunny, cloudless morning in Los Angeles. Niccolò, wearing a light jacket and a backpack, sets off on foot from LAX. He glances at the taxis and wonders if any of the drivers are former priests. There are a number of ground transportation options available to him, but it's only a two-hour walk to Venice Beach, and the mercury is already on the rise. The forecast for this day in early February calls for a high of 19 degrees Celsius.

Niccolò's stride is more brisk than usual. But he is not in a hurry. In fact, after 40 minutes or so of walking along Lincoln Boulevard, he makes a detour on LMU Drive and heads for the Sacred Heart Chapel on the campus of Loyola Marymount University. His heart beats faster as he rounds the Sunken Garden on Ignatian Circle. The white chapel and its clock tower are intact, even though the university itself is no longer affiliated with the Catholic Church.

Niccolò approaches the three portals, and then hesitates. He quickly removes his shoes and socks, and slips on a pair of old, worn out sandals. Then, he steps inside the chapel. He is not surprised to discover that its interior no longer bears any vestiges of its religious past. Instead, it is a popular student lounge. Pews have been replaced with sofas, chairs, and tables. The altar has been converted into a juice bar. Niccolò winds his way through the maze, approaches the bar, kneels, and silently addresses the Lord in prayer. He ignores the reaction of those around him.

After he is done praying, he rises to his feet, directs his eyes beyond the bar to the sanctuary wall where a crucifix was once affixed, and, with an air of determination, turns about to leave.

"This is no longer a House of God," ventures one student, somewhat sympathetically.

"It's a House of Heathens," laughs another, sipping on a drink.

"You can't do that sort of thing in here anymore," scorns a third student.

Niccolò raises his eyebrows. "Young man, I'll pray as I please."

"Oh yeah, what gives you the right, *old* man?"

"This House used to belong to a very close friend of mine. And I intend to buy it, and give it back to Him."

"By the looks of you… Hell, you don't have that kind of money!"

"Believe me, I will. Now, if you please? Get out of my way. I must follow my faith. And, right now, it leads out that door. Because that's where the money is." Upon that, Niccolò heads towards the vestibule. But the heathens get in the last word.

"What an old fool!"

"Where the hell is campus security, anyway? The guy's obviously a tramp!"

"Papa needs a new pair of shoes!"

Niccolò doesn't waste time finding Choc Tawpie. The youth hostel is a bit pricey, but it is conveniently tucked away in an impasse somewhere in the heart of Venice Beach.

Chertsey O'Brien, the "chambermaid," is a fairly attractive young lady with dark fishtail hair and "chocolate chip" nail polish. She takes obvious pride in her British accent. Unfortunately, she does not enunciate well. This is due to her efforts to speak around the wad of black licorice gum on which she so laboriously chews, day and (presumably) night.

Nicolò follows Chertsey—wearing nothing but a pink bandeau bikini, cocoati earrings, and morganite bangles—down a narrow corridor from Scot's Cookies to the door of Chamber 3, which is momentarily deserted.

"You have the top bunk. That one over there, in the corner by the window. The sheets are a bit tatty, but they're clean. I'll punch your pillows, if you like."

"Thank you, Chertsey. That won't be necessary. Who has the bottom bunk? Anyone?"

"Not just *anyone*. It's the redhead from Rotterdam. *Share the Huana.*"

Niccolò furrows his brow.

Chertsey smiles. "That's her credo…. Look, Niccolò. I'd tell you her name—but, I assure you, she needs no introduction."

Niccolò sets his backpack down beside a gray metal storage locker decorated with travel decals, some of which have been half peeled off. There are three doors, side by side, each with a handle lock.

"Middle one's yours. The one on the right is for linen."

Niccolò turns the handle, but the door does not open.

"It seems to be locked."

"Lock doesn't work. Around here, it's the honor system. If you have valuables, there's a rental safe in the office. Just give it a tug."

Niccolò yanks hard on the handle, and the metal door swings open with a terrible clatter. Immediately, Niccolò is overwhelmed by a peculiar—but vaguely familiar—odor. He is also taken aback by the clutter inside.

"Just tell the strawberry to move her stuff. She's not allowed to have a monopoly on the lockers. I'll bet she's in the linen closet, too."

Niccolò struggles to close the metal door. But it is warped and resists his efforts.

"There's a trick to it. Here let me show you." Chertsey twists the handle, puts pressure on the lower corner of the door with her right foot, and slams the door shut with her left hip.

Niccolò is duly impressed. Chertsey executes a curtsey.

"You could bruise yourself doing that." Niccolò points to the locker.

Chertsey smiles broadly. "I don't think so. Bust the door maybe." She slaps her thigh and winks.

"Care if I open the window?"

"You'd have to pull out a few nails first."

Niccolò wrinkles his nose as he steps towards the window. His curiosity is not rewarded, though, because there is nothing to see but a brick wall.

"You'll find a slice of blue sky out there. But you have to look up."

"Ah!" Niccolò offers a glint of satisfaction.

"Speaking of *up*. Think you can climb into bed tonight?" Chertsey points to the top bunk.

Niccolò backs away from the window. "No problem. I may be getting *up* in years, but I'm not stiff in the joints. Does she snore?"

Chertsey accidentally swallows her gum. It momentarily alters her voice. "I don't think so…. But they say she knocks on the wall now and then. With the back of her head. But no one really complains. After all, she's the chamber quean. And by the way, that's *quean with an a*."

Niccolò nods, but he's not sure what she means exactly. "Well, I'm intrigued."

Chertsey approves. "If you need anything, go buy it or do without. I'll be in the cookie shop."

"There *is* one thing."

"Yeah, what's that?"

"I hear there's an itinerant priest in the area. A Catholic priest. I don't know his name. He keeps a low profile for obvious reasons. But he has a loyal following. Mostly locals, I think. Do you know where they meet? I'd like to join the congregation."

"You'll have to ask around."

Niccolò heeds her advice. He spends the rest of the afternoon on the oceanfront, stopping various passersby and prodding them for the exact location of the church. He also asks the shopkeepers. But all he gets are shrugs, insults, and false leads.

At one point, he is attracted by an old van parked behind a vendor's stall. On display are incense burners, trinkets, crosses, posters, and hippie love stuff. The sign reads "Lucy's Crossroad Accessories." But it's the van that interests him most. Painted on the side is a crossroads that appears to incorporate religious symbolism. But Niccolò is hungry, and the vendor is nowhere to be found. He decides to check out a hot dog stand he's already passed by a few times. A good American hot dog–smothered in ketchup, mustard, and pickle relish! He's living the dream....

Wiping the mustard from his chin, Niccolò is determined to strike gold on his first day in Venice Beach. Throughout the evening, he queries people with friendly faces along the Ocean Front Walk. He shuns the tourists, who are ignorant, in favor of would-be informants–namely, those who appear to be local residents. In particular, he targets middle-aged women, hoping to persuade them with his Italian charm. But it's the same story. The locals are either uncooperative or downright hostile.

Having interrogated the shopkeepers earlier in the day, Niccolò now hits the vendors and street entertainers. But he only succeeds in arousing suspicions. Up and down the oceanfront, rumors fly. Niccolò is a spy. But he doesn't give up hope—not just yet. He accosts every public servant he crosses. At his own risk, he stops joggers, bikers, skaters, and pogo stick riders. He even dares to interrupt the course of personal transporters of the gyroscope or maglev variety—all to no avail.

That night, in his top bunk, amidst the quiet chatter and muffled commotion of fellow bed seekers, Niccolò reviews the situation. He comes to the obvious conclusion that since he has failed to break through the beach community's conspiracy of silence, he must continue his investigation elsewhere. Niccolò therefore begins to explore his options. He settles upon one of them, which inspires a smile of confidence, and gently drifts off to sleep, the peaceful continuity of which is only briefly interrupted by the late night arrival of the so-called chamber quean. Niccolò turns over in bed, adjusts his pillow, and picks up his dreams where they left off.

The next morning, after a brief chat with Olivier on Chertsey's computer, Niccolò tries to contact Cardinal Renato Nastors. Although they have never met, they have been in communication with one another on several occasions, mostly by way of social media. In any event, there can be no doubt about it. The former Church official will recognize the Pope. And since he is a sympathizer, he will deliver the information upon which Niccolò's mission so desperately depends. Niccolò reasons that even if the cardinal is not in the loop, he will agree to inquire in the Pope's behalf.

Although his numerous attempts to contact the cardinal fail miserably, Niccolò does succeed in pinning down the address of the cardinal's private residence. He has no other choice but to pay Cardinal Nastors a personal visit. Niccolò uses public transportation to cross the city, and completes the journey on foot. A Reise Security patrol car slowly passes him by as he approaches the gate in front of the cardinal's home, but it doesn't stop. Apparently, Niccolò is not deemed a threat to the neighborhood. Glancing at the security camera mounted on the gate post, Niccolò presses the intercom button. Nobody answers.

However, the gardener has been alerted to Niccolò's presence at the gate. "Nadie en casa. Nobody home." The gardener–who wears a baseball cap and a stubby mustache–wields a rake in one hand, and waves prohibitively with the other.

"I understand. But I am a friend of Cardinal Renato Nastors. Can you give him a message?"

"No, but I can call Security."

Niccolò glances at the patrol car, which is still in view. It has just entered a roundabout.

"The cardinal is in good hands. You are obviously a man of devotion."

The patrol car makes a full circle. It then pulls over to the curb and parks. Niccolò watches out of the corner of his eye as the security officer lowers the window and rests his arm on the sill.

"I am devoted to my work."

"Then you are a slave to money. What a pity!"

"I do not work for pay."

"Then you will eat the fruit of your labor. Blessings and prosperity will be yours."

The gardener is utterly confused. "I don't eat the fruit. I just pick it, and throw it away."

"And why is that?"

"Because it makes a mess in the yard, that's why!" The gardener tightens his grip on the rake.

"I happen to know that the cardinal is quite fond of persimmons, lemons, and avocados."

The gardener mumbles something to his rake. Niccolò is able to make out two consecutive words: "pinche culero."

"I beg your pardon? I don't speak Spanish." Niccolò feigns ignorance in order to give the gardener a chance to redeem himself.

"I said we don't have that fruit here!"

"That is unfortunate. But, my friend, what truly counts in this world is the fruit of the spirit. Love, joy, peace, goodness, faith–"

"¡Vete a la mierda!" This time, the rake's handle grinds a hole into the gravel at the gardener's feet.

"Sorry, no hablo español." This time, Niccolò does not fail to cross his fingers.

"I said don't preach to me!"

"I apologize. I have a habit of doing that, I'm afraid. But you are clearly a man of sound heart and mind. A man who prides himself on doing charitable work for the Church, am I correct? I do hope the cardinal has found a way to–"

"I told you before. The cardinal is not here."

"Well, then. I won't trouble you any further." Niccolò makes an open gesture with his right hand, and whispers, "Che Dio ti benedica." He turns his back on the gardener.

The gardener hesitates, and then stamps his rake. "¡Espera!"

Niccolò looks over his shoulder.

"Who sent you here?"

"I was sent here by the Lord."

The gardener nods with dissatisfaction. "Let me tell you something. Every day, they send one–a 'priest impersonator.' And they always say the same thing." The gardener spits on the ground. "¡Vete a la verga puto!"

Niccolò is unfazed. "You are right to stand your ground, amigo. And I give you warning. Beware of false priests which come to you in black robes, for they are nothing but vermin in the eyes of the Lord."

"You do not wear a robe. But that means nothing. How do I know you are not one of them? How do I know you are a true man of God?"

Niccolò sighs. "You cannot know. You simply must believe."

"That is too much to ask, señor."

"Please, call me padre."

"I cannot talk anymore, *impostor*. I have work to do."

"Go to it, then. Rake up the soil. And tend to the plants and trees. But hear me, good man. One day, you shall stand before kings."

Niccolò realizes he is pouring on the religious syrup. But the gardener is obviously not a man of great refinement.

"Look at your hands. What do you know about work?"

"I do spiritual work. I am the Lord's groundskeeper."

"And I am the Pope! ¡Adiós!" The gardener turns on his heels and, using his rake as a staff, briskly walks away, cursing under his breath.

Niccolò is left to ponder the situation. But he is keenly aware that he is being watched. So he doesn't ponder for long. He gives the officer a friendly salute, and leaves the way he came.

Before Niccolò reaches the first cross street, the patrol car pulls up alongside him, flashing its yellow lights. The security officer lowers the passenger side window.

"May I have a word with you?" inquires the officer politely. He is a robust Hispanic man in his early 40's. But unlike the gardener, the officer has a face that promises intelligence and compassion.

Niccolò approaches the open window. "Officer, I just wanted to see an old friend."

"If you were an old friend, you and Dany would be catching up on old times in the garden right about now. He's worked for the cardinal since he was a boy."

Niccolò is forced to acknowledge the truth. "I have never actually met the cardinal. Not in the flesh, anyway. But we have exchanged views on a host of matters over the years—mostly religious matters, of course. Especially those of particular concern to the States. So perhaps 'old friend' is a bit of an exaggeration. But I think it's fair to say that we are well acquainted. Am I to understand that you know the cardinal personally?"

"We've shared a few bottles of Bonardi." The officer reflects for a second. "But I'm surprised he's never told you the story of Dany Ocampo."

"I'm afraid he has not."

"I'll be glad to tell it, if you like. Do you have identification?"

Niccolò produces his passport, and passes it through the window.

"Alberto Cambrusso." The officer scratches his chin. "You are going to laugh. But if you ever shaved that off, you could almost pass yourself off as the Pope."

"Cardinal Nastors once told me the same thing." For the second time in less than half an hour, Niccolò crosses his fingers.

"My name is Officer Salmono. But before I was hired by Reise Security to patrol the neighborhood, I was better known as Bishop Salmono. I was an auxiliary bishop, and this neighborhood used to be in my pastoral region. Anyway, that's how I know the cardinal."

"Back in Italy, people address me as Monsignor Cambrusso. But you can call me Alberto."

Officer Salmono smiles, and opens the door. "Hop in, Alberto. Maybe I can help you. Care for some coffee?"

"I prefer wine," admits Niccolò as he gets in the car.

"As a former man of the cloth, I can assure you that I prefer wine as well. But I'm a security officer now. And I'm on duty."

Somewhere in East L.A., two devout Catholics are seated in a coffee shop, reminiscing about the good old days. One is Officer Salmono, formerly known as Bishop Salmono. The other is Niccolò di Montachiesa, fictitiously known as Monsignor Cambrusso. But here, they drop all formalities in favor of their first names, Tomás and "Alberto." Tomás drinks a caramel macchiato. Alberto's choice is a mocha cappuccino.

"I can tell you the exact date. It was March 13, 2013. The irony of it is that my parents had moved from Buenos Aires to Los Angeles the year before. So I missed the hoopla."

"But you were just a kid."

"Yes, but I understood the historical significance of it. And it inspired me. From that day forward, my goal was to join the priesthood. What about you? When did you decide?"

"I had a revelation of sorts during a road trip to Paris. Nothing spectacular, really. To be honest, I don't even remember the date. As far as I know, it didn't coincide with any ground-shaking event."

"But there was a Pole in the Vatican?"

"Indeed there was." Niccolò smiles.

Tomás looks at the time. "I have to make another sweep of the neighborhood. Come on."

"Are you going to patrol the cardinal's street again?"

Tomás nods. "Yeah, I'll drop you off at the corner. But I'll fill you in first. That's a promise."

Niccolò dabs his mustache with a napkin, and they leave.

"So he went to Peru," explains Tomás. He swivels his bucket seat forward to check the advisory panel. The patrol car is set on auto-drive, and it has made an unscheduled stop in front of a convenience store. "Override. Inform the clerk that subject is harmless. I'll pay for the beer." Tomás swivels back towards Niccolò. "The clerk's a new hire. He called in the neighborhood drunk."

"You know him?"

"We've had a few chats. He told me once he'd rather be an alcoholic than a Catholic. And I had to break the news...."

Niccolò rubs the back of his neck. "So the cardinal went to Peru? That explains what I heard on the plane. That Shepherd One had reportedly landed in Cusco. I guess there was a grain of truth in it."

"It was a charter flight. And the cardinal was traveling incognito. So it's not that far-fetched. Especially when you consider the fact that the Pope was responsible for the archbishop's appointment. The cardinal could have easily been mistaken for the Pope."

"And, of course, there's the papal villa."

"Exactly. In fact, you've hit the nail on the head."

"What do you mean?"

"Cardinal Nastors had no intention of meeting with the former archbishop. He was merely seeking refuge in Peru. He'd received a number of death threats, and he feared for his life. The general consensus here in L.A.–and everywhere else, for that matter–was that the Church should be held accountable for its long and sordid history of committing crimes against humanity. That made the cardinal a convenient scapegoat for malcontents. But it also made him a target for assassins. The cardinal wished to 'escape the crosshairs,' as he put it. So, he fled to Peru. His objective was to reclaim the papal villa."

"But of all places on earth, why the papal villa? I mean, isn't that a bit too obvious? There's no way he could maintain anonymity there."

"Exactly."

"So he failed to reclaim the villa. Otherwise, we'd know his whereabouts."

"Or he succeeded–"

"And found himself in the crosshairs after all."

"That's right. But it would be hard to sweep that under the rug. Even in Peru. So, I think the first scenario is the more likely of the two. Especially in light of what the locals told the authorities. They claimed that the cardinal never made it to the papal villa. Because he had become so paranoid that he was convinced he was being followed. The guide was only too happy to believe him. So there was a change of plans. They headed for a remote village in the jungle. And that's where the cardinal went completely loco. He told his guide that God had appeared in his dreams. And that God had revealed to him the true purpose of his trip to Peru. The cardinal, it seems, was destined to receive a new set of commandments. These commandments would reflect modern Christian ethics that would not only reinvigorate the faith, but would create a new foundation upon which the Catholic Church could be rebuilt."

"It's not such a bad idea," interjects Niccolò. "To resurrect the Church, I mean."

"I'm with you on that, Alberto. And perhaps God does have a plan of action. But I don't think it has anything to do with carving a new set of tablets, and handing them down to a half-crazed cardinal perched on some jungle mountain in Peru."

"Is that what he did? Climb a mountain?"

"That's what the locals say. The cardinal paid his debt to the guide, and dismissed him, saying that he would now follow in God's footsteps. When asked to what mountaintop they would lead, the cardinal replied, 'God only knows.' And that's where the cardinal is today."

"He never came down from the mountain."

"That's the story. But whether it's true or not, one thing is certain. The cardinal has vanished."

"And so has the Pope. But one or the other may reappear."

"I hope so. Dany is convinced the cardinal will come home. But not until it's safe. And that could be a while. In the meantime, he takes care of the place."

Tomás points at the virtual display that wraps around the interior of the patrol car, and then activates the passenger side window so that Niccolò can swivel about and get a real world view of the home of Cardinal Renato Nastors. There is nobody at the gate.

"Do you ever stop to talk with Dany?"

Tomás shakes his head. "Sure. Almost every day, in fact." The patrol car continues past the gate towards the roundabout. "I'm about the only person he trusts anymore. That's because we have a mutual goal, which is to protect the cardinal's home from vandalism. Everyone else gets the rake treatment."

The patrol car completes the loop, and once again passes in front of the cardinal's residence. Upon reaching the cross street where its driver unknowingly picked up a papal passenger, the patrol car pulls over to the curb and stops.

"I can let you off here, unless you want a ride back to the hotel. Where are you staying?"

"In a youth hostel in Venice Beach."

"A youth hostel–are you kidding me?"

"There's no shame in humble quarters. And besides, it's all I can afford."

Tomás understands. These days, the clergy is no stranger to bankruptcy. And even those who find employment are forced to tighten their belt. "So how do you like Venice Beach?"

"It's great. But I'm not there to hang out and feed the gulls. I'm trying to locate the 'band of rebels' everyone is talking about. I want to join the congregation. That's actually the reason I wanted to speak with the cardinal in the first place. I thought maybe he would know where it meets."

"It's possible, but I doubt it. We're the old guard. I'm pretty sure the rebels would not want us to contaminate them."

"I hadn't thought of that," admits Niccolò.

"So what do you say? I'd be only too happy to swing by Venice Beach. And besides. I still haven't told you the story of Dany Ocampo."

"I'm anxious to hear it, but if you don't mind, I'll take a rain check."

"Sure." Tomás makes a gesture in front of the control panel, and the passenger door opens. "Listen, Alberto. Let's do stay in touch. You can reach me anytime at Reise Security. Or right here on the street, if you don't mind waiting a bit."

"Thank you." Niccolò waves goodbye.

"Be safe!" The door closes, and Tomás drives away.

Niccolò digs out his passport, and ponders the photo of Alberto Cambrusso. "I'm sorry, but I can't lead a double life. I'm sticking with Nic." He slips the passport back into his jeans pocket. "And that, Tomás, means you are out of the picture."

The sun is low in the western sky as Niccolò starts his long journey home.

6 THE POPE AND THE POT OF GOLD

A week after his arrival in the States, Niccolò is no closer to tracking down the elusive "band of rebels" than he was on day one.

The media, in an effort to rekindle interest in the story, now refers to the rebels as the Catho Novas, which, on the surface of it, simply means they are the New Catholics. But the notion of "seduction" is not lost on the public. Clearly, the church is seeking to grow its membership, and that is to be expected. But there have been unconfirmed reports that sex is being used as a recruitment tool. And so, the new name coined by the media is considered not only clever, but also fair play.

From the outset, the media has played on the "point of worship" mystery. Due to the itinerant nature of the church, the meeting place has been officially dubbed the Venetian Blinds, as all of the meetings are presumed to be held in Venice at a blind address known only to the membership. A recent survey asked the question, "When you hear the term Venetian Blinds, do you think of slats or sluts?"

"Hope you find your pot of gold today. In the meantime, have a rainbow cookie." Chertsey takes one from the cookie counter, bags it, and hands it to Niccolò. "You like almonds?"

"I grew up eating Jésuites. It's an almond cream pastry. So, yes, I like almonds. Thank you."

"If you write that down for me, I'll pass it along to Scot. Anyway, good luck."

Niccolò shakes his head. "I've decided to give my search a rest, so—"

"On the seventh day…?"

"I hadn't thought of that. But the truth is I've simply run out of ideas. So I'm going to do some reading and writing."

"Oh? Let me see."

Niccolò shows Chertsey a medium-sized paperback, whose title she cannot read, because he's holding the book upside down, and covering some of the title's letters with his fingers. He also clutches a green plastic clipboard, with a blue ballpoint pen dangling from it on a string, and an unopened package of loose leaf paper.

"A bit old-fashioned, eh? I can loan you a tablet, if you like."

Niccolò offers an appreciative smile, but also a wave of the hand that conveys polite refusal. "I prefer pen and paper, thank you."

"Well, have a good day at the beach."

"Maybe I'll feed the gulls."

To Niccolò's delight, the ocean breeze is so light that it only occasionally disturbs the paper on which he is writing. Now and then, he consults the paperback. His toes continually labor the dry sand, as if they are the engine that fuels his thoughts. His ankles are getting a bit of sun, because he has rolled up the legs of his faded blue jeans.

The rhythm of the sea, with its breaking waves and whispering swash, plays against the constant squawking of seagulls and the clamor of surfers, sunbathers, and beach strollers. The sun is high in the sky, and its light is only rarely interrupted by a fleeting cloud.

"Good afternoon. I was just noticing that book you're reading."

The book's cover, which is bent up at the edge due to frequent handling, features a washed out photo of St. Peter's Basilica wrapped in a black ribbon. Below the illustration is the title, written in thin red letters: *The Vatican: Terminal Cancer.*

The author is given as Sam Diamos.

Niccolò glances at the dog-eared book, and then lowers his sunglasses and looks up. An attractive lady in her late twenties or early thirties is bent over him, hands upon her knees.

"Of course, I downloaded it. Nobody buys paperbacks anymore."

"Have you read it?" inquires Niccolò.

"Cover to cover–so to speak. We've all read it."

The lady, wearing a ruffle-trimmed daisy print tankini beneath a sheer red tunic, picks up the book and flips to Chapter 17. "There's a whole chapter here on Venice. Look."

She points to the heading, "The Venice Cell," and reads: "Although it is quite popular to believe that the Catholic resistance movement is alive and well, and holding regular, albeit clandestine, meetings in Venice, California, some pundits suggest that the holdout congregation has already folded, or even go so far as to claim that it never really existed in the first place."

"That's an interesting passage." Niccolò stands up, and brushes the sand off his jeans. "But the author plays it safe. He presents the facts, but never offers an opinion. At one point, though, he does chastise a reporter's mock interview with Father Crockett–a name which is obviously meant to evoke the Alamo."

"Yeah, I saw that interview. What a crock of shit!"

Niccolò frowns.

"Pardon my French. Are you a writer?" The lady flips back her wavy black hair, and directs his attention to the clipboard in the sand.

"Everyone's a writer these days," replies Niccolò in a dismissive tone of voice. "So I'm giving it a try. I thought I'd tackle the Church."

"Hey, you're not Sam Diamos, are you?"

Niccolò snorts, but not quite with laughter. "No. And neither is he. Sam Diamos is a pen name. His real name is Clipper Davis."

The lady plops down in the sand. "Really? He writes horror stories. I just read one called *The Cactus Snatcher*. It was really good!"

"He's been successful in the genre," admits Niccolò, reseating himself. "But I guess he's trying something new."

"By the way, I'm Lucy. I think I've seen you walk by a few times."

"Lucy's Crossroad Accessories?"

Lucy gives Niccolò two thumbs up. He half expected her to cross her arms, or her fingers.

"That's me. What's your name?"

Niccolò takes a deep breath. "My full name is Niccolò di Montachiesa—"

"Oh, that's hilarious! That's the Pope's name!"

"Ah! You know that."

"Look, can you keep a secret?" Before Niccolò can respond, she spits it out. "I'm a Catholic. Stop by the shop, and you'll see. I sell all sorts of religious stuff. I even sell pictures of the Pope."

"Then it can't be much of a secret."

"Selling is one thing. Believing in what you sell is another."

"Believing is one thing. Practicing what one believes is another," echoes Niccolò, taking it one step further.

Lucy lowers her voice. "Now you're getting into dangerous territory."

"You're right. It's none of my business."

"Not really, no." Lucy plays with the book, then adds, "Do you live around here?"

"Can you keep a secret?"

Lucy nods, and a grin spreads across her face. "Well, I suppose it's none of my business."

"I'm staying at a youth hostel. Until the money runs out, that is. After that, I'll find a nice bench somewhere."

"Hard times, huh? But maybe you'll strike it rich with that book you're writing."

"Maybe."

"But you can't use the Pope's name. Even if it's your name, too. You'll have to find a catchy, uh—what do they call it?—a nom de plume."

Niccolò is about to say something, but Lucy stops him. "Come on, Poppy, 'pen name' sounds too pedestrian."

"Poppy?"

"You don't honestly expect me to call you Nickelo d'Montachusetts, do you?"

"Di Montachiesa. But you can call me Nic."

Lucy considers it for a second, then gives Niccolò the up and down look. She finally settles on the green eyes. "That is really funny, you know? You do look a helluva lot like the Pope!"

Niccolò rubs the hairs on his chin, indecisively. Perhaps he can confide in just one person. After all, Lucy may be a Catho Nova. She has hinted as much. And his inquiries have gotten him nowhere.

"Do you want the honest-to-God truth? I *am* the Pope."

Lucy rocks back and forth in the sand. "That is priceless!" she laughs, beside herself. "You're kidding, right? It's like your favorite joke."

"I'm not joking, Lucy." Niccolò's voice is dead serious.

Lucy interrupts her laughter, and frowns, as if confronted by a lunatic. She picks up the clipboard, somewhat nervously. It takes a moment before her eyes disengage from Niccolò's.

"What is this, Italian?"

"Yes. That's my first language."

"That's funny. You don't have an accent."

"You can thank my American tutor for that. He was quite strict. I can speak German, French, and Spanish, too. I also know my Latin."

"Say something in German," challenges Lucy.

Niccolò raises an eyebrow. "My German accent is a bit off, but here goes: "Wo ist Ihre Kirche?"

Lucy is duly impressed. "Not bad! So tell me. What does it mean?"

Niccolò is taken aback. After all, it should be easy for a speaker of English to decode such a simple phrase–especially when the words are so nearly identical. "It means, 'Where is your church?'"

"Nice try! But, okay. Let's say you can speak German, and all those other languages, too. That still doesn't make you the Pope. It just makes you a Polyglot. But you're serious, right?"

"I'm the Pope," states Niccolò matter-of-factly.

"And I'm the Queen of Sheba. But, hey! Who cares? The other day, I ran into Merlin the Magician. So why not? But at least he's well fed."

Niccolò plays the pity card. "I had a cookie this morning."

"What? A cookie? Nothing but a cookie? That's it! You're coming with me, Poppy. You can't write on an empty stomach. You'll starve to death before you finish the last page. Come on. Get up. I have a couple of sandwiches in the van."

Niccolò's prayers have been answered. While they break bread in the van, Lucy talks about her faith, and before long she admits that it was a fellow vendor who first introduced her to the Chapel Vaneti—what the press calls the Venetian Blinds.

"That's when I met Father Deutkes. He's really—"

"So Father Deutkes runs the church?"

"Father Deutkes is a—how can I say it?" Lucy thinks hard, then smiles with satisfaction. "It's a nom de pulpit."

"Well, I'd like to meet him. Can I come with you on Sunday?"

Lucy wipes some crumbs from her bottom lip. "I'm afraid that's too soon. I have to get permission, and that usually takes a couple of weeks. Can you pass a background check?"

Niccolò shrugs.

Two weeks later, Niccolò checks out of the Choc Tawpie. Lucy has offered him a place to stay. And he's down to his last dime.

"I'm sure the strawberry would pay to keep you around." Chertsey searches for something on the cookie counter. "Ah! There it is…. I have something for you. Close your eyes and hold out your hands."

Niccolò complies, and Chertsey slips him something flaky. Niccolò feels the triangular shape, and smiles broadly. He knows what it is.

"Go ahead. Try it. Tell me what you think."

Niccolò takes a bite. "It's heaven!"

"You won't find a Jésuite anywhere else in Venice Beach. So now you'll have to come back."

"You *wanna* bet?"

Chertsey laughs, accidentally launching a glob of black licorice gum over Niccolò's shoulder. "Near miss, eh? Anyway, you'd better say goodbye. She'll be smokin' hot if you don't."

The Pope and the Pot of Gold   51

Lucy takes Niccolò under her wing. Not only does she allow him to sleep in the van at night, but she also proposes a way for Niccolò to earn some spending money—enough to pay for food and keep himself clothed. In exchange for helping her set up shop every day, Lucy will allow "Poppy" to set up a confession business.

Niccolò, who sometimes refers to Lucy as his "angel of mercy," gets to work. He paints "SOS Confessions" on the side of the van. Lucy uses it to transport merchandise and display stands, but once emptied, the van undergoes a conversion that allows "Poppy" to hear confessions at five dollars per session. Niccolò continues to wear blue jeans, but he soon buys a black t-shirt with a rhinestone cross on it, a crimson tie-dye headband, and a pair of white Nike's.

The "SOS" comes from Niccolò's "swap meet" Social Security card, which is numbered 505-33-0666. Lucy bought it for him. Needless to say, Niccolò is not too happy about the three sixes on the card, but he considers the 33 as a counterweight of sorts. He initially misreads the 505 as SOS. Lucy was greatly amused by this, but quickly pointed out that only license plates and computer passwords mix numbers and letters. Social Security cards do not. But she finds "SOS" a very appropriate name for Niccolò's confession van business. After all, people are desperate to confess, and "Poppy" might even save a life or two. Especially if he can convince people that he really is the Pope.

At first, "SOS Confessions" is not as successful as either Lucy or Niccolò had hoped. It merely feeds off Lucy's clientele. Then Lucy hits upon an idea, inspired, she says, by the warnings of the church prophet. She puts her artistic talents to good use, and creates a large placard that reads, "THE END IS NEAR. CONFESS HERE!" Lucy's idea works like a miracle, and soon

Niccoló is profiting from word of mouth. The general opinion on the Ocean Front Walk is that "Poppy" is a religious wacko, but one with an entrepreneurial spirit. Niccolò's claim to the papacy is seen as a running gag. But people find him charming. And they feel better after they've confessed.

Then, one Friday afternoon in March, a courier arrives at Lucy's Crossroad Accessories. Some whispering ensues. And then Lucy makes the announcement. Niccolò has been invited to church. She cannot reveal the location, but she assures him that it's within a short walking distance.

And so it is. Despite reports to the contrary, Sunday mass is held weekly. This one is held in an old dance studio. To avoid the curious, a sign is posted in the window, and the curtains are drawn. The sign reads: "For Lease." But no phone number is provided.

"Good morning. I'm Father Helgeberger." The priest is a handsome black man.

Lucy turns to Niccolò. "His real name is Sherman Priestley. So he always uses an alias."

"A nom de pulpit," interjects Niccolò, reminding Lucy of their first conversation in the van.

Lucy smiles. "That's right! Last week, it was Father Spitzer."

Meanwhile, Father Priestley is offering the congregation a preview of his lesson.

"Phone book?"

"Ouija Board."

"Hmm...."

Niccolò turns his attention to the pulpit as Father Priestley calls upon Burt, the church "prophet." Burt reminds everyone that the Big One is going to strike, and that California will soon fall into the ocean. However, he must return to the "Prophet Tree" in order to pin down the date. Lucy reminds

The Pope and the Pot of Gold

everyone that Poppy proclaims daily that "The End is Near." The congregation blesses the Pope (Niccolò finds himself in the awkward position of blessing himself–but with little enthusiasm), even though he is qualified as MIA. Niccolò tries to convince those around him that he *is* the Pope, but they think he's a loony, and therefore a perfect addition to their congregation. They criticize the Pope for the downfall of the Catholic Church (Niccolò finds himself in the awkward position of defending his papacy–with forced conviction), but nonetheless declare themselves his defenders. At the end of the sermon, the churchgoers eat Oreo cookies and pour a pink powder into a glass which is filled with water. Finally, the priest accepts contributions towards their annual pilgrimage into the desert, and asks Jeffrey, their resident ufologist, to give a funding report. Then he turns to Franklin for the weather forecast (which is very meteorologically laden with scientific jargon, but also concludes with divine explanations; seems his parents named him after Ben Franklin). But the pilgrims must first save themselves from the Big One, so their first priority is to leave L.A. on their "fact finding mission" to the mountains.

  Over the course of this and subsequent Sunday masses, Niccolò catalogues the wackos in the church. He is particularly amused by Charlotte, a fat lady whose mongrel she dresses up in his finest Sunday clothes. The dog participates in the Eucharist, and barks whenever the congregation says an "Amen!" The dog is named Ramon after her brother, who died of an illness. Ramon (the dog) was offered as a remembrance, and to cheer Charlotte up.

  Then there is Tiffani, who is known as the church slut who whores for God. She fancies herself a "fisher of men." Tiffani always brings a pie and three randomly chosen "Wise

Men" to church services. The one who chooses the slice of pie with the magic bean in it will be her sex partner for the next three nights. The first time Niccolò witnesses the little ceremony, a black man named Hershey gets the bean. He, of course, receives a round of applause. And Father Priestley blesses the union. On a subsequent visit, a man brings his family, and they applaud when hubby/daddy is chosen. It's the only way they can get his butt in a "pew" (usually a lawn chair).

    An opium addict, and former soldier, named Barry hallucinates in church. Not only does he see the Virgin Mary in almost anything, he proclaims his love for her, and unzips his trousers to expose his Jojo, at which moment he is thrown a towel. Sometimes, an event will trigger a military reaction. "Duck! Hit the trenches! Return fire!"

    Barry isn't the only one with a vivid imagination. A man named Brad always brings his mother to church, and speaks to her often during mass. When the congregation rises, she forgets to sit down afterwards, and Brad will scold her kindly, "Sit down, mother!" The thing is, Brad's mother is a ghost.

    This doesn't bother Edgar, a deathly thin "dirty old man" who believes firmly in Brad's mother. He expects to die soon, and "sees" Brad's mother as a possible partner in the afterlife. He often takes Brad's mother aside for a little chat. Edgar is the ultimate conservative. His favorite expression is, "In my day..." He shakes his head disapprovingly of certain church members like Barry, the opium addict. But, mainly, he questions the liberal bent of the new church. Whenever he is particularly worked up over an issue, or is presented with a provocative female display that stirs what's left of his testosterone, he will suddenly clutch his heart, jitter his eyes, wheeze, and turn deathly pale. The priest will rush a cookie to him. "Quick! Take this!" Then he'll wash it down with the pink liquid. This is just the cure

The Pope and the Pot of Gold 55

for Edgar. He calms down, straightens up, and proclaims, "I'm okay." He has cried wolf so many times that the day Edgar does finally croak in church, the assembly will applaud with great relief.

One of the "female displays" that particularly excites Edgar is Eva, the bimbo nudist. Eva wears nothing to church but a thong with a fig leaf print and a feather boa wrapped around her shoulders, which, along with her long blonde hair, more or less hides her breasts. She believes that she is the reincarnation of Eve, and she is always on the hunt for Adam. Of course, every man is eager to identify himself as Adam, and she falls for it every single time. When it comes time for the Eucharist, the priest always slips her a Fig Newton.

Sometimes, a man named Sam ("the storyteller") will entertain the congregation with a "true tale." It is invariably far-fetched but inspiring. Eva, of course, believes his stories–lock, stock, and barrel. She always gives Sam a big hug when it's over, and Sam never complains. It would appear that Sam is a homeless person who is not quite right in the head.

The only Asian in the congregation is Kimberly, the bling! bling! girl. She's in her mid-50s, a rich widow. She dresses provocatively, like a teenager, with short skirts and high heels. Among women, she is condescendingly known as "Pussy Skirt." The wimpy men she attracts are referred to mockingly as "Jellyfish." Kimberly doesn't mind. She's more concerned with her appearance than with her reputation. She frequently refreshes her lipstick. She carries a bag of jewelry with her, and at any moment swaps them out depending on who she wishes to impress. She will thrust her hands in a church member's face and, with her Asian accent, say enthusiastically, "Five thousand dollars! Plus tax!" (One day, a disapproving church member wears an oversized black t-shirt embossed with "$8.50 + Tax" in gold and silver letters beneath a traditional red and blue taegeuk.)

Kimberly has been known to wear a fur coat in summer. She is a shop-a-holic. She is also the church lotto player and casino aficionada. However, though she frequently brings back casino winnings, she has yet to buy a winning lotto ticket.

Church music is provided by Carlos, Rosita, and their seven children. They are conservative Catholics. When they enter, Edgar can be heard to whisper, "Here come the singin' pepitos!" The Hispanic couple typically starts out singing (somewhat off tune) in English, but drift despite themselves into Spanish. The children scream along with them. Everyone applauds. Almost.

During the mass, Father Priestley, or whatever alias he's using on that day, often addresses God. He then throws his voice towards a hidden amplifier, and "God" replies in a Scottish accent that is reminiscent of Sean Connery. Sometimes, Father Priestley and God will get into an argument. Is this a strategy to encourage the veracity of God's presence? Or is the priest that daft?

After the first mass, Niccolò steps "backstage" to chat with the priest, who has gathered children around him. "Father Priestley…?"

"*Helgeberger*, please. You're Poppy?"

"I'm Pope Ignatius I. My real name is Niccolò di Montachiesa."

"Nice to meet you, Poppy."

Niccolò resigns himself for now. He examines the crumbling ceiling of the somewhat decrepit dance studio.

"How do you do that? You know, the thunderous Godspeak thing."

"We're the last Catholic church on Earth, brother. God is paying attention. He's focused on us. And He blesses us with His presence at every Sunday mass."

The Pope and the Pot of Gold   57

The Pope steps back and watches as the priest takes a Jesus dummy out of a highly decorated canvas chest, and begins to discuss religion with the children, many of whom are Hispanic. Frequently, he uses his ventriloquist skills to his advantage, turning to the dummy, saying, "Now what would Jesus say?"

Niccolò mutters to himself, "How can something so absurd be so engaging? It's actually quite clever."

But when Niccolò is asked to participate, he respectfully declines.

7 THE POPE AND TWO LADIES

The afternoon before their departure for the Sierra Nevada, Lucy suddenly comes down with the flu. She is the latest victim of the public restrooms, where the sanitary conditions are generally deplorable. After a customer makes a comment that she is shivering despite the heat, Lucy turns to Niccolò.

"I think I'm about to faint," she says. "Can you please help me to the van? I need to lie down."

Niccolò lays his hand gently on her forehead. "Feels like forty," he says.

"Forty?"

"Sorry. One hundred and four. You should see a doctor." Niccolò accompanies Lucy to the van.

Lucy shakes her head. "No, I'll be fine." She steps into the van. "Would you like a beer?" She takes a chilled bottle of Heineken out of the van's mini-fridge.

"No thank you," replies Niccolò.

Lucy laughs. "Look. A couple of months ago, Father Priestley used Heineken as an alias. So it must be okay." She thrusts the green bottle in Niccolò's face.

Niccolò accepts, almost as a defensive gesture. "Why don't you go for a cool swim in the ocean?"

Lucy considers the idea. "I don't have a bathing suit."

Niccolò shrugs. "Eva—"

"Poppy, this may come as a shock to you. But I'm not a brainless beach bunny with a box office bod, okay?"

"I wasn't suggesting you skinny dip," retorts Niccolò. "I have an extra t-shirt. And it was Eva who gave it to me."

"Eva gave you a t-shirt?" Lucy laughs. "It must be from her throwaway collection. Eva stops at the donation box every other week with a truckload of clothes. Mostly, men's underwear. We told her that Catholic Charities went out of business, and that no one is servicing the box. It's being used strictly as a dumpster."

"I think you're right, Lucy. Eva told me this t-shirt belonged to Adam 71520. When she found out his real name was Skye, she dumped him."

"But not the t-shirt, apparently. You're a lucky man, Poppy." Lucy giggles, and takes a good hard swig of beer. "Let's see it."

Niccolò breaks out the t-shirt and unfolds it before Lucy's eyes. The t-shirt features a multi-colored sea-goat on a black background, and the word "Capricorn" appears above it in colorful wavy letters.

"I told Eva I'd never wear it because I do not subscribe to anything astrological. And besides, the goat–"

"I like it," says Lucy, taking another swig of beer. "Are you a Capricorn?"

"No."

"Then why did you accept it? You could have just said no."

"I accepted it because Burt was there when she gave it to me. And he predicted I would have a need for it."

"Well, Burt was right. And, by the way, I *am* a Capricorn. And Burt knows it." Lucy finishes her beer, sets the bottle aside, and motions for Niccolò to pass her the t-shirt. She presses it against her body, takes note of the length, and says, "Okay. I'll go for a swim. But let me take a nap first. I'm feeling a bit achy."

"If you go for a swim first, you'll feel more relaxed afterwards. And that means you'll fall asleep faster, and rest better, too."

Lucy nods. "Okay, fine. But you're coming with me. In case I faint or something. You don't want me to drown out there, do you?"

"Someone has to mind the store," objects Niccolò.

"Come on, Poppy.... Be a sport! Tell you what. You can perform a saltwater baptism on me. What do you say?"

A short time later, a "Will Return" sign sits on the sales counter of Lucy's Crossroad Accessories. There is a simple handwritten note posted on the confession van. It reads, "God Will Answer Your Prayers. But I Will Be Back Soon."

Despite the vendor's absence, the shop continues to draw the occasional would-be customer. One middle-aged woman acts particularly suspicious. She appears to be waiting for a moment when nobody is paying attention.

Across the way, the owner of a bicycle shop, known to everyone as Mr. Crane, stands in the doorway. He is quietly observing the parade of tourists and locals that pass by on foot. But between passing bodies, he catches a glimpse now and then of the woman, who is trying on various crucifixes and flipping through display boxes full of large plastic-wrapped postcards of famous religious paintings. She lingers on *Saint Sebastian* by Andrea Mantegna, then returns to the crucifix display. She looks over her shoulder. Mr. Crane is watching her as best he can.

A hundred feet away, a crowd has gathered around two street entertainers. One of them introduces himself as Tom Wilkes, Indian Fighter. The other one proudly proclaims that he is a great warrior named Chicken Hawk. Both are wearing leather outfits. Tom Wilkes boasts a pair of silver six-shooters in studded leather holsters. Chicken Hawk has a primitive bow and a leather quiver full of feathered arrows strapped on his back. In their opener, Tom Wilkes and Chicken Hawk challenge themselves to a duel. Chicken Hawk begins by juggling tomahawks, then tossing them one at a time at Tom Wilkes. Tom juggles them behind his back, and tosses them back to his partner. The audience rewards the performers with ample applause.

A young couple, apparently not interested in the Wild West, stops to chat with the bicycle shop owner. This is the break the woman has been waiting for. The passersby are totally oblivious to her. She slowly removes a beautiful 24-inch wooden crucifix carved with rose flowers and thorns, opens her plastic shopping bag, and begins to slip it in.

Suddenly, an arrow whizzes through the air, narrowly missing the woman's head, and plants its tip in the trunk of a nearby palm tree. The shoplifter is so startled that she drops the bag, but clings onto the crucifix. She turns in the direction of the Wild West show.

For a moment, she clutches the crucifix as if it will protect her from the red devil who is taking aim with another arrow, as if going for the kill, but when some Wild West enthusiasts begin shouting "Scalp her!" she panics. She drops the crucifix and takes off running. In so doing, she trips over a dog leash and falls flat on her face. Mr. Crane rushes over to help her up, but manages to detain her until the crowd encircles them. Minutes later, Security arrives on the scene.

Meanwhile, Niccolò and Lucy are swimming a hundred feet or so offshore. They are riding the gentle waves, their heads slowly bobbing up and down as they talk. The sun is high in the west.

"It's a six-hour drive," protests Lucy.

"It's okay. I can drive it," reassures Niccolò.

"Okay, but I'll be barfing in the back. I hope the other passengers don't mind."

"You'll be fine, Lucy. Believe me."

"It's going to be chilly up there."

"Just take some warm clothes. The mountain air will do you good."

"You obviously haven't been to the Sierras. You can't see the peaks for the haze."

"According to Franklin, we'll be camping above the haze."

"Poppy, you just don't get it. Look at me. I'm sick as a dog! Do you know what I want? I want to stay home in my little doghouse. I want to spend the weekend in my doggie bed. I want to wrap myself up in a big blue doggie blanket. And I want to rest my head on my doggie pillow–the one with the pink apple blossoms. I need to be near the bathroom and the kitchen."

"You need friends," insists Niccolò.

"I have them–my refrigerator, my medicine chest, and my cable TV. Those are all the friends I need."

"Then I'll stay with you."

"No, no. No, Poppy. You are going. Father Hopfenbeck or Plochnitz–or whatever!–will find a ride for you. This is something you don't want to miss. Burt is going to prophesy. He's going to finally get the nitty-gritty from the Prophet Tree. Determine the exact date of The Great Seismic Event. I guarantee you, as much as I'd like to go–"

Suddenly, up from the depths surges a tangled mass of red hair. For a brief moment, Niccolò is awed by the virginal image of a Dutch Madonna aureoled by the sun.

"Ingeborg!?"

"How are you, Nicky?" she replies. Twisting her red hair around, she comes face to face with Lucy. "Hey!"

Lucy is stunned. She fails to respond right away.

"We met at the youth hostel," explains Niccolò. "I thought you would be back in Holland by now."

"Two more days," replies Ingeborg.

"I didn't catch the name," mumbles Lucy.

"Ingeborg Grutter," intervenes Niccolò.

"Call me Inge. Everyone else does."

"Nice to meet you. I'm Lucy."

"Oh, I *love* 'Lucy'! It's a great name. Is it short for Lucille?"

"Oh, I could have a *ball* with that one!" answers Lucy sarcastically, noting the blank look on Ingeborg's face. "Never mind…. It's Lucy. Just, you know, plain old Lucy."

"That's great!" She turns to Niccolò. "You know, I couldn't believe my eyes when I saw you, Nicky. I'm right over there!" She points towards the beach. "You see the backpack? That's my beach towel right beside it."

"Well, you certainly know how to pop in on people," says Lucy.

"You don't look too good," replies Ingeborg, ignoring Lucy's remark.

Lucy glances at Niccolò. "I'm sick. And I must warn you. What I've got is very contagious."

"She has the flu," explains Niccolò.

Lucy gives Niccolò a very harsh look.

"Oh, that's nothing. But you know what? I have just the thing for you in my backpack. Take my word for it. You'll snap right out of it! Come on. You can lie on my beach towel. Soak up the sun. What do you say?"

"You can tell Lucy about your experience on the river," suggests Niccolò, attempting to stir up a little intrigue.

"I told Nicky that story in bed," says Ingeborg. "We laughed all night long!"

Niccolò quickly explains. "I had the top bunk. She had the bottom."

Niccolò, Lucy, and Ingeborg wade out of the water. Lucy notices that Ingeborg is younger, firmer, and more physically endowed. Lucy feels a bit frumpy in her black Capricorn t-shirt, which is long enough to hide her panties and upper thighs, and so loose fitting that it fails to cling to her breasts, even though it is dripping wet. Ingeborg, who takes the lead, wears a skimpy green bikini that barely covers her female assets.

No doubt onlookers consider Niccolò—who is obviously quite fit for his age—a very lucky man. But they are probably a bit puzzled as well. After all, despite his sexy entourage, he is wearing a souvenir t-shirt from San Luis Obispo and a ragged pair of cutoff jeans.

Lucy sits down on the beach towel as Ingeborg begins to rummage through her backpack.

"Humph! Looks like I used it all," concludes Ingeborg after a few minutes. "You catch things on the road."

"Ingeborg hitchhiked all the way from Boston Harbor," explains Niccolò.

"I had a few adventures," smiles Ingeborg.

"Oh?" murmurs Lucy, who is not really all that interested.

"Sexual adventures," specifies Niccolò.

"Hmm!" replies Lucy.

"I had a lot of offers. But I was very careful. Not too young, not too old. Well dressed. Nice car. Warm smile. Honest eyes. And except for that guy in Missouri, it all went like a dream. I ate in fancy restaurants and stayed in the best hotels. Of course, I had to give them a little something…. You know!"

"Tell her what happened in Missouri," nudges Niccolò.

Lucy lies flat on her back and closes her eyes. "I'm listening."

"I was hitchhiking out of St. Louis, heading southwest along the interstate. I thought I'd take the southern route through Oklahoma, New Mexico, and Arizona. Anyway, I'd already turned down a few rides, mostly truck drivers, but also this one guy driving an old Buick convertible with two nervous German shepherds in the back seat."

"Whoa, doggies!" interjects Niccolò.

Lucy opens a critical eye, then snaps it shut.

"Well. I just said, no thanks! And you know what? The guy jumped out of the car! He wouldn't take no for an answer! His dogs jumped out, too! So I took off running. Backpack and all! I didn't know which way to go."

"Cross the highway," suggests Lucy.

"That's a bright idea! I would've either caused an accident or ended up road kill!"

"Head for the woods."

"You mean, the rapist's playground? You don't watch many movies, do you?!"

Lucy shrugs. "So what happened? You got chewed up by the dogs?"

"That's a good one!" Ingeborg laughs.

"She was rescued by a Harley," says Niccolò, trying to move the story along.

"Yeah. Well, Harley was my knight in shining armor. But Melvin? I swear, that biker was built like a Clydesdale! He didn't have enough sense to wear a helmet, so when he turned around to see what he'd caught, I got my first look at his face. And it was a real shocker!"

"Ugly old bear?" suggests Lucy.

"Are you kidding me? Melvin? He may have been a redneck biker from the sticks, but I'm telling you, he had the face of a Chippendale! You simply cannot imagine! For a moment, I thought I was living in a Harlequin romance! I kid you not! I was riding down that highway in hog heaven! And, baby, I was hangin' on tight!"

"You forgot the part about Buick and his dogs."

"Well, I don't know what Buick had in mind. But he looked the porno type, you know? Anyway, I looked over my shoulder as I rode away. I can tell you, this Buick guy was furious. He flipped me the bird. And then he whistled. I couldn't hear it, but he had two fingers in his mouth, and I saw his dogs turn back. Anyway, Buick and his dogs jumped back in the car, squealed the tires, and gave chase!"

"So you ended up with the guy in the Buick?"

Ingeborg shakes her head. "Melvin took an exit. Buick missed it. And we never saw him again."

"So let me guess," sighs Lucy. "You had corn dogs at Bonnie Lee's diner. Checked into a sleazy motel by the lake. And had a torrid night of redneck sex with Melvin, the Chippendale biker with the Clydesdale dick."

Ingeborg laughs. "That's a good one!"

Lucy pops open an eye. "Okay, so what happened?"

"He took me to a river landing. There was a canoe rental, and also a general store. Mainly, they sold fishing gear, groceries, and liquor. Melvin rented a cabin, and Miss Ingeborg cooked."

"Not bad," says Lucy.

"I'm not one for pork chops, let alone biscuits and gravy. But I was really hungry. So we had dinner. I let Melvin eat the fruit pies. Those are disgusting!"

"You must be going somewhere with this. Did you get the Harlequin treatment?"

"He wanted to go swimming in the river."

"That sounds romantic. Were you naked?" asks Lucy.

"Let me put it this way. Those backwoods boys can peel the hide off a squirrel."

"I get the picture. And what about Melvin?"

"Stiff as a log."

"Perfect! So let me guess. You find a private swimming hole at the base of a mossy bluff. A full moon reflecting on the water, smooth as glass. All is quiet except for the whispering of riffles downstream and the gentle rustling of oak leaves above your head. And there you are. You and Melvin. He with the yearning flesh. And you with the fiery passion that only a redhead can feel. And then, suddenly, he grips your buttocks, and pulls you in tight. You put a grip on his massive shoulders as his powerful outboard begins to churn the water. And then you splash around like a fish on a hook."

"What novel are you reading?" asks Ingeborg. "We spent the whole time swinging out on this inner tube and dropping into a cold spring. After the fourth drop, all I wanted to do was wrap myself in a dry blanket and sit by the fireplace."

"At least the cabin had a fireplace."

"I'd already used the fireplace for cooking. Anyway, the logs were still burning."

"I hope one of them was Melvin's. All he had to do was light the powder keg."

"Maybe, but he said that a cold swim was just the ticket after a long haul on a bike. So he left me by the fireplace and went to bed."

"And you crawled in with him?"

"Around midnight. But he slept–"

"Like a log!" guesses Lucy.

"That's right. And in the morning, he dropped me off in town. This guy saved my life, and I never had a chance to thank him. He was really an angel."

"Hmm! Well, it's a nice story. But I don't see all that much humor in it," says Lucy. "I mean, seriously, you two actually laughed all night? I don't get it."

"I guess it was the marijuana," admits Ingeborg.

Lucy is flabbergasted. She sits up, swings around on the beach towel, looks Niccolò in the eye, and whispers, "What?!"

"Did I turn down your Heineken?"

"No, but–"

"I can't explain it right now, Lucy. But biker stories take me back. And, well, let's just say that in the flower of my youth, I was no stranger to weed."

Lucy breaks into laughter. "But wait, wait, wait! You're the *Pope*, right?"

Niccolò nods. "Yes. But I wasn't *always* the Pope."

"I don't believe it!" Lucy laughs so hard, her eyes flood with tears.

Ingeborg is amused, but also confused.

"What does she mean, 'you're the Pope'?"

"I told her I'm the Pope. And she doesn't believe it."

"Oh."

Ingeborg dismisses her confusion. She turns to Lucy. "By the way, I forgot to mention. The key to the story is that Melvin was a born again Baptist without much of a brain. He wanted to play with fire. But he was too afraid to jump in. Religion can do that to a man. Even a redneck hunk like Melvin."

Niccolò is about to make a comment when Mr. Crane, the bicycle shop owner, suddenly appears, accompanied by a policeman.

"Lucy! This is Officer Bickford."

"Yes?"

"Willie's been arrested."

"Is that what all that ruckus was about? We saw the crowd up there, but—"

"Guillermo Flores. Do you know him?" asks the officer.

"Yeah, that's Willie. He's the guy that plays Chicken Hawk—" begins Lucy.

"What's the charge, officer?" interrupts Niccolò, who knows Willie to be a God-fearing man, having confessed him on more than one occasion.

"Assault with a deadly weapon. He shot an arrow at one of Lucy's customers." He points at the palm tree, where the arrow is being painstakingly removed by another officer.

"Is the customer okay?" asks Ingeborg.

"Other than a few abrasions, yes. She'll be fine." Officer Bickford turns back to Lucy. "Do you know a Mrs. Helen Blythe?"

"No…."

"That's the name of the customer. We have reason to believe she was shoplifting."

"I was watching her," confirms Mr. Crane. "She was attempting to steal a crucifix. The wooden one with the rose carvings."

"Your full name is Lucy Ferguson?" asks Officer Bickford.

"Yes."

"We need you to make a statement."

"But I didn't see anything."

"That doesn't matter. We have witnesses. You'll need to come down to the police station tomorrow afternoon. Identify the suspect, Mr. Flores. Give us some background on him. And also confirm that you do not recognize Mrs. Blythe. She may have been a customer of yours in the past."

"But I'm leaving for the weekend. First thing in the morning!" protests Lucy, suddenly changing her mind about the trip to the Sierras.

"I don't think so," replies Officer Bickford.

Lucy faints.

8 THE POPE GOES CAMPING

A convoy of eight vehicles pulls into a parking lot across the street from a local restaurant. Thirty-one weary travelers gather together under a crystal blue sky. The Owens Valley haze has been cleared out by a recent thunderstorm, and so Mount Whitney can be seen towering in full splendor above the town of Lone Pine, California. According to Father Priestley, whose current alias is Wickett, the cathedral-like spires that highlight the jagged peak make it the crown jewel of the Sierra Nevada. It is lunchtime, and after a brief stretching of legs, the group crosses the street to the restaurant. Father Priestley opens the door, and steps up to the "Wait to be Seated" sign. His sheep fall in line behind him. A waitress greets them, and after a few tables are cleaned and pushed together near the window booths, the travelers are all seated together.

Niccolò sits next to Tiffani in a window booth opposite Hershey and Sam. Although Niccolò was reluctant to accept Tiffani's offer to accompany them on the trip, Hershey didn't object, and Sam insisted. Sam and Niccolò rode in the back seat. As for Hershey, a strikingly handsome black man with an infectious smile, the days of the magic bean are over. He and Tiffani are just friends now, although Hershey occasionally stretches the limits of friendship with an intimate touch here and a sexual tease there. Tiffani doesn't seem to mind, but Niccolò has a feeling that she invited Niccolò and Sam along to ensure that Hershey doesn't engage in too much sex talk.

"So where are you folks all heading?" asks the waitress.

"Onion Valley," answers Father Priestley. "We'd planned on stopping in Independence for lunch, but it's getting late."

"You must have called ahead. The road is usually closed this time of year. But we haven't had much of a snow. Are you fishing?"

"Wilderness camping. And I didn't call ahead. Franklin here keeps tab on the weather and current road conditions."

"If we had more time, we'd visit the Alabama Hills. Or maybe even head up to Whitney Portal," adds Franklin.

"It's a beautiful drive," says the waitress. "Are you ready to order?"

Niccolò, who has overheard this brief exchange of words, leans towards Sam. "So why isn't it called Union Valley? At least that would make sense."

Niccolò is alluding to Sam's story of the Battle of Cherbourg, which he told en route from Baker as they headed up Highway 395. The story came up because prominent geographic features in the Owens Valley region are named after the two ships involved in the naval battle. The Alabama Hills, a movie-friendly landscape featuring granite rock jumbles, was named after the CSS Alabama, the confederate ship under the command of Captain Raphael Semmes. Kearsarge Lakes, Peak, Pinnacles, and Pass were all named after the USS Kearsarge, which was captained by John Ancrum Winslow. The CSS Alabama was defeated and sank off the coast of Normandy in 1864.

"I can't answer that, but it's a good question."

After Sam's table has ordered, the resident storyteller adds, "In case you're wondering, it was Burt who named Ancrum Cave. It's a tribute to Captain Winslow."

"Burt said it's not really a cave," objects Niccolò.

"That's correct. A more accurate term would be 'fissure'—but Burt calls it a cave because it loses the sky about half way in. It zigzags back into the mountainside a ways, then dead ends. But it makes an excellent depository, and it can shelter up to ten people."

Niccolò has already made some inquiries. Burt explained to him that Ancrum Cave is located between Dragon Peak and Kearsarge Peak, but closer to the former. The cave is difficult to find, and, in any event, the fissure doesn't invite a closer look. It is a perfect hiding place for sacred documents, relics, and the supplies the church will need for the Final Days. Those days are drawing near, but are not as imminent as The Great Seismic Event, whose date will finally be revealed by the Prophet Tree. As for the tree, Burt would only say that it stands just outside Ancrum Cave, and that it cannot be distinguished from the other trees of the same species that surround it.

About half way through lunch, Burt stands up and addresses the membership.

"I just want to remind you that we'll be camping at the trailhead tonight. We'll have plenty of time to relax, but you'll need to make your preparations for an early morning departure. Breakfast will be served at dawn, so I suggest you hit the sack as soon as possible. We have a long hike ahead of us, and it's not an easy one. We'll follow the trail to Golden Trout Lake for a while, but after that we blaze our own. There is no set route. And that is intentional. The exact location of Point B must remain our little secret. So tree notches and cairns are strictly forbidden. Father Wickett and I will guide you every step of the way. And don't worry. We'll get you there and back in a reasonable amount of time, regardless of the challenges of the terrain. And that includes any snowdrifts we may encounter. If all goes according to God's plan, we'll arrive late afternoon. We'll set up camp immediately, make an early dinner, and take care of church business before the evening prayer service. Monday morning, we'll grab a breakfast and head back to the parking area. Some of you have taken off Tuesday. Those who haven't, you should try to get some sleep on the trip back to L.A."

By mid-afternoon, the convoy of eight is driving alongside Independence Creek. Thanks to a relatively dry winter and an early call for the plows, Onion Valley Road is remarkably free of ice and snow. The sun has disappeared behind the Sierras by the time the convoy reaches the parking area and campground at road's end, but the sky is still a bright blue.

Barry is in charge of setting up the tents. But he cannot do it alone, so Niccolò volunteers to help. Back in L.A., Niccolò was surprised that nobody owned a van or camper. As the tents go up, Hershey arranges the firewood in preparation for the evening meal. With a little advice from his mother, Brad will do the cooking. Jeffrey and Franklin are in charge of picnic baskets and coolers, and the food and drink they contain. Due to the size of the group, the two picnic tables are used for serving, not for eating. One is supplied with drinks, napkins, utensils, and condiments. The other is a self-serve buffet table. Tiffani and Kimberly are in charge of setting everything up.

Several members of the congregation have not made the trip. Edgar stayed home because his heart would not be able to endure the physical challenge of such an arduous journey into the mountains. Eva declined to join the group because her naked body would not endure the cold. Charlotte knew she couldn't haul her fat body up the mountain, but used her dog Ramon as an excuse for not coming along. As for Carlos and Rosita, they refused to leave their seven children at home, or in the hands of a babysitter.

That night, Niccolò shares a tent with his road buddies. Niccolò and Sam take the sides; Hershey and Tiffani take the middle. Each camper has a sleeping bag, and those who do not have an inflatable pillow simply fold their clothes and slip them beneath their head. Modesty is observed to the fullest extent possible. Twenty-nine campers sleep in their briefs and panties. Two campers do not. One of them is Kimberly, who shares a women only tent. She claims she only wears lipstick to bed. The other one is Hershey, who not only sleeps in the nude but also does not bother to zip up his bag, leaving his ebony body tucked out of sight but well within Tiffani's reach, should her curious hands wish to grope his manhood in the darkest hour of the night. It also opens up an opportunity for Hershey. He reckons that even if Tiffani does not take the initiative, her breasts, which are barely covered, will be receptive to his touch if he takes care not to disturb her sleep.

"Poppy," whispers Sam after everyone has settled in for the night.

"Yes, Sam?"

"I'm thinking that Lucy must have had a rough day of it."

"Officer Bickford said he'd make it quick and painless. He knows Lucy isn't feeling well. She fainted right in front of him."

"I just hope that bug knows when his twenty-four hours are up. You should have had someone spend the night with her. Or at least check on her."

"She'll be fine, Sam."

"What was the name of that Dutch lady?" asks Tiffani, yawning.

"Ingeborg," whispers Niccolò.

Yawns are infectious. Sam yawns, and so does Niccolò. Hershey is unaffected. He is aroused by the prospect of spending the night at Tiffani's side.

"What was her cure for the flu? Do you know?" asks Tiffani.

"I don't know. Something herbal, I guess." Niccolò yawns again.

Hershey leans over to give Tiffani a goodnight kiss. She accepts it with a smile, but adds, "Don't get any ideas, Mr. Wise Guy. Okay? I need my beauty sleep."

Hershey returns her smile reassuringly. A few hours later, he suddenly kicks his sleeping bag open. "What the–?" He sits up, and draws his legs up to his chest.

Tiffani jerks awake and sits up, clutching the bag against her breast. Niccolò breaks out of a dream, rubs his eyes, and fishes for the penlight in his jeans pocket. Sam–who merely grumbled when a corner of Hershey's sleeping bag brushed his face–remains fast asleep.

Niccolò activates the penlight. At first, all he sees is Tiffani's bare back, but then he leans forward and aims the light (discreetly) towards Hershey.

"There's something in my bag!" says Hershey. "Shine the light down here." He peels back the partially open sleeping bag, revealing a ball of fur. "What is that–some kind of rat?" he asks in a voice that is embarrassingly shaky.

Tiffani leans in for a closer look, using Hershey's right knee for support. "Oh, come on, Hershey! Don't be such a wuss! That's a chipmunk!"

"Definitely a chipmunk," echoes Niccolò.

"What's it doing in my bag?" complains Hershey.

"Spending the night, I think," says Tiffani.

Hershey quickly slips on his mini brief and slides the sleeping bag out from under his body.

"Maybe it has rabies or something!"

"It obviously popped in during dinner," chuckles Niccolò.

"Or maybe even during the night. You left your bag unzipped," notes Tiffani.

The chipmunk doesn't move. It is petrified.

Hershey pushes the sleeping bag gently towards the door of the tent. Niccolò, who has not removed his t-shirt, hands the penlight to Tiffani, crawls towards the door, unzips the flap, and flings it back towards the outside. "Scat!" he says.

The chipmunk is happy to comply. It darts out of the tent and disappears into the night.

Hershey refuses to get back into his bag. Tiffani returns the penlight to Niccolò, falls back upon her pillow, turning her back to Hershey, pulls the sleeping bag up under her chin, and closes her eyes.

Seconds later, the entire congregation is awakened by a scream.

"There something furry in my bag!" The voice is Kimberly's.

There is a general commotion, followed by the sound of running feet.

Suddenly, Kimberly shoves her head in Niccolò's tent, whose door flap he has forgotten to close and zip. "Make way. I'm coming in!"

There is a shuffling of bodies inside the tent. Niccolò can't really make anything out in the dark, but clearly Kimberly has taken possession of Hershey's sleeping bag. She squeezes in somewhere.

"Hey! I'm freezing here!" protests Hershey.

"Then get in!" responds Kimberly.

"Not a chance!" says Tiffani sharply. "Climb over, Hershey. You're with me!" She unzips her bag.

Hershey slips into Tiffani's bag. It is a very tight fit, but he doesn't mind at all.

"Oooh!" he exclaims, feeling Tiffani's body pressed against his. After a few seconds, he begins fumbling for his mini brief.

"Leave it on, please," says Tiffani, who wriggles in her bag until she is once again facing Niccolò. Tiffani and Hershey fall asleep in the spoon position.

Once again, a head pops into the tent.

It is Father Priestley. "What was all that about?" he asks.

"The chipmunks are cold tonight," replies Niccolò. "Just turn the other cheek and get some sleep."

Despite the disruption in the night, those assigned to prepare breakfast do so in time for sunrise. The hikers find a seat wherever they can. Only one picnic table is needed for serving, so the other one is free. Some of the hikers sit on stones. Others spread a blanket on the ground, or else just sit in pine needles or grass.

Niccolò, Tiffani, Sam, and Hershey are on the ground. They are joined by Kimberly, the last person out of their tent (Sam fetched her clothes), and her three former tent mates, Jessica, Daphne, and Marlene. All three are barely past twenty years of age, and they are inseparable. They are new to the congregation, so Kimberly promptly introduces them as they eat breakfast, which consists of scrambled eggs, sausage doused in maple syrup, and coffee for some, but granola cereal, cinnamon toast, and hot chocolate for others. With each introduction there is a shaking of hands or a salute, depending on the distance between the parties involved.

"This is Jessica Parks," says Kimberly. "Her boyfriend calls her 'Jurassic Park.'"

Jessica flashes her teeth and wiggles her fingers, all of which have long natural nails.

"The rest of the world just calls her Jess…. And this is Daphne Cordillera."

"Good morning," says Daphne, her voice bright and cheery. "My friends call me Daffodil."

"Daphne is from Figueres, Spain," adds Kimberly. "She's practically an expert on Salvador Dalí. She speaks both Castilian and Catalan."

"And English," adds Daphne, smiling.

"And here we've got Marlene Schlick. She's got her own bar, Schlick as a Whistle. Right across from Sweet Cutterlee's, where Daphne works."

"Yes, but we met at the beach!" laughs Daphne.

"Shopping for sunglasses," explains Jessica. "By the way, my boyfriend is Barton O'Connor. He played the role of Richard Chesterman in a biopic last year–"

"*In a Moment of Divine Sophistication*," interrupts Marlene. She turns to Jessica. "It's a good film, actually. But strictly underground. I'm sure they've never heard of it. Or your boyfriend."

"Get over it!" chimes in Daphne.

"I know all about Richard Chesterman," says Niccolò. "Church massacres rarely escape my attention. Especially when it involves a Catholic church."

"This is Poppy," says Kimberly. "I don't know his last name, but he thinks he's the Pope. And this is Sam Rayburn. He's got no home, so he lives inside his stories. This is Tiffani Putnam. She whores for God. And this is John Punter, her latest trick."

Sam laughs. "That's a good one!" he says, à la Ingeborg. He winks at Niccolò.

"Don't let her fool you. I'm Hershey Woods. And we prefer to think of Tiffani here as a 'fisher of men.' That makes me her latest convert." He puts his arms around Tiffani.

"Hershey and I were attacked by big angry rodents last night," says Kimberly. The girls, of course, know better.

"Don't chipmunks have burrows?" asks Hershey. "Not that I'm complaining!" He squeezes Tiffani affectionately.

"They do," confirms Niccolò.

"God works in strange ways, right Poppy?" says Sam, glancing at Hershey and Tiffani.

"According to Father Priestley—" begins Niccolò.

"Wickett," corrects Sam.

"That's right. I spoke with Father *Wickett* this morning. He had a very simple explanation for what happened. Last night, Burt was eating peanuts in the sack. And he's in charge of the sleeping bags. Father Wickett said that Burt likes to change bags on every trip because he doesn't like the feeling of peanuts between his toes."

"Burt works in strange ways," concludes Sam.

9 THE POPE AND THE PROPHET TREE

The hikers, who now call themselves the Wicketeers, stop for a lunchtime snack in a meadow somewhere along the Golden Trout Lake trail in the Kearsarge-Gould-Dragon area northwest of the trailhead in Onion Valley. Further up the trail, the valley forks. To the left is the trail to Golden Trout Lake, which lies beneath the crags of Mount Gould. To the right is the trail to the unnamed lakes that reflect the lofty summit of Dragon Peak. According to Hershey, who has a topological map in his backpack, the lake-pocked valleys make the area resemble a giant scrotum. Father Priestley, who is fond of reading clouds, prefers to think of the area as a wishbone. Burt likens it to a wisdom tooth. Secretly, the hikers agree with Hershey.

Every now and then, a chipmunk is spotted scurrying about curiously. But they prove to be quite shy, and few hikers are willing to part with anything but a few crumbs to test their boldness with respect to approaching humans. The chipmunks remain indecisive. Finally, Burt empties a bag of peanuts a few steps away from the group, and several chipmunks find the courage to snatch them up for their cache. Everyone but Niccolò is satisfied. The hikers rise to their feet and slip on their backpacks, but, as they do so, Niccolò asks Burt from a few yards away if he can spare another bag of peanuts. Burt shrugs, and tosses him a bag. Niccolò catches it, walks to a large flat stone, seats himself, empties the peanuts into one hand, then pours half of them into the other, bows his head, and waits. The peanuts lie in the cup of his palms, which rest atop his extended legs. Less than a minute goes by before one of the scampering chipmunks makes a dash for Niccolò's offering. It runs up his leg, stops at his right hand, and begins to nibble away. Seconds later, another chipmunk appears, and before anyone can find the time to scratch his head in amazement, it is eating out of Niccolò's left hand. The chipmunks remain perched on Niccolò's knees until all of the peanuts have been consumed, and then they rush off across the meadow.

"That was amazing!" says Tiffani, speaking for the entire group.

"Oh, I had monks of one type or another eating out of the palm of my hand for many years," replies Niccolò.

"That's a good one!" says Sam, who seems to have adopted the expression.

The Wicketteers hike throughout the afternoon. They steer right at the fork in the trail (dubbed "Dragon's Fork" by Burt), but soon abandon the footprints of others and climb up towards a grove of naked aspens.

"Point B," confirms Burt.

The group sets up camp in a clearing near a jagged rock face, and breaks out their dehydrated dinners, the most popular of which is a vegetarian chili kit. A "Which way you goin'?" hiker named Billy Phillips, who packed in a couple of propane cylinders, is given the task of entering Ancrum Cave in order to retrieve the propane skillet, which is sealed in a waterproof nylon bag. Jessica, Daphne, and Marlene follow him into the fissure. They have volunteered to fetch the picnic canisters, which contain, among other essentials, plastic utensils, tumblers, and melamine bowls, as well as salt and pepper shakers and spice, herb, and seasoning jars.

As Billy enters the "cave" section of Ancrum Cave, he verifies with his flashlight that nothing has been disturbed, including the sealed tubs containing such items as water filters, first aid kits, bear repellent, personal hygiene kits, space blankets, and extra clothes. Church documents and relics are stored inside stacked aluminum chests at the back of the cave. Not only are these chests, which are about four feet long, individually padlocked, they are bound together by a chain (also padlocked) that runs through the ring-shaped handles as well as a single large steel eyebolt anchored in the stone wall.

Father Priestley reminds the group that no campfire will be built, and that candles will not be permitted during the prayer service, as they do not want to draw the attention of other hikers in the area. Flashlights with dimmers are permitted inside the tents, but only if used discreetly. Burt adds that, God willing, the waxing moon will shine brightly. Franklin confirms that it will. The powwow is interrupted by the return of "Jurassic Park," "Daffodil," and "Schlick" bearing the oversized picnic canisters, and by the departure of Niccolò, who says he needs to pee. No sooner have the girls set down the canisters than a high-pitched scream resounds from within Ancrum Cave, followed by a deep scratchy growl.

"My God, it's a mountain lion!" shouts Billy in a hoarse voice trembling with fear. "Get me the hell out of here!"

Barry responds with the instinct of a soldier. He runs to his backpack, rips it open, grabs his loaded .357 magnum by the handle, unsnaps the holster flap, and flings the holster aside as he charges towards the fissure. He nearly trips over Niccolò, who has prostrated himself at the front of the cave entrance and is praying that Daniel will be delivered without harm.

"Who are you talking about?" says Kimberly sharply. "That's Billy in there!"

"I'll give you 'five thousand dollars' to shut up!" scolds a female hiker.

"Cash me out, Caitlan!" ripostes Kimberly.

A second later, two deafening shots are heard. Niccolò calmly stands up, but is brushed aside by Billy, who exits the cave in a frenzy. Niccolò sees the shock on everyone's face. The cave is dead silent, and they fear for Barry's life. Niccolò takes it upon himself to enter the cave. A few minutes later, he and Barry walk out of the cave to a collective sigh of relief.

Barry has a triumphant look on his face.

"I'm telling you, Barry, I had that totally under control!" insists Niccolò.

"Hey, guys! We're having mountain lion for dinner!"

"Don't ask me to say grace!" grumbles Niccolò.

As a matter of fact, nobody wishes to eat wild cat meat, unless it's made into jerky. That doesn't dissuade Barry, who is a survivalist at heart. He pokes around in the picnic canisters, nods with approval, and heads back towards the cave, unsheathing his hunting knife....

After dinner, it's time to attend to church business. Burt puts on a stocking cap and calls everyone to attention. "Some of you may be asking yourself, 'Why here?' First of all, this is a stand of quaking aspens."

Niccolò looks around. No one is particularly surprised by the silly implications of this statement.

"Several years ago, I was birding here in the Sierras. I was particularly interested in getting photographs of the belted kingfisher. One night, I was shaken by a strange dream. A certain well-known fisherman revealed to me that the Quaking Aspen had supplied the wood for the cross of the crucifixion. At first, I refused to believe it. I objected that it must have been a Cedar of Lebanon, or perhaps an Aleppo Pine."

Niccolò glances at his watch, and then ponders the leaf that dangles on a branch of the tree—a different tree this time, if one is to believe Burt's story. Niccolò scans the trees nearby. Not one is scarred by anything remotely resembling a cross, at least not from this vantage point.

"I therefore carved a cross in the tree—and waited! I spent two more nights in Ancrum Cave. The Fisherman continued to visit me in my sleep. But he did not speak to me. He simply watched over my dreams and ensured they were peaceful.

"Finally, on the third morning of the fourth day spent among the aspens, I saw that the cross had indeed vanished, and that the Prophet Tree now proudly displayed the first leaf of the year. I made several efforts to listen to the tree's voice. I put my right ear to its bark and plugged the left one with my finger. And then I switched ears. But if the Prophet Tree were speaking, its voice was too faint to be heard. I was quite discouraged."

"You hear a spirit with your mind, not with your ears," points out Niccolò.

Burt hears this remark, and smiles. "In fact, I was going about it all wrong. In a sudden moment of inspiration, I plucked the leaf off the branch, rolled it up tightly, and stuck it…"

"Up your ass," suggests Niccolò, but only with his lips.

Burt takes off his stocking cap, and continues: "…in my ear!"

"Which one?" asks Niccolò.

"First one, then the other," replies Burt. "In each ear, a different prophecy."

Niccolò accepts the answer with indifference. "Okay."

"In fact," continues Burt, "the leaf served to amplify the voice of the Prophet Tree. The tree spoke to me for only a few minutes. The first thing it said to me was that I would join a church, and that the Fisherman's cave would become a depository for that church. The cave would also be a sanctuary for the church membership in the Final Days. Then the tree warned me that a great fire would ravage the land, and that many people would die in its flames, including a member of my family. Later that summer, Southern California was indeed engulfed in flames, and my Aunt Trudy, who was an invalid, was one of its first victims. It was later confirmed that the cause of the fire was arson. I made several attempts to notifying the media before the fire was set, but nobody would listen."

Niccolò shrugs.

"Every year, I consult with the Prophet Tree on the anniversary of my first visit. And every year, the prophecy is fulfilled. Father Wickett is my witness. He has accompanied me on virtually every trip I've made to Point B, and it is his faith in the miracle of prophecy that has led him to fulfill the first one concerning Ancrum Cave. As the membership grows, we will bring more supplies to the cave. Most of you brought along a little extra something on this trip. Father Wickett and I packed a couple of miniature radiation detectors. Brad brought a variety of laxatives upon the advice of his mother. Sam is contributing a couple of sewing kits. Kimberly loaded up on chopsticks. Those are for the picnic canisters. And the girls here brought cosmetics."

Niccolò's thoughts turn for a moment to Lucy. Since she was unable to make the journey, she gave Niccolò a plastic bag full of individually wrapped crucifixes, and also several boxes of Indian incense. This was her offering to the cave.

"Last year, the Prophet Tree warned me of a Great Seismic Event. It provided me a precise date, but I couldn't quite make it out. The voice was too weak. I tried to adjust the leaf, but it slipped out of my ear. When I stuffed it back in, the leaf turned gold, withered, and crumbled into bits. Some of you were here to witness that truly unfortunate moment. Needless to

The Pope and the Prophet Tree

say, we returned home thoroughly disappointed. But, well, here we are again. More numerous than before, and more determined to get the facts. Tonight, as the moon rises, I will consult with the Prophet Tree, and it will reveal to me the exact date of The Great Seismic Event. I am sure of it."

He holds up his stocking cap. "I will pull this cap down over my ears to secure the leaf. And with this many witnesses, the voice is sure to be strong!"

Niccolò once again surveys the group. Nobody seems to doubt a word that Burt, their prophet, has said.

"And now, it is time!" announces Burt. "So please, gather round."

It is obvious to Niccolò that Burt will be unable to reach the leaf. It is too far off the ground. But Burt has foreseen this. He motions for Barry to approach. Barry knows what to do. He assumes a crouching position, and Burt climbs onto his shoulders. Moments later, Burt is able to pluck the Prophet Tree's leaf amplifier. Barry neither staggers nor grunts. He is a strong man.

"Couldn't one of the girls have done that?" asks Niccolò.

Everyone frowns, as if to say, "What a ridiculous idea!"

Burt pinches the leaf between his fingers, and carefully rolls it up. Clearly, he has never smoked weed. He is quite awkward at the task. After confirming that everyone is focused on him, Burt sticks the leaf into his right ear and pulls his stocking cap down over it. Everyone awaits the first prophecy with bated breath. After a long three minutes, during which time he gently nods, Burt pulls the stocking cap up over his ear and extracts the leaf. He then repeats the process with his left ear. Finally, satisfied that the Prophet Tree has expressed itself in full, Burt exhibits the leaf. It turns gold, withers, cracks, and falls into bits. Burt spills the remains of the leaf onto the ground.

"Ashes to ashes," confirms Father Priestley.

"Amen!" respond the Wicketteers.

"And only the tree barks," quips Sam, making an obvious reference to Charlotte's dog, Ramon.

"Eva could use a leaf like that," whispers Brad to his mother.

The Wicketteers laugh, but only for a moment, as they are eagerly awaiting the results of Burt's consultation with the Prophet Tree.

"The Great Seismic Event will occur on the morning of April First," reveals Burt, speaking into a digital recorder handed to him by Father Priestley.

Niccolò can hardly contain his outburst of laughter. He disguises it with a cough, and puts his hand over his mouth. Several of his fellow churchgoers turn to look at him. Niccolò makes a gagging sound, and excuses himself quietly. He digs the penlight out of his jeans pocket and makes haste to the fissure, into which he disappears. He regains his composure after stifling a few giggles, and nonchalantly heads back into the cave proper. Near the chests, Niccolò spots the bloody remains of the mountain lion, which Barry has promised to remove first thing in the morning. Niccolò makes the sign of the cross, pinches his nose, and then makes an about face.

"Are you okay, Poppy?" asks Sam upon his return to the group.

"I think my dinner and I had something of a disagreement. But I feel fine now."

Sam pats Niccolò on the back. "You missed all the seismic details."

"I heard the date. That is all I need to know," replies Niccolò.

Sam nods. It simply does not occur to him that anyone would be foolish enough to doubt the validity of the prophecy.

The Pope and the Prophet Tree

Niccolò, on the other hand, knows the difference between well-grounded faith and blind acceptance of utter nonsense. Nevertheless, he is able to maintain a straight face. He does manage to cast a disparaging glance at Burt, though. The prophet is busy scribbling notes in a pocket calendar and chatting with a number of inquisitive, but nonetheless gullible, devotees.

"What about the second prophecy?"

Sam bites his lip apprehensively. "The Prophet Tree predicted that a tragic accident will result in the untimely death of one of our dearest brethren. That came as something of a shock to us all."

Barry, who has just finished reloading his .357 magnum, carelessly waves it in Niccolò's direction as he wipes the barrel with a chamois cloth.

"And did Burt name this unfortunate soul?" asks Niccolò, calmly shifting position.

"No, but he said it would be the work of the devil."

Niccolò searches his mind for an appropriate response. But Sam backs away, and turns his attention to Father Priestley, who, after a few private words with Burt, has taken center stage, and is preparing to announce the evening's prayer service.

Sam beckons Niccolò to his side, gives him a friendly nudge, and then points discreetly to the sky.

The moon shines brightly, just as Franklin predicted.

10 THE POPE ON PALM SUNDAY

April Fools' Day comes and goes, and the great fault lines of California sleep right through it. Not even the most insignificant temblor is recorded that day. As expected, Burt faces questions from the congregation at the next church meeting, which is scheduled to focus on preparations for Easter Sunday following the sermon. Burt explains that the Prophet Tree did not specify the year.

"It makes perfect sense," he says. "After all, the Prophet Tree first spoke to me of The Great Seismic Event last year. Obviously, we are being given advance warning. And that gives us time to prepare. We've been informed of the epicenter, and we know the extent of the damage the earthquake will cause. We also know that we can count ourselves among the survivors if we evacuate the area the day before. What we don't know yet is the year. I suspect the Prophet Tree will share that information with us at next year's consultation."

Niccolò raises his hand. "Perhaps, in order to raise church funds, we could have someone manufacture some Prophet Tree brooches. Aspen brooches with a single leaf."

"A synthetic emerald, probably cubic zirconia, set on white enamel," adds Lucy, who figures she could sell them at Lucy's Crossroad Accessories.

Burt shakes his head. "I'm sorry, I must reject that idea. The Prophet Tree is a not-for-profit tree."

After some hushed exchanges in the congregation, Father Priestley returns to the podium. "If there are no more questions, I would like to turn our attention to a new guest here today. Please welcome Livy Viagara."

Livy stands up. "Thank you, Father Weingarten. And thank you, Caitlan Silberstein, for inviting me." She bows towards Caitlan, who is sitting right beside her.

"Livy and Caitlan are renting an apartment together," whispers Lucy to Niccolò, as Livy shakes the hand of worshippers seated nearby.

Niccolò observes the two ladies, both of whom are in their thirties. Caitlan is a dishwater blonde. Livy has short black hair. Caitlan is the more feminine of the two.

"Caitlan never mentioned that on the hike," replies Niccolò.

"You don't really know her, do you?"

"Not in the Biblical sense," admits Niccolò.

"Livy is from New York," concludes Father Priestley.

"That's true," adds Livy, "but I'm definitely not a New Yorker. I've lived in L.A. too long!"

Father Priestley smiles. "We also would like to report that Officer "Bic" Bickford, who declined our invitation to be here today, was able to get Willy Flores off the hook. Most of you know Willy as Chicken Hawk. Lucy informs me that he and his partner, Tom Wilkes, the Indian Fighter, are once again performing on the Ocean Front Walk."

"Helen Blythe walked," whispers Lucy, as she waves to the congregation.

"But that's a good thing," replies Niccolò. "Because she came back and bought the crucifix."

"Okay, so I told you that already. But what you don't know is that I doubled the price."

Niccolò frowns at her.

"Okay, so the devil made me do it!"

Niccolò is about to comment, when Barry, who is seated just behind them, stands up suddenly and shuffles sideways to the aisle. He is adjusting his binoculars. "You, sir! Over there, by the minesweepers. Identify yourself at once!" he shouts.

"Back on the opium," whispers Lucy.

Father Priestley glances at Jeffrey, who seems to be the target of Barry's binoculars.

"At ease, soldier! I'm Lieutenant Jeffrey Sayles. I, uh, have a message from UFO headquarters. All is quiet on the Martian Front."

"You may deliver your report to General Mills," replies Barry.

"Thank you! And you may return to your post!" replies Jeffrey, trying to keep a straight face.

"Well, then!" says Father Priestley. "Let us proceed with today's sermon."

"*The Tree of Knowledge*," states Burt, who figures that between all the questions, comments, and interruptions, the congregation may have lost sight of the subject.

"Yes, thank you, Burt. We are all familiar with the events in The Book of Genesis, which was written and compiled by Moses in the Wilderness of Sinai. The prologue alone encompasses the Creation, the Garden of Eden, the Great Flood, the Nations descended from Noah, and the Tower of Babel. One of the pivotal moments in the early chapters of Genesis takes place in the Garden of Eden. You know it as the Temptation and the Fall of Humankind. Please open your Bibles to Genesis, chapter two, verse eight."

"Mom, open your Bible!" whispers Brad. "Genesis, chapter two, verse eight!"

Father Priestley begins to read from the New King James Version:

> The LORD God planted a garden eastward in Eden, and there He put the man whom He had formed. And out of the ground the LORD God made every tree grow that is pleasant to the sight and good for food. The tree of life was also in the midst of the garden, and the tree of the knowledge of good and evil.

"I might add here that Franklin once questioned how a tropical garden could thrive in the desert where rain is a meteorological rarity. The answer lies in the following passages where Moses explains that the Garden of Eden is watered by a great river, which then splits into four.

"Now, please turn to chapter three, verse one."

> Now the serpent was more cunning than any beast of the field which the LORD God had made. And he said to the woman, "Has God indeed said, 'You shall not eat of every tree of the garden'?" And the woman said to the serpent, "We may eat the fruit of the trees of the garden; but of the fruit of the tree which is in the midst of the garden, God has said, 'You shall not eat it, nor shall you touch it, lest you die'." Then the serpent said to the woman, "You will not surely die. For God knows that in the day you eat of it your eyes will be opened, and you will be like God, knowing good and evil." So when the woman saw that the tree was good for food, that it was pleasant to the eyes, and a tree desirable to make one wise, she took of its fruit and ate. She also gave to her husband with her, and he ate. Then the eyes of both of them were opened, and they knew that they were naked; and they sewed fig leaves together and made themselves coverings. And they heard the sound of the LORD God walking in the garden in the cool of the day, and

> Adam and his wife hid themselves from the presence of the LORD God among the trees of the garden. Then the LORD God called to Adam and said to him, "Where are you?" So he said, "I heard your voice in the garden, and I was afraid because I was naked; and I hid myself." And He said, "Who told you that you were naked? Have you eaten from the tree of which I commanded you that you should not eat?" Then the man said, "The woman whom You gave to be with me, she gave me of the tree, and I ate." And the LORD God said to the woman, "What is this you have done?" The woman said, "The serpent deceived me, and I ate.

"There are several points of controversy that arise in the reading of this text. What exactly was the Tree of Knowledge? What or who was the Serpent? Why did God plant the Tree of Knowledge in the first place, if it bore forbidden fruit? After all, as we read in chapter two, God planted only trees that were 'good for food.' That seems to be a contradiction. And why was the Serpent allowed in the garden? Why was it given the gift of speech? Some of you may recall Balaam's donkey in the Book of Numbers. But it was God who 'opened the mouth of the donkey' so that she could address her master, who had struck her three times when she turned away from the sword held by the Angel of the Lord, who stood in her path. Today, we will attempt to address these points of controversy.

"First, let us discuss the Tree of Knowledge."

Eva stands up and proudly displays herself to the congregation. She is wearing her fig leaf print and feather boa. Nothing new there. But in something of a bold move in church, she unwinds the boa and sweeps back her long blonde hair to expose her breasts. Upon each nipple is an apple pasty, one gold, one red. Beneath each pasty is a word written in glitter of the same color mixed with sprinkles of black. Together, the two words read: *Eat 'em!*

"The Tree of Knowledge was an apple tree. So today I'm wearing apples! This one is a Golden Delicious!" explains Eva, turning slowly for all to see. "And this one is a Red Delicious! They're my Adam's apples!"

"And they're delicious," whispers Brad to his mother.

"I think you mean *Eat 'em* apples," says Kimberly in a corrective tone of voice.

Eva raises her eyebrows in self-defense. "Only *Adam* can eat 'em, okay?"

Edgar makes a "squeeze the fruit" gesture with his hands.

"Edgar? Did you have something to say?" asks Father Priestley, who thought Edgar was asking to speak.

"No…. Oh, well, yes, sure! You know the old saying? 'An apple a day keeps the doctor away.' Well, it doesn't keep my doctor away!"

"At the risk of turning this mass into something, shall we say, soft core, can you please hide your apples, Eva?" asks Father Priestley.

Eva complies, but a few men are heard to groan with disappointment.

"I'm sure I speak in behalf of the entire congregation, Eva, when I say that we all applaud your total devotion to all things Adam and Eve," remarks Father Priestley.

In fact, Eva is something of an apple fanatic. She bakes apple pies, smothers her crêpes in apple sauce, and drinks apple cider. Needless to say, her favorite electronic toys bear the symbol of an apple on them. She listens to Beatles music. And her favorite painter is Magritte. She has several large posters of his work, including *Le fils de l'homme* ("The Son of Man," which depicts a man wearing an overcoat and bowler hat, his face largely obscured by a hovering green apple) and *Ceci n'est pas une pomme* ("This is Not an Apple," a still life which denies that it is the popular fruit). Eva also finds pleasure in shooting plastic apples that sit on various pieces of furniture in her apartment. She does so with a bow and arrow she bought in a toy store. The arrows have suction tips, and they rarely find their target....

Father Priestley spends a moment pondering the Bible passages on the podium beneath his eyes.

"But I would like to point out that although the Tree of Knowledge is commonly depicted as an apple tree, the Bible remains vague on this point."

Sam stands up. "Father Weingarten."

"What say you, Sam?"

"I believe it was a pomegranate tree, which is native to the area where the Garden of Eden was presumed to be. Pomegranate means 'seedy apple,' and the fruit is associated not only with Hades, but also with fertility."

"'In pain you shall bring forth children,'" quotes Father Priestley.

Eva frowns.

"Be fruitful and multiply," says Sam. "But listen, Father, I don't want to derail your lesson, so I would simply suggest that you read up on the Greek myth of Persephone. I would also suggest you look up the *Madonna della melagrana*, or 'Madonna of the Pomegranate,' by Sandro Botticelli."

"Mary's insemination by God," suggests Father Priestley, who is somewhat familiar with the painting.

"The seeds of Christianity," states Sam.

"I have no problem with your theory, Sam. But, as I said before, the Bible does not name the tree."

"You are mistaken! The Bible is very clear on this point!" The thunderous voice from the "rafters" is that of God, speaking in his Sean Connery voice.

"Welcome to the House of the Lord!" responds the congregation, well trained in such visitations.

"Please enlighten us," replies Father Priestley.

"It states clearly in verse seven that Adam and Eve made coverings for themselves by sewing together fig leaves. The tree of the knowledge of good and evil was therefore a fig tree. If it had been a pomegranate tree, they would have sewn together pomegranate leaves. You know the tree by its leaves."

"Pick a leaf, any leaf! Go ahead, pick another!" mumbles Eva, lowering her voice to imitate the serpent.

"But, Lord, are you saying then that the forbidden fruit was a fig?" inquires Father Priestley.

"A tree is also known by its fruit," replies God.

"Lord, I am reminded that Matthew, Mark, and Luke all related the parable of the withered fig tree."

Father Priestley flips quickly to the New Testament, and within seconds locates the desired passage. Niccolò is sure that it has been bookmarked.

"I am reading from The Gospel According to Matthew, chapter twenty-one, verses eighteen through twenty-two."

> Now in the morning, as He returned to the city, He was hungry. And seeing a fig tree by the road, He came to it and found nothing on it but leaves, and said to it, "Let no fruit grow on you ever again." Immediately the fig tree withered away. And when the disciples saw it, they marveled, saying, "How did the fig tree wither away so soon?" So Jesus answered and said to them, "Assuredly, I say to you, if you have faith and do not doubt, you will not only do what was done to the fig tree, but also if you say to this mountain, 'Be removed and be cast into the sea,' it will be done. And whatever things you ask in prayer, believing, you will receive.

"The lesson is that you must have faith in God's answer to our prayers, and that we must repent of our sins," summarizes Father Priestley.

A cavernous voice, somewhat indistinct, yet also quite loud, rudely interrupts the conversation between God and Father Priestley. It causes the church candles to brighten. "He doesn't give a fig about that!"

"Bite your tongue!" replies God, dimming the candles.

Father Priestley makes the sign of the cross. "Where God walks, Satan is sure to follow!"

"The Devil needs no introduction!" replies Satan.

The candles once again glow brighter. In fact, the candles brighten and dim in accordance with who speaks, God or the Devil. At other times, the flames assume their normal luminosity.

"Father Weingarten is quite right to quote this passage," says God. "In this parable, Jesus was looking for the fruit of repentance. The fig tree had none to offer, so it was made to wither away. The fig tree was like unto Jerusalem, which professed its faith in Me, but without spiritual conviction. And so the Temple, which had become a den of thieves, was destined to be cleansed, just as Jerusalem itself, if it did not repent, was destined to be destroyed."

"Thank you, Lord. But I am confused." Father Priestley scratches his head. "You confirm that the forbidden fruit was a fig. But if that is the case, then Adam and Eve, in fact, ate of the fruit of repentance. But their only sin was to eat the fruit. Surely it is not a sin to repent!"

"They disobeyed my command," argues God.

"Who do you think you are? Bluebeard?" taunts the Devil.

"Were you not such a pitiable creature, I would rip out your tongue. Such poor attempts at sarcasm are embarrassingly childish," retorts God.

"Is it not within your power, O Lord, to banish Satan from this church forever?" asks Father Priestley.

"Yes, but it is within the Devil's power to resist. And so he does," sighs God. "But you are confused. Hear me out. The fig tree is more than a tree, but 'more' doesn't mean 'same.' In the parable, we are talking about faith. In the garden, we are talking about morality. Faith and morality are not the same. But they do intertwine. And so you are right to draw a parallel between the two fig trees. For in each case, the fig tree serves to illustrate a lesson."

"Lordy, all this faith and morality mumbo jumbo is just making things worse," says Satan. "Let me make it simple for you. It was a fig. But not an ordinary fig. It was big and gnarly, and it bore the fruit of knowledge. And, I'm quite proud to say that the fig tree was the Devil in disguise. And that the fruit spoke the Words of the Devil. Words of wisdom, I might add. I taught Adam and Eve the difference between right and wrong!"

"That's right," mumbles Eva, squinting with reassurance.

"Why do you think Jesus cursed the fig tree on his way to Jerusalem?" asks Satan pointedly. "It was payback, pure and simple! God is vengeful, and he doesn't give a fig about parables!"

There is a moment of silence.

"Father Weingarten."

"What say you, Kimberly?"

"I say there is a rotten apple in every barrel, and a rotten tree in every garden. Don't listen to this pack of lies!"

Father Priestley understands that Satan is a bad apple, but he seems to be at a loss to address this point in a meaningful way. His eyes float up to the rafters.

"Kimberly is correct," says God, who is never at a loss for words. "Satan is telling you lies. The fig tree was not the Devil in disguise. It was the Devil cursed! I turned him into a fig tree for all eternity so that he would behold the wonders of creation without the ability to intervene. But Satan was clever, and said that Man and Woman were ignorant and ungrateful. He claimed they were no different than any other creature, except that I had created them in my own image, which he claimed was an act of shameless vanity. In this, he was wrong. And he knew it, though he said otherwise. And though I felt his assessment of Man and Woman was in great error, he spoke his mind truthfully. Therefore, the burden of proof was upon me. So I struck a bargain with the Devil. And I said to him, 'Because you dare challenge me at every turn, you are henceforth cursed! You shall become a fig tree in my garden! And you shall see my purpose. And mark my word, you shall remain a tree for as long as your fruit remains untouched. I have faith in Man and Woman. I will forbid them from tasting your fruit, and they will obey. For they are respectful of God's love and do not wish to taint it. And they will not defy me in the least. For in their heart, they thank the Lord for the many blessings they receive! And so, you shall be proven wrong. And the price you shall pay is this. You will remain a fig tree until the end of time!' But, as I have said, Satan was clever. As clever as a snake!"

Father Priestley ponders for a moment. He flips a few pages in the Bible, seeking an earlier passage. "Let us once again turn to Matthew. I am reading from chapter twelve, verses thirty-three through thirty-seven."

> Either make the tree good and its fruit good, or else make the tree bad and its fruit bad; for a tree is known by its fruit. Brood of vipers! How can you, being evil, speak good things? For out of the abundance of the heart the mouth speaks. A good man out of the good treasure of his heart brings forth good things, and an evil man out of the evil treasure brings forth evil things. But I say to you that for every idle word men may speak, they will give account of it in the day of judgment. For by your words you will be justified, and by your words you will be condemned.

Father Priestley points his finger towards the floor in accusatory fashion. "Satan, you are the worst kind of viper! You have an evil heart. You speak nothing but lies! And your fruit was poison!"

"Calm down!" replies Satan. "I was not a bad tree. And neither were my figs poisonous. I simply offered Man and Woman a means to discern good from bad, right from wrong. I opened their eyes so that they could see all things clearly. They were blind and ignorant. If it weren't for my precious figs, we would all be naked imbeciles!"

Eva stands up. Her convictions are in disarray. She is devoted to the Lord, but finds the Devil to be quite persuasive. She opens her mouth to speak.

"Sit down, Eva!" orders Kimberly in a loud whisper, her hand cupped to her mouth.

"And I am not a viper!" adds Satan, who has perhaps been considering Eva's state of mind.

"Not in the literal sense," agrees God. "But as I gave speech to the donkey, so did you give speech to the serpent, who you persuaded to act in your behalf."

"It was the only way to tempt the Woman," admits the Devil.

"As I have said, you are very clever. And to your cleverness we owe the Original Sin. You are responsible for the misery that has spoiled the great joy of my creation."

"You punished Adam and Eve and all who came after. Not me!"

"I hold you in contempt!" thunders God.

"This is a church. Not a court!" bellows the Devil.

"Father Priestley is looking a bit pale," says Niccolò to Lucy.

"Let me be the judge of that!" The candles flicker dangerously.

"Permission denied!" The wax candles are practically engulfed in flame.

"You are dismissed!" The church teeters on the edge of darkness.

"I object!" The intensity of the light causes the membership to shield its eyes. Sam slips on his sunglasses.

"Overruled!" The candles are snuffed, and the church is suddenly pitch dark. The congregation, which moments before was flooded in murmurs, is now hushed.

"Oh! Lord, you have thrown out the Devil once again!"

"Let there be light!" replies God, softly. The candles come back to life. They shine moderately, in reverence to God. "Good," says God, satisfied.

"So what are we to believe, Lord?"

"Have faith in what I have said."

There is a long moment of silence.

"God has spoken," says Father Priestley.

"Not only does he play God, he also plays the Devil's advocate," whispers Niccolò to Lucy.

"Amen!" chimes the congregation.

Ramon barks.

Father Priestley picks up a bottle of sparkling water sitting on a table near the podium, and takes three long drinks. He punctuates his appreciation of each drink with the customary expulsion of breath. His face regains its color. "And now let us turn our attention to Easter Sunday. Charlotte chairs the Easter Committee. What have you to report?"

"Father Weingarten—"

The candles brighten just a bit. Ramon jumps off Charlotte's lap and begins running in circles, barking furiously.

"Hush! Hush, Ramon!" reprimands Charlotte.

"Excuse me. I forgot one detail," says Satan, silencing Ramon.

"And what was that?" asks Father Priestley.

"For the agony that is childbirth, you have no one to blame but God. And for the ecstasy that is sex, you have no one to thank but me. I hear my sweet minions calling. Farewell!"

Eva bites her lower lip. Ramon returns to Charlotte's lap.

And Niccolò turns his thoughts to Francine, and sighs, "Those were the days!"

11 THE POPE AND THE KISS OF LIFE

For Niccolò, now that he has been stripped of his papal duties, Holy Week is a time for reflection. Not so much related to the last days of Christ, but to his own failure to save and restore the Catholic Church. For Lucy, Holy Week presents an opportunity to double, perhaps even triple, sales of religious merchandise. She sets up shop early Tuesday morning as dawn breaks. Niccolò, who usually busies himself inside the confession van once he has helped Lucy with the sales counter and display stands, acts upon his need to reflect, and goes for a solitary walk on the beach instead. He slips on his sandals and cuts across the sand to the shoreline, where tongues of water soon lap at his feet. Lucy's eyes follow Niccolò compassionately. As he slowly shrinks into the distance, Lucy returns to her thoughts.

Having been prohibited by Burt from reproducing the Prophet Tree as a brooch, Lucy now revives an old idea she once had about producing and selling a miniature Tree of Knowledge. The idea dates back to a telephone discussion of her childhood memories that she had with her mother while adorning the small artificial Christmas tree in her apartment. Every year, in the days before Christmas, she would set up a nativity scene on a coffee table in the living room. Now, Lucy sells miniature nativity sets at Christmastime. And they are quite popular. Lucy is quite sure that the Tree of Knowledge would enjoy equal success, perhaps

The Pope and the Kiss of Life 107

even eclipsing sales of the Nativity because it would be marketable year round. She never acted upon her original idea because of the costs involved, but now she encourages herself to take the risk. She must be entrepreneurial if she is to achieve her goal of one day owning a brick and mortar shop on the Ocean Front Walk. So she once again considers the idea, this time around with modifications suggested by the duel between God and the Devil that she witnessed at the Palm Sunday mass.

  First, she envisions the fig tree, which she imagines to be about ten inches high. Then she adds the figurines, appropriately scaled. Eve is seated on a bench swing, supported by a twisted bough of the tree. One hand is placed invitingly on that part of the bench seat which is unoccupied, while the other offers a fig to Adam, who stands beneath the tree's canopy, but a quarter of the way around the trunk. Coiled around the branch above his head, but with its headed extended downward, is the Serpent, watching intently. Standing just beyond the tree opposite the bench swing is God, his back turned. In the trunk of the tree is a small door which can be opened to reveal the Devil inside. The question she asks herself is whether Adam and Eve should be anatomically correct. She also runs through a mental gallery of images depicting the Devil. Her thoughts are interrupted by Mr. Crane, who waves at her from across the walk. He is unlocking the door to his bicycle shop. A young man is in his company. He is wearing a t-shirt depicting a gerbil.

  As Lucy mechanically arranges her wares for the day's clientele, Niccolò strolls at water's edge, head bent downward, completely lost in thought. He blindly approaches a young couple, accompanied by a German shepherd. The dog has been freed of its leash, which is loosely coiled around the woman's hand. As a result, the dog begins to stray. This is not unexpected. The man whistles, and jiggles a bright red ball above his head, commanding the dog's attention. The German shepherd knows the game well, and is always an eager player. He barks with excitement, whips the sand as he races to the game master's side, and begins to jump for the ball, which is not out of reach, but which manages to elude his snapping jaws.

"Is Mitchell taunting you, Taylor?" baby talks the lady.

Taylor barks in the affirmative.

"He wouldn't have it any other way," assures Mitchell with a wink and a smile. After a few false moves, he turns on his feet, and passes the red ball to his game partner, who steps back and catches it with her free hand. "Go to Stacy!" urges Mitchell, but Taylor is already on his way. However, Stacy quickly tosses the ball back to Mitchell. This doesn't prevent Taylor, who is mommy's boy, from jumping on Stacy and digging his front paws into her shoulders. This lasts only for a moment. Taylor pushes off, and darts back towards Mitchell, fully aware that the much anticipated moment has arrived. Mitchell hurls the red ball far out into the ocean. Taylor barks, as if to say, "I'm on it!" and bounds into the surf. He swims rapidly out to the floating ball, scoops it up, and heads back to shore.

In the meantime, Niccolò passes by the couple. They wish him a good day, but Niccolò fails to respond.

The couple shrugs.

"Come on, Taylor!" shouts Stacy as the dog wades back towards her.

"Come to papa!" shouts Mitchell.

Further up the shoreline, a jogger splits his attention between the playlist selection in his ear and the sight of a couple playfully wrestling a red ball from the mouth of a German shepherd. He notices that the dog did not bother to shake off the water once ashore. No doubt the dog knows that once he has surrendered the red ball, he will return to the ocean to fetch it again. The jogger is a man in his late forties, or perhaps early fifties. He is wearing the mandatory jogging outfit. A sun visor is strapped to his balding head. The strap has been personalized at the factory. The letters spell out the name Joel.

"Go fetch!" shouts Mitchell.

As expected, these words trigger an immediate reaction on the part of the German shepherd. Taylor barks enthusiastically, and takes off like a bullet. He plunges back into the surf, and cuts a straight path through the waves towards the coveted game piece which, having described a lazy arc across the morning sky, and plopped into the ocean, now rides the gentle blue swells.

Joel's eyes follow the dog as he makes the final lunge for the ball, snatches it, and heads back to shore. He then turns his attention for a moment to the contemplative man who walks towards him at a snail's pace. Until now, he has only been vaguely aware of this solitary figure. Since Joel is the one primarily responsible for closing the gap between them, he considers this man to be little more than an obstacle around which he must make a polite detour in order to continue his route along the shoreline.

Taylor barks wildly. Stacy and Mitchell clap their hands. Niccolò sighs softly. Joel wobbles his head to the music in his ear, and silent words pass over his lips. All the while, the moment of Joel's planned evasive maneuver draws near. However, he is suddenly faced with a far more urgent situation. The world begins to turn dark around him. A sharp pain jabs him in the chest. And he breaks his stride.

A few yards further, and Joel stumbles, and falls to his knees. He clutches his heart, and gasps for breath. His eyes make out a pair of sandals in the sand. They belong to the man he'd hoped to avoid. Joel feels a warm and comforting hand resting upon his shoulder.

"Here is one man who recognizes the Pope," says Niccolò with calm satisfaction. "And for that, I offer my deepest gratitude. May the Lord bless your soul!"

Joel strains to say something, but his tongue does not cooperate. He looks up at Niccolò pleadingly, but stops short of the compassionate green eyes that are directed towards him. Instead, he fixates on Niccolò's t-shirt. Set against a white background is a portrait of Christ the Savior, his long black hair flowing loosely from beneath the crown of thorns upon his head.

"Perhaps you would like to confess?" Niccolò raises his voice, suspecting that the earphones are preventing the jogger from hearing his words. "Can you hear me, son?"

Joel, suddenly convinced that he is about to draw his final breath, allows himself to succumb to the veil of semi-consciousness, and collapses at Niccolò's feet.

Niccolò suddenly realizes that his vanity has misled him. This man is suffering from a heart attack, and is about to die unless he intervenes. Now, it is Niccolò's turn to fall to his knees. He clasps his hands together in prayer, and implores God to save the dying man's life.

Meanwhile, Taylor, who is in the midst of another round of the fetching game, drops the red ball, and comes running. He senses that something is dreadfully wrong.

"Taylor! Taylor!"

The couple is confident that their dog will hear and obey them, and so does not give chase. Instead, they are content to whistle and flap their arms, much to the amusement of a nearby beachcomber, who examines and then rejects a scallop because it is chipped. A bit further up the beach, three teenage boys, dressed in sleek black and yellow neoprene, spot a religious man bent over a jogger in prayer. They drop their surfboards and rush to the scene. They understand what is happening. So does the dog that is licking the jogger's face. But, apparently, the man with the crown-of-thorns t-shirt is hopelessly out of touch with reality. How foolish to think that prayers can save a man's life! Results come from action, not words....

"Hey! Get out of the way! We know what to do!" shouts one of the surfers.

Stacy and Mitchell exchange a look of dawning realization that a life and death drama is unfolding before their eyes. They and the surfers converge on the scene at the same time.

"Stand back!" commands Niccolò. "And let me do God's work." Niccolò resumes his prayers.

The surfers look at each other in bewilderment. Then, without uttering a single word between them, they reach the same conclusion. They must overpower the religious fanatic who refuses their assistance.

"We're trained in CPR!" one of them insists in a last ditch effort to avoid a skirmish.

Taylor's red ball lands unexpectedly near Mitchell's feet. Mitchell turns about and nods towards the beachcomber that threw it. He then picks the ball up, and tries to interest Taylor in a new game of fetch while Niccolò prays. But to no avail. Mitchell shrugs it off, and glances at Stacy, who is busy describing the situation and their location to a 911 operator.

"An ambulance is on the way!" confirms Stacy.

"Amen!" says Niccolò. He stretches out his open-palmed hand, halting the advance of the three teenage surfers, who have begun to execute their plan to push him aside and restrain him. But although Niccolò's peremptory gesture is effective (at least temporarily), it's not until Taylor begins to growl at them menacingly that the surfers fully abandon their plan to forcibly intervene. As soon as they back off, Taylor turns his attention back to the jogger in order to continue lathering his face.

Niccolò, however, nudges the German shepherd's muzzle aside, opens wide the jogger's mouth, and begins to administer mouth-to-mouth resuscitation, taking deep breaths between each strong exhalation. The self-proclaimed CPR experts look at each other nervously. "That's the old way!" one of them complains. "You're supposed to do chest compressions! Here, let me show you!"

"I know what I'm doing," replies Niccolò sharply.

Taylor backs him up with a show of teeth.

"Come here, Taylor! Come, boy!"

Taylor not only ignores Mitchell's command, but stubbornly resists all subsequent efforts to pull him away. As a result, Mitchell abandons any further attempt to gain control of his dog. "Have it your way, Taylor."

Too embarrassed to sustain the accusatory glare of the surfers, Mitchell turns towards Stacy. Perhaps she can… But she is already heading up the beach towards the parking area to meet the ambulance, whose siren now blares in the distance.

Taylor, drooling with conviction, returns to his duties. His tongue, though, is indiscriminate–licking both the face of the jogger and that of his devoted resuscitator. Much to the surprise of Mitchell and the surfers, Niccolò is not particularly bothered by this. In fact, he doesn't even bother to wipe the dog's saliva from his face or the jogger's. Instead, he continues to offer his patient the kiss of life, and grants the dog's tongue free reign….

And then something amazing happens. The jogger begins to stir. He has regained his pulse. Shortly, he opens his eyes. Blue iris meets green iris, and a silent exchange passes between them.

The ambulance arrives. Stacy points the way, and two paramedics hit the beach in great haste. But by the time they reach the patient with their equipment, Joel is sitting up, his arms wrapped around Niccolò's back, and his head resting on Niccolò's chest, face to face with the Savior.

"Thank you for coming," says Niccolò to the two paramedics, who are both relieved and somewhat perplexed.

Ten minutes later, the ambulance is gone. The three teenagers—still shaking their head in disbelief—head back up the beach to reclaim their surfboards. Stacy and Mitchell sit in the sand, holding hands, quietly going over what they have just witnessed. The beachcomber, examining with great satisfaction the jade turbo shell he has just fished out of the receding foam, glances amicably at Niccolò, who is pacing up and down the shoreline, Taylor at his side.

"There is a tug-of-war between the Lord and the Devil," explains Niccolò, looking down at his canine companion, whose head is turned upwards. "Just as there is a tug-of-war between man and beast. But one game is more serious than the other."

Taylor whimpers.

"That's right," says Niccolò. "I am a servant of God. I play on his side. But I have failed Him. I have failed the Church. And I have failed in my mission. Even so, God does not abandon me. I prayed with every ounce of faith in my soul that the Lord might reach down and save Joel's life, and He answered my prayer without the slightest hesitation."

Taylor's brown eyes reveal that he understands completely.

"I was once a great shepherd. But I have fallen on hard times. I have lost my sheep."

Niccolò turns about and begins walking in the other direction. He glances at the young couple sitting in the sand.

"Mitchell is a good man. Stacy is a good woman. And yet they turn their back on the Lord. They refuse to believe that a simple man can give the kiss of life to another. Perhaps they would think the Pope capable of such a feat, but they ignore who

I am, and would not believe me if I revealed myself to them. They would simply scoff, as do my best friends, who think they know me well."

Taylor slurps his tongue, and blinks his big brown eyes.

"But whether there is any hope for me, I can at least take great joy in knowing that today a man's life has been saved."

Taylor begins to pant.

"And yet…" Niccolò shakes his head. "And yet, I fear for his soul."

Niccolò comes to a halt, bends his knees, and assumes a crouching position. He looks into Taylor's eyes. "You believe I am the Pope, don't you?"

Taylor gives Niccolò a quick lick on the face. Niccolò, in turn, hugs the German shepherd and wipes a tear from his eye. "Then perhaps there is hope."

On that note, Taylor leaps away and rejoins Stacy and Mitchell, who welcome him with open arms.

Niccolò smiles, looks at the sun rising in the eastern sky, and turns back towards his point of departure, Lucy's Crossroad Accessories. It is some distance away. But he feels that a burden has been lifted, at least in part, from his shoulders. He has found consolation, and that lightens his step.

Behind him, he can hear Taylor's joyful bark.

12 THE POPE CELEBRATES EASTER

At some risk, Easter Sunday is celebrated at the home of Kimberly Young, and the public is invited to attend. The home, which is located in an established upper class neighborhood of L.A., is of typical American architecture, but exhibits a bit of Korean influence in the way it is dressed. For example, the window panes which frame the double entry have as their motif blue songbirds and green-leafed bamboo canes on a background of frosted yellow glass.

Inside, the house is quite spacious and luxuriously appointed. Although the furnishings are somewhat eclectic, the artwork is predominantly a mix of modern and traditional Korean. An étagère is loaded with Asian glass figurines. Next to an ashtray studded with gems is a large jade dragon. Bamboo canes and a variety of living indoor plants are arranged in porcelain vases. In short, the interior properly reflects Kimberly's taste for all that is expensive and flashy. It's all a bit overwhelming.

Today, the interior has been bastardized by colorful wicker baskets filled with beautifully painted eggs, pink and blue streamers hanging from the walls, and a giant egg that sits in one corner. The hollow egg consists of Mylar, printed with a colorful array of Easter themes, stretched over two halves of a balsa wood frame. The egg sits on an appropriately sized bamboo egg holder. Propped up against the wall behind it are bamboo canes that serve as carrying poles. This is, in fact, a type of gama intended to transport the egg and its human occupant to the garden in celebration of Easter.

Father Priestley and Sam carefully lift off the top of the egg for Brad and his mother to inspect. Inside the egg chamber is a round cushion, a plastic stepstool, and a long Mylar strip that will conceal the egg joint once the egg is occupied.

Kimberly's backyard is generous in size, and consists of a well maintained garden with two rock fountains. Pear, apple, peach, and cherry trees are all harmoniously arranged in rivers and islands of shrubbery, flowers, and grass. There is a "temple" in one corner that is probably nothing more than a storage shed for garden tools, and a very ornate stone lattice screen in another which hides the air conditioner and utility meters. To catch the wandering eye, Kimberly has incorporated into the garden a number of wind chimes and mobiles featuring traditional dragon designs. Located near the back of the garden is a broad wooden table, intricately carved with scenes representing food gathering. The pavestone patio on which it is situated favors diamonds and ovals over squares and meanders, as do the pavestone pathways that weave through the garden. In addition to the table's eight wooden chairs, seating is provided here and there by wooden benches and smoothly cupped boulders. In short, the garden is a miniature paradise.

Today, however, paradise has been invaded by church members and guests. The guests are predominantly Hispanic families who have responded to Charlotte's bilingual "Easter Egg Hunt" flyers, which have been taped to vans selling frozen desserts in Hispanic neighborhoods, and posted by various ocean front vendors on their stands and counters. Charlotte, Kimberly, Tiffani, and Rosita, who comprise the Easter Committee, congratulate themselves on such a good turnout.

The Pope Celebrates Easter 117

Everyone awaits the beginning of the festivities. Some children are playing with Ramon. Others sit by the fountains, dipping their hands or feet into the cool water. As a precaution, Kimberly has brought the goldfish inside the house. The seven Piñeda niños busily distribute bunny headbands to all of the adults gathered in the garden. Niccolò reluctantly dons a pair.

Most of the adults are socializing while they serve themselves at the buffet table. Tiffani has purchased an assortment of cobblers, pies, and cheesecakes for the occasion. Kimberly has provided the beef and chicken satays, the multi-colored eggrolls, and the fortune cookies, which have been poured into a large popcorn bowl. Charlotte has brought the plates, cups, and utensils, and keeps the punch bowl filled nearly to the brim. Rosita has brought the tortilla chips, red and green salsas, and a spicy bean dip. She has also brought some large coolers. Kimberly uses an "Easter wagon" (which actually belongs to Ramon) to bring bags of crushed ice from the house. Rosita prepares the coolers, which Charlotte then stuffs with soda cans, juice boxes, and bottles of flavored mineral water and green tea.

Wagon in tow, Kimberly winds her way through the crowd. One of the wagon's wheels bounces over a man's shoe.

"Sorry!" shouts Kimberly over her shoulder, without slowing down.

A little girl jumps in the wagon.

"Amelia! No!" shouts the man.

Kimberly turns around.

"Hello. I'm Joel Marzoff. And these are my three grandchildren, Ivan, Tonye, and…"

He points to the little girl in the wagon.

"Amelia."

"Second, first, and pre-K," says Ivan.

Joel picks up Amelia, and Kimberly, shaking her head, resumes her wagon pull, heading for the kitchen door.

Amelia grabs a small gift wrapped box in Joel's hand.

"Here, let me help you with that," says Joel, setting Amelia down on the ground. He gives the wagon a boost from behind, rolling it over the threshold.

"Thank you. I didn't catch your name," says Kimberly.

"Joel Marzoff."

Kimberly's hand rises to her mouth. She has just realized who this man is. "You're the man that Poppy saved on the beach, right?"

"That's right. My ex-wife wasn't too happy about that," he laughs. "But I don't jog anymore. I just walk."

Kimberly parks the wagon near the freezer. "What's this?" she asks, noticing the gift in Amelia's hands.

"Oh! That's a little something for the hostess." Joel crosses his arms.

"Kimberly Young," says Tonye, who has obviously practiced the name.

Kimberly corrects her grimace with a friendly smile. "Well, that would be me. And it's pronounced *yoong,*" she says, tapping Tonye affectionately on the nose. "It's a Korean name."

"Oh, I'm very sorry." Joel is embarrassed. He motions for Amelia to give Kimberly the package.

"Don't be sorry. I'm Korean," winks Kimberly as she accepts the package from Amelia.

"Open it!" insists Tonye, excitedly. "I picked it out myself!"

"No, you didn't!" scolds Ivan. "We all picked it out!"

Amelia shrugs.

"Well, I'm sure it's a wonderful gift." Kimberly plucks off the white bow.

"Do you know Tae Kwondo?" asks Ivan.

Kimberly rolls her eyes, but disguises her reaction by pretending she's looking for a pair of scissors.

"I'm taking lessons this summer!" Ivan is quite proud of himself.

"I'm sure you'll enjoy it," says Kimberly, who begins to tear at the wrapping. Inside the box she finds…

"An egg timer?" Kimberly is somewhat perplexed.

"Kids!" shrugs Joel, amused.

"You can set it for thirty minutes or whatever you want," says Tonye. "How long does an Easter egg hunt last, anyway?"

"As long as it takes," replies Kimberly. She gives all three children a cold hug.

Lucy and Niccolò enter the kitchen at this precise moment.

"Joel. We're so glad you came." Niccolò extends his hand to shake Joel's.

"Are these your grandchildren?" asks Lucy.

Outside in the garden, there is a commotion. Some people are gathering around the punch bowl, straining their eyes, and raising their voices.

"What's wrong with you people?" grumbles Barry, frustrated by the crowd's apparent blindness. "She's right there! In the middle of the bowl!"

Kimberly pops her head outside. Father Priestley is already heading for the kitchen door. Rosita is jumping up and down, waving her arms frantically for help. Jeffrey, Hershey, and Sam are trying to get to the punch bowl before it's too late, but it's a tight crowd. Some of the children have joined their parents, who hoist them upon their shoulders so that they, too, can see.

"Mommy, I can't see!" complains one little girl.

Her mother lifts her up. "Look in the punch bowl, Dulce! You have better eyes than I do. All I see is the reflection of a tree. Maybe *you* can see the Virgin Mary."

"Hail Mary!" shouts Barry, addressing the bowl.

Kimberly bulldozes her way through the gathering children, a wet kitchen towel in her hand. She is followed closely by Father Priestley.

Barry has already unzipped his fly. Now, he slips his hand into his pants, pulls down the elastic band of his boxer shorts, and grips a hot barrel of flesh.

Jeffrey, Hershey, and Sam begin sliding the bowl away from Barry, which isn't easy on a wood-carved table. Barry tries to follow, repeating one "Hail Mary!" after another.

"No, Barry! No! Put it away! Right now!" shouts Kimberly, jabbing onlookers with her elbows. Rosita meets Kimberly in the midst of the fray. She grabs the other end of the kitchen towel.

"You can't stop Jojo! Go, Jojo! Go!" shouts Barry, masturbating rapidly.

Kimberly and Rosita work together to wrap the kitchen towel around Barry's lower abdomen, and begin pushing him away from the table. Meanwhile, the punch bowl sloshes to a stop at the far end of the table, accidentally splattering several guests with fruit punch.

Kimberly and Rosita kick and shove Barry towards the temple, losing the towel in the process. Billy responds to their urgent call for assistance. He and Rosita restrain Barry while Kimberly opens the door, and then push Barry into the temple, where he falls onto a stack of bags filled with potting soil, and then crashes into some gardening tools. He jumps to his feet, and bangs his head on the underside of a shelf. A box of seed packets spills on his head.

"Jesus!" screams Barry.

Kimberly locks the door, and then turns around, wiping her forehead and exhaling a sign of relief. Not unexpectedly, the guests are in shock. All eyes are riveted upon her.

From inside the temple, there is a crescendo of grunts and groans, followed by heavy breathing and silence. And then a sweet voice pleads, "Let me out, please! In the name of God, please let me out!"

The guests turn to one another, mouths agape.

Kimberly clears her throat. "This is very embarrassing," she admits.

Father Priestley quickly intervenes.

"Barry absolutely adores the Virgin Mary," he explains. "He just has a funny way of showing it. Let us pray that he finds another way. Dear Lord–"

Some of the guests put on a hard frown. Others chuckle discreetly.

"Has anyone seen Chantelle?" asks a mother, interrupting Father Priestley's prayer.

"She's playing in the fountain with Uriel," says an older boy.

"Thank you, Trent." The mother steps out of the crowd. "Chantelle! We're leaving!"

The majority of the guests stay for the Easter egg hunt, which starts promptly. Barry continues to knock softly at the temple door, begging to be released from his prison. After a few reassuring exchanges, including an affirmation that he has zipped up his pants, Kimberly capitulates.

"Keep an eye on him, Rosita. I have to go to the bathroom." She dodges one egg seeker after another, enters the house, and slips past Niccolò and Lucy, who are chatting with Edgar.

"From now on," says Edgar, clutching his heart, "I'm sitting with you!"

Kimberly enters the bathroom. "Oh! Charlotte..."

The bathroom is unisex, and can accommodate up to three people. In fact, there are three semi-private toilets, three hand washing basins, and a communal shower. The toilet stalls are comprised of the back wall, two 36-inch walls atop which rise thin frosted glass panes similar to those at the entry, and a curtain of strung glass beads that must be parted to gain access to the toilet. The toilets are each a different color, but all of them have toilet seat covers featuring fire-breathing dragons. Charlotte heads for the Blue Toilet, which is furthest away from the bathroom door. She squeezes through the somewhat narrow opening, causing the beads, which are arranged in patterns of different shades of blue, to swing wildly. She plops down on the toilet with great fanfare. Kimberly quietly picks the Red Toilet, which is next to Charlotte's, if for no other reason than to engage her bathroom partner in small talk. The Green Toilet near the bathroom door remains unoccupied.

"If you need anything..."

Meanwhile, Joel has taken center stage among the adults in the garden. He is telling his audience in details that do not necessarily fit the facts how Niccolò saved his life, and how, after much soul searching, he has decided to devote his life to God. At the end of his story, Joel motions for Niccolò to join him. Niccolò leaves Lucy's side and steps into the circle, where he is welcomed with open arms and cheers.

"God is love!" declares Joel.

"Love Jesus," recommends Niccolò afterwards. "But fear the Lord."

The children continue hunting for chocolate Easter eggs, which are not hard to find due to the colorful foil in which they are wrapped. However, the eggs are becoming scarcer.

Ivan, Tonye, and Amelia return to their grandfather, who is now standing with Father Priestley, with their baskets.

"We can't find anymore," complains Tonye.

Father Priestley calls Sam, and whispers something in his ear.

Back in the bathroom, Charlotte and Kimberly are washing their hands. Kimberly has removed her rings, whose precious stones, as she is apt to remark, are as genuine as they are expensive.

"Eva?" shouts Sam, entering the bathroom cautiously, after casing the main areas of the house.

"She's not in here," replies Kimberly.

"She took *everything* to the bedroom." Charlotte tilts her head, her eyes full of insinuation.

"Which one?" asks Sam.

"Oh, that would be the first bedroom on the left.... And be sure to knock before you enter, Sam," advises Charlotte, reaching for a hand towel.

"She could be naked! I mean, *really* naked!" laughs Kimberly, inspecting the glitter on her fingernails.

Charlotte shrugs. "Who cares? I was thinking of *Adam*."

"Ah!" laughs Sam. "I didn't think there were any Adams left. She invited one to the party?"

"No, no. It's just another one of those random encounters. But, as you know, Eva's a far cry from the Virgin Mary. So you can imagine what they're up to in there," winks Charlotte.

"Just say hello. And don't look at 'em!" says Kimberly.

Sam and Charlotte give each other a funny look.

"At them," enunciates Kimberly, rolling her eyes.

"Kimberly, do me a favor," says Sam.

"Don't say another word," replies Kimberly with a slight puff of exasperation. Then, with her rings dancing in the corner of her eye, she adds, "I'll be right back."

As soon as Kimberly leaves the bathroom, Charlotte snatches up the rings and dumps them in her handbag. She turns to Sam and gives him a big "thumbs up."

"Well played, Sam!" she says, hurrying out of the bathroom.

"I'm tired of this game, Charlotte. I won't play it again!"

Kimberly knocks on the bedroom door. Eva opens it just a crack.

"It's Kimberly."

Eva swings the door open wide. "Come in, Kimberly. Look! I'm all ready to go!"

"What?" Kimberly searches the bedroom. Not a sign of Adam.

Eva smiles, and pulls her in.

Outside in the garden, children are anxiously awaiting the arrival of the Easter Bunny. Some of them have already begun eating their chocolate Easter eggs. Others have simply passed their small baskets to their parents, who are beginning to look at their watches. There is still plenty of food and drink, but the parents are primarily here for the entertainment.

Brad and Carlos are busy opening up boxes of chocolate Easter bunnies. They hand the packages of chocolate bunnies to Livy and Caitlan, who have spent the whole time chatting with Jessica, Daphne, and Marlene, but who now are in charge of the serving carts. Each of them is covered with a cloth sprouting green tinsels, simulating grass.

"Mother, you're just in the way!" scolds Brad, as he tries to hand some chocolate bunnies to Caitlan.

"You should respect your mother!" snaps Carlos.

Livy is trying to build a pyramid with her packages. Caitlan simply stacks hers.

"Father Schäftwaller," hails one of the parents. "I thought maybe you would be in the bunny outfit this year."

The Pope Celebrates Easter 125

Father Priestley looks at Joel, and adjusts his bunny ears. "The Easter Committee had someone else in mind."

"Here comes the Easter Bunny now!" shouts Edgar, pointing towards the open garden gate. Hershey and Billy, gripping the bamboo carrying poles, slip through the gate. They are transporting the giant Easter egg, which is nestled in its egg holder.

Kimberly exits the kitchen door and joins Father Priestley.

"Have you seen Charlotte? I think she took my rings!"

Father Priestley shakes his head no. He watches as the giant Easter egg is set down beside the carts. As soon as Hershey and Billy have removed the bamboo carrying poles, the children gather round.

"This year, we have quite a surprise for you!" announces Father Priestley.

Ramon runs to where Charlotte is hiding, behind the stone lattice screen. But before he can bark, Charlotte picks him up. "Shh!"

Kimberly is searching everywhere for Charlotte. Her face is turning red, and her mouth is dry. She stops at the punch bowl for a drink. Charlotte watches as she picks up a cup and ladle.

"Everyone, please welcome Livy and Caitlan. They're new to the congregation."

Livy and Caitlan bow.

"Are you ready?" they ask the children. The children respond with a collective, "Yeah!" They wave their hands excitedly.

Livy and Caitlan remove the Mylar strip that conceals the crack where the two egg halves meet.

"On the count of three, let's all say 'Easter Bunny!'" instructs Caitlan.

"Shout it out!" encourages Livy.

"One... Two... Three!"

The top of the Easter egg pops off, but unexpectedly flops over onto the serving carts, knocking most of the chocolate Easter bunnies to the ground.

At the same moment, Kimberly plunges her hand in the fruit punch.

"My rings!" she gasps in horror.

Eva, wearing nothing but a pink body suit, bunny ears, painted whiskers, and a cottontail, jumps up from inside the egg. The children have all rushed to the pile of chocolate bunnies on the ground, disputing the packages even though there are plenty to go around. Only the parents notice Eva, and they are stunned.

"This is obscene!" mutters one mother. Her husband pays her no mind.

Kimberly rushes into the house with her rings. She heads straight to the kitchen sink.

Ramon, who is normally a well-behaved dog, begins to wiggle uncontrollably in Charlotte's arms. Apparently, he is excited by the children, who have fallen into a dog pile as they continue to fight over the chocolate bunny packages.

Barry, who has been roaming around the garden, stumbles on an Easter egg that no one has found.

"Grenade!" he shouts.

He picks it up and throws it towards the garden gate. Instead, it strikes a man who is entering the garden. Barry hits the ground and covers his head.

Niccolò greets the stranger.

"I'm Andy DeLuca with the ACLU. We're here to shut down this operation!"

"This is private property!" replies Niccolò. "You can't do that!"

"No?"

He signals for his men. A half dozen of them join him.

"Step aside," says Andy. "We're going in."

As they approach the general mayhem over which Eva is presiding, Kimberly rushes out of the kitchen door.

"Charlotte! I'm going to kill you!"

Barry spots an Easter basket full of chocolate eggs. He dives for it, and begins to throw them at the ACLU, which he takes for the enemy.

Imagining that the grenades are exploding, but that more enemy troops are pouring into the garden, Barry grabs one of the bamboo carrying poles and charges….

An hour later, the garden is deserted, and the bunny ears have come off.

Niccolò has brought Kimberly and Charlotte back together. This isn't the first prank one of them has pulled. But Kimberly felt this one was a bit too harsh. Sam denies any involvement.

Kimberly wanders back to the table. She gives the punch bowl an accusatory look, then picks up a fortune cookie. She breaks it open, and squints to read her fortune.

"You have won the lotto." She serves herself a cup of punch.

Suddenly, it hits her. "Oh, my God! The Sunday Lotto!"

She rushes back into the house, finds the remote, and turns on the TV. She punches the numbers that call up the news channel. She begins reading the banner that streams across the bottom of the screen. And there it is: the winning lotto number!

Kimberly repeats the number to herself as she dashes to a golden Buddha sitting on a small round table, lifts it up, and snatches her lotto ticket. As she listens to herself repeat the winning lotto number, she sees that she could just as well have been reading it directly off the ticket.

"Oh! My god!" She kisses Buddha on the head, and runs to the kitchen, where Rosita is wiping the counters.

"I've won the lotto!" she screams, waving her ticket.

Father Priestley is in the garden chatting with Burt.

"I couldn't get a single news reporter on the phone," he tells Father Priestley. "So I went around to every news station and began knocking on doors. But I knew it was a waste of time."

Father Priestley is about to voice his relief when Kimberly barrels out of the house. She literally throws herself into his arms.

"Father…"

"Schäftwaller."

"Schäftwhatever! Look!' She thrusts the lotto ticket in his face. "I have the winning ticket!"

Father Priestley is dumbfounded, but fifteen minutes later he calmly addresses the congregation. Everyone has stayed behind to help clean up, and to attend a brief prayer service. They also expect a report from the Easter Committee.

Brad leans into the giant Easter egg and pulls out Eva's body suit. He looks around.

"Brad told me earlier today that his mother had a dream. Brad?"

"That's right, Father," replies Brad, tossing the body suit back into the egg. "Mother said she dreamed that we were all celebrating Easter Sunday in a magnificent church."

"Well, Brad, I apologize if I didn't give your mother the benefit of a doubt. Kimberly?"

"I have a major announcement to make," says Kimberly, her eyes sparkling. "Every week, I play the Sunday Lotto in an effort to raise money for the church." She holds up her ticket for all to see. "I have here in my hand the winning ticket!"

Everyone gasps in disbelief.

"I've never given up faith," assures Father Priestley.

"Father Schäftwaller and I have agreed to accept the winnings in a lump sum payment. And with this money, we will build a church. A real church! Our very own church! So, I'm sure you will all stand with me when I say, "Fuck the ACLU!"

Niccolò turns to Lucy, and groans, "I think I'm going to be sick."

13 THE POPE'S SLIPPERS

A personalized picture frame—upon which can be read, "Kimberly Young, AuD"—shuffles through photos of the Easter egg hunt. The photos were taken by Franklin using Crapp (camera remote app), an interactive program allowing him to operate a number of high definition digital cameras located throughout the garden for the occasion. One camera was mounted in a small drone that hovered above the party. With the app, Franklin, who milled around the garden totally absorbed in his assigned task, was able to see a live feed from any camera selected, and to manipulate its lens, zoom, and menu of optional features for the desired snapshot. The photos were downloaded to a folder on Kimberly's home computer, which can share the folder's contents with various home media, including picture frames.

Two home security cameras were also making their passive sweeps of the garden during the Easter egg hunt. Their software includes "smart" features that allow them to ignore familiar faces and predictable events, thereby eliminating false alarms. However, for something as "alert prone" as a party, the "smart" functions are totally disengaged, and the cameras simply record.

Kimberly is seated in front of her TV set, drinking a bottle of hybrid Korean-Irish beer, and viewing the same photos that appear on the picture frame, but in large format, when the

The Pope's Slippers 131

doorbell sounds a cascade of pleasant chimes. A second later, her security system communicates with her TV, which announces in a soft voice that Adriano Bonamici is at the door, while at the same time opening a window on its screen showing a close-up of the gentleman caller as captured by the video camera that has temporarily halted its sweep of the front of the house.

Kimberly wipes her mouth with the hand clutching her beer, sets the bottle down on the bamboo floor, walks to the entry, checks herself in the mirror, and opens the door, smiling.

"Adriano, please come in."

Adriano and Kimberly exchange a long kiss before closing the door. The security camera transmits the scene to the TV's open window, so that Adriano, looking over Kimberly's shoulder, can watch himself kissing her from the back.

"Won't you have a seat? I'm looking at photos from the Easter egg hunt this afternoon. But we have so much to catch up on.... I'll just turn it off."

"N'Ear Beer?" Adriano points to the beer bottle as they approach the sofa.

"Closer than you think. I print my own labels. It's actually McCafri Lite."

"Then I'll have a couple of those."

Kimberly makes a U-turn and heads for the kitchen. The TV continues to shuffle through the day's photos. But Adriano doesn't pay much attention to them. A few minutes later, Kimberly returns with three beers in a bucket of ice.

"I have all this left over ice," she explains.

The ice has been printed into various shapes, including Easter egg shapes that look like they're made of loosely wrapped crystal yarn, and "mummified" Easter bunnies in overlapping coils of ice-cloth. Some of the ice shapes have been crushed.

"Here we are. Two for you, and one more for me." She sets the bucket down on the floor, picks up the beer bottle that is two-thirds empty, finishes it off quickly, then fishes two cold bottles out of the bucket. She hands one of them to Adriano, pinches up her skirt a bit, sits down on the sofa, and cozies up next to her out-of-town lover.

"I thought you were coming to Chicago this year," says Adriano, twisting off the bottle cap.

Kimberly turns off the TV.

"I'm coming. But not until July. That's when TympoGear is having its open house. They're introducing the new Aurora model this year. That's why I'm going."

"Oh?"

They entwine their arms and take a drink out of each other's bottle. Kimberly giggles.

"So, you're in L.A. Your sister's wedding?"

Adriano takes a long drink. "My sister, yes."

"Does your sister have a name?" prods Kimberly. She has always noticed his reluctance to discuss his family.

"Chiara."

"Chiara Bonamici." Kimberly likes the sound of it.

"Not anymore," corrects Adriano between gulps.

"So who's the lucky man?" Kimberly wraps her arm around Adriano's neck, clutching her beer bottle, from which she attempts to take a drink. Instead, she kisses Adriano on the ear.

"I like it when you do that," admits Adriano.

"Just giving you a checkup, dear…. What did you say his name was? The man your sister married?"

"Luigi," sighs Adriano.

"So your sister is now Chiara Luigi," whispers Kimberly, who is now licking his ear.

Adriano tries to shake his head. But he's in a headlock. "Luigi is his first name."

"Of course it is," smiles Kimberly.

"Okay. I might as well tell you. Chiara married a man by the name of Luigi"–Adriano swallows, giving him a second to think–"Luigi Bologna…. He's fifteen years her senior. Luigi is a business man here in L.A. But he really hates this place." He drops his empty beer bottle to the floor.

Kimberly blows in Adriano's ear, then withdraws her affectionate embrace.

"Anyway, it doesn't matter much because Luigi owns a country villa somewhere between Torino and Milano, and that's where he plans to retire."

"You'll miss your sister when she moves to Italy," says Kimberly. She offers a second beer to Adriano.

"It's family, you know." He grips the twist-off cap, sets it aside, and raises the bottle to his lips appreciatively.

"Adriano. Listen. Your sister can marry it. I don't care. But if you're going to feed me *baloney*, there isn't much hope for us. If I'm going to be in your family someday, you need to open up a bit. Come on. Tell me about the wedding."

Adriano takes a long drink. He hesitates, taps his fingers on his knee, and sighs.

"Kimberly, I'm not really at liberty to discuss it. I've told you before. We're a very close-knit Italian family. And until you're a member of it, family matters must remain private."

"Cousin Gianni escaped from the loony bin, and he's got a gun. Is that it?"

Adriano laughs nervously.

"Well, at least I know your sister's name. Is that her *real* name?"

"Yes, that's her real name. Why don't you show me your photos?"

"I didn't take them," admits Kimberly. She activates the TV. "One of our church members, Lincoln Sausage, took them. Here." Kimberly gives Adriano the remote. "You can look at them while I refresh the beer." She takes the bucket and heads back to the kitchen.

While Kimberly empties the bucket of its water and replenishes the ice, Adriano begins to click through the photos. As he does so, he hesitates on a photo, as if recognizing a face. He dismisses the idea, and continues. But then the face reappears, this time at a better angle and closer up. He spots Kimberly returning out of the corner of his eye, and continues to click.

Kimberly and Adriano continue to look through the gallery of photos while drinking their beer. Kimberly makes a comment here and there, but does not identify anyone by name. Finally, Adriano can't resist the question that nags at him.

"Who is the man there with the 'Resurrection' t-shirt?"

Kimberly, believing herself to be clever, simply replies, "Oh! That's the Pope."

Adriano nearly gags on his beer. "The Pope? Here in L.A.?"

Kimberly gives Adriano a queer look. "What! You didn't know? Come on. You're Italian. And being Italian, you're probably a good Catholic, too, right? So how come you didn't know the Pope was here? But I guess you didn't. Otherwise, your family would've invited him to the wedding. Instead, he came to my Easter party. And, to be honest, dear, he was quite sexy in those bunny ears!"

Adriano shifts his position on the sofa. "He really is the Pope?"

Kimberly rolls her eyes. How can Adriano be so naïve?

"What name does he go by? Niccolò?"

"We call him, Poppy. Why?"

"Okay. Let's settle this. Luigi's real name is . . . Luigi da Vigoni. Now, what's the Pope's real name?"

"I just told you! It's Poppy!"

The next day, a man approaches Lucy after she has finished with a customer. His eyes are focused on the van's sign, "SOS Confessions."

"I'm Lucy. Can I help you?"

"It's nice to meet you, Lucy. My name is Adriano. I'm looking for someone named Poppy. A friend of mine said I could find him around here somewhere. And I was just noticing the van...."

"Well, you've found him. Poppy does confessions in there. Would you like to confess?"

"Do I need an appointment?"

"Poppy is taking a nap."

"It's urgent."

Lucy shrugs. "Okay. I'll wake him up. Just give me a second. Do you need a privacy screen?"

"No."

Lucy slides open the van's door, and leaves it open while she rouses Niccolò.

"He'll be just a few minutes," says Lucy upon exiting the van. She slides the door shut.

"Thank you. I'll buy one of these."

"Step in, please," begs Niccolò, a few minutes later, sliding the van's door open.

Adriano steps into the van. Niccolò motions for Adriano to take a seat.

Adriano immediately falls to his knees.

"Your Holiness!"

"Please. I don't care for sarcasm."

"Aren't you Niccolò di Montachiesa?"

Niccolò is stunned, but just for a second. "You almost had me fooled," he laughs. "Everyone knows the Pope's name."

"I'll tell you what I know," says Adriano. "I know you had more than just a 'business relationship' with the Calecchio family. Every year, Alec and Chani invited you to their daughter Sofia's birthday party. That was common knowledge. But they also invited you to meet Princess Amatoli. It was a very private soirée. The press never got wind of it. Alec saw to that. But I know all about what happened that night between the Pope and the Princess. Or, should I say, between Niccolò and Lavinia?"

Niccolò is clearly troubled. "Who have you been talking to? Signor Aponti?"

Adriano snorts dismissively. "No, no. This isn't hearsay. What I know comes straight from the horse's mouth. Lavinia married Luigi da Vigoni, and she told me everything after Luigi divorced her. It's funny, he just married my sister!"

Niccolò rubs the hairs on his chin. "Where is the Princess now?"

"Wherever she chooses to be, I guess. Definitely not in L.A., though. She'll never set foot in this city again. Luigi gave her the villa in Saint-Jean-Cap-Ferrat. But I don't think she's there right now. Spin the globe, and find a spot on the opposite side of the Earth from L.A. Most likely, that's where she is. I'll find out soon enough. Do you want her phone number?"

Niccolò shakes his head. "This wedding you speak of, was it here in L.A.?"

"It's Luigi's turf. He's the local *papa nostro*. He married my sister Chiara in a chapel on some property he has in one of the canyons. Later, we all gathered at his estate in the valley. I used to run errands for Barbi down here. That's how I know Luigi."

"And Lavinia," adds Niccolò.

"Yeah. One day, Luigi asked to see the family photos in my wallet. When he saw my sister's photograph, he invited her down to L.A. And that was the beginning of the end for Lavinia."

"Perhaps you have an interest in her," fishes Niccolò.

"Lavinia? No. I have an interest in someone else. Someone you know…."

Niccolò leans back. "Someone I know?"

"Kimberly Young."

The impact of this name on Niccolò is evident, especially because Adriano has correctly pronounced her name.

"Kimberly gave an Easter egg party yesterday. Why weren't you there?"

"I was at the Cappella della Madonna giving away my sister."

"What are your intentions exactly?" asks Niccolò. "And why are you here?"

"I want Kimberly's hand. But I know she won't have anything to do with me. Not if she learns I'm working for the Cosa Nostra."

"You're right," agrees Niccolò. "But why tell me?"

"Because you know who I am."

"I don't know for sure, but I suspect you are Adriano Bonamici."

Adriano nods. "I used to work for Alec Calecchio. Then I worked for Barbi Rizzo. But now I work for Antonio Donati. He owns auction houses in L.A., Chicago, Philadelphia, New York, and Miami. It's a different assignment. But it all boils down to the same company."

"Who was at the wedding?" asks Niccolò pointedly.

"Why does it matter?" shoots back Adriano.

"Do you want me to help you?"

Adriano drops his guard. "Well, uh, Barbi Rizzo and his wife Ascalia were there. So were Antonio and Vitolia Donati. Let's see. Who else? Alec and Chani Calecchio, of course. And their daughter Sofia. She's matured into a beautiful young woman. The bridesmaids were Carlotta Licci and Tea Barbiera. Most of the women were widows. Giorda Giacometti. Paola Canaoli. Most of the men were in the business. Like me. There was—"

"That's enough." Niccolò raises his hand. "I have one question for you. If you can answer this one question, I will help you. Who is Signor Aponti?"

"You're an old friend of Bruno Gratiano. Ask him."

"You don't know?"

Adriano heaves a sigh. "His real name is Carmelo Acampora. And he's marked."

"And do you believe his claim that the Vatican was behind the assassination of Elronde Hatheborne?"

"That's the word."

"Where is Carmelo?"

"I don't know. He's a ghost. Once we fingered him, he disappeared off the planet."

"Like me," says Niccolò.

"I won't say anything," assures Adriano.

"I don't care about that," admits Niccolò, much to Adriano's dismay. "Nobody here believes that I could possibly be the Pope."

"And that's the problem," says Adriano. "I need you to come with me to the auction house tomorrow. That's where I plan to make the announcement. You're the only person who can see me safely out of the Cosa Nostra."

"In case you haven't noticed, I've lost my papal cross," points out Niccolò. "And I have no more favors to cash in."

"They still respect you," assures Adriano. "But they have to see you. Otherwise, they will never believe that I have your blessing. Antonio is meeting with Alec and Barbi tomorrow. Luigi will be there, too. At least, that's what Chiara told me."

"It would not be a good idea for me to interrupt their meeting," cautions Niccolò.

"All you have to do is attend the auction. By the way, your slippers are on the auction block. Maybe you'd like them back?"

"My slippers? Are you sure of that?"

Adriano nods affirmatively.

Niccolò is taken aback. All he can find to say is, "Can you return them to me?"

"If you help me, yes. The slippers have to be auctioned off, mind you. We've already published the auction list, and they're on it. But you can bid on them while I'm making my pitch in the back room. If everything works out, Antonio will reimburse you."

"How will they know I'm not an impostor? Maybe they won't bother to verify?"

"Then I'll be a dead man. But I'm sure they'll check you out. I've always played it straight with them. And, anyway, even if they think I'm on coke or something, or that I've brought in the FBI, they will still want to make sure before they pull the trigger. So trust me. They'll check. In fact, I wouldn't be surprised if Alec doesn't step out onto the floor. He might even come sit with you. After all, you're *almost* family."

"I applaud your desire to quit the Mafia," says Niccolò. "But let me ask you something. Do you carry any burdens on your shoulder? Can you walk away free of guilt?"

Adriano looks down at his hands. "I've done things. God knows I've done things."

"Would you like to confess?"

Adriano nods.

"I'm listening."

The next day, a messenger comes to see Niccolò. "Adriano sent a car."

Niccolò turns to Lucy. "I'm closed for the day. I'll see you back at the apartment." Lucy formulates a question, but Niccolò dismisses it with a wave of the hand. He then follows the messenger to a black Nissan Altima, which is parked around the corner on Speedway.

Niccolò's eyes brighten. "My favorite car!"

"I know. Get in, please." The messenger opens the back door. Niccolò slips inside. The messenger walks briskly around the back of the car, opens the opposite door, and takes a seat beside Niccolò. "Drive," he says.

The driver doesn't say a word, but occasionally looks at Niccolò in his rearview mirror. Niccolò doesn't ask any questions. He peers out of the tinted window and watches as the car makes its way to South Venice Boulevard, where the driver makes a left turn....

An hour later, Niccolò is seated on the main floor of the auction house. It is located in a nondescript building behind a popular Italian restaurant called Pasta Donati. Niccolò waits patiently while the auctioneer introduces one item after another.

Finally, Adriano enters the building. He spots Niccolò, and sits down beside him. He looks at his watch.

"Antonio will send for me," he informs Niccolò. "When he does, I'll have your slippers put on the auction block. That's our man up there." Adriano glances at the auctioneer. "He knows you're here. He knows what you want. And he's waiting for the signal."

Before long, a young lady approaches them.

Adriano lowers his voice. "Tea Barbieri.... One of the bridesmaids at the wedding. She's an assistant to the auctioneer. She and I have dallied a bit. But nothing worthy of a confession."

Tea leans down and whispers something in Adriano's ear. Adriano nods, and Tea departs.

The Pope's Slippers

"Wish me luck," he says. As Adriano heads towards a side door, he flashes a signal to the auctioneer, who very discreetly acknowledges it.

After the current item is removed from the auction block, a male assistant brings out a large four-legged box decorated in golden arabesque. The box is set upon a table, tilted back a bit, and its lid opened. Inside, nestled in red velvet, are two slippers.

"And now we have the slippers of Pope Ignatius I. This is all that we have left of the papal accoutrements. Inside the lid of the box is a sleeve in which we have slipped the certificate of authenticity."

The male assistant opens the lid a bit further, and indicates the sleeve with his finger.

"These slippers are handmade. The vamp is composed of red satin, red silk, and gold thread. It is decorated in gold braid, and features an embroidered gold cross decorated with rubies. The soles are made of the finest Moroccan leather. We are opening the bid at five thousand dollars."

"Plus tax!" thinks Niccolò aloud, imitating Kimberly's accent. A few heads turn his way. He shrinks in his seat, quiets himself, and waits patiently while a handful of bidders enthusiastically pit their wallets against each other.

Tea reappears and sits down beside Niccolò. "Are you bidding?" She rests a hand on Niccolò's knee.

"I'm waiting to see where it goes. Do you know who is bidding?"

"I know the name and background of every bidder in the house."

"And who am I?" He wiggles his knee, but Tea's hand just rides it.

"You're the Pope."

"Does that surprise you?"

"Should it?"

Niccolò shrugs. "Who is the man over there? The one who just bid eight thousand five?"

"That's Ulrich Cholubski. He's with the Church of Scientology. He's in a bidding war with the man in the blue suit. That's Edward Dunham. He's from the LDS Church. Both are well funded. Adriano said not to worry about placing a bid. The sky's the limit."

"That is very generous. But I am going to impose a limit on myself. I know what these slippers are worth."

"It's hard to put a price on sentimental value," says Tea.

"I never wore the slippers," replies Niccolò. "And even if I had, I would not bid one dollar more than the cost of their manufacture. The slippers are rightfully mine. But I know how much the Vatican paid for them. And that price will be my final bid."

The bidding war continues. Niccolò enters the fray at eleven thousand dollars, but eventually drops out.

"Sold for fifteen thousand dollars to the gentleman in the white suit."

A dispute arises. Edward Dunham hails the auctioneer, and claims that his last gesture was overlooked. Ulrich Cholubski challenges his Mormon adversary, and the auctioneer dismisses the complaint. As a result, Dunham storms out of the auction house.

"Bye, Edward!" shouts Cholubski, the Scientologist.

The auctioneer motions for his assistant to whisk the box away to the claims desk. As the next item is placed on the auction block, Tea pats Niccolò on the knee, and then departs. A half an hour later, Adriano returns.

"You let them go?" questions Adriano, referring to the papal slippers.

"Sometimes, you have to let go," replies Niccolò. "Material things most of all."

"And the past?" asks Adriano.

"We cannot abandon the past," admits Niccolò.

"Well, I'm trying to! Here…." Adriano hands Niccolò a card. It is a Pasta Donati card which can be punched for a free pizza on the tenth visit.

Niccolò turns the card over, and reads a handwritten note on the back of the card. "What is the name of Sofia's bird of paradise?"

"You have to answer the question," urges Adriano. "I hope you have a good memory."

Niccolò smiles. "I know the answer. May I borrow your pen?"

Adriano lends Niccolò a gold-plated pen. On the back of the card, beneath the question, he writes "Ciendra," and hands it back to Adriano, who once again heads to the side door.

Meanwhile, Niccolò glances at the claims desk, where Ulrich Cholubski is signing a payment voucher. Niccolò decides to pay Ulrich a visit.

"Ulrich Cholubski?"

"Do I know you?"

"No. But your slippers do. I'm the Pope."

"Look, mister. I don't know who you are. But you're not the Pope. You're the third bidder. And you lost. So, I'm sorry. But the slippers are mine."

"Look me in the eye. I am the Pope."

Ulrich, who is waiting for the slippers to be handed to him, gives Niccolò a moment of thoughtful scrutiny. "You do resemble the Pope, sort of."

The claims desk manager hands Ulrich the red box. Ulrich opens the box, verifies that the slippers are inside, brushes

Niccolò aside, and begins to walk towards the exit. A bodyguard is waiting for him at the door.

"May I ask you a question?"

"Just one," replies Ulrich.

"Why do you want the slippers?"

"Are you kidding? To the victor belong the spoils."

"But the Church of Scientology had nothing to do with the fall of the Catholic Church."

"I'm speaking in behalf of all churches. Now, if you'll excuse me."

Ulrich is joined by his bodyguard as he reaches the exit. The bodyguard opens the door, and Ulrich steps outside, where a limousine awaits.

"I never wore them," says Niccolò. "It's a hollow victory."

"Look, Cinderella. You want the slippers? You can't have them! And I'm warning you. If you take one more step, I'll have Malcolm here squash you like a pumpkin!"

Niccolò watches as the bodyguard helps Ulrich into the limousine, which speeds away with its prize. The door closes, and Niccolò turns around. Adriano is fast approaching. He is grinning broadly.

"The boss wants to see you," he announces.

"About the slippers?"

Adriano dismisses that with a wave of the hand. "He just wants to meet you. In the pizzeria. In about fifteen minutes. It will be just the three of us. Alec and Barbi are escorting Luigi back home. They plan to give him a royal send-off. Chiara is packed and ready to leave on a midnight flight. It's their honeymoon. Alec said he would look you up in a few weeks. I think he wants to rescue you. But first, he has some urgent business to attend to. Phoenix. Naples."

"Are you out?" asks Niccolò, after a moment of contemplating the consequences of a so-called rescue.

"I'm out. And I owe you a great debt. But I have another favor to ask."

"You would like for me to preside over the marriage?"

"And pray at my funeral. You know, in case Alec changes his mind."

Antonio Donati welcomes Niccolò to the Pasta Donati.

"Your Holiness," says Antonio, with deference. "Please have a seat." He snaps his fingers, and a server brings over a bottle of wine. Antonio fills the three glasses half way.

"This is California wine," observes Niccolò.

"When in Rome," replies Antonio.

"I regret not having an opportunity to see Alec," sighs Niccolò.

"Alec appreciates your dethroning Maldiavos," says Antonio. "He will always be a faithful friend and ally. He sends his best regards."

"I appreciate that." Niccolò plays with the wine glass. "What about Adriano here?"

"Adriano works for me. And I had the final word on this matter. He is free to pursue a life outside the family. I think Luigi is happy with this decision because it will frustrate Lavinia, who favors him. She won't be allowed to see him again."

"And will Adriano be able to stay in touch with his sister?"

"Absolutely. Luigi insisted on that. But on his terms, of course."

Niccolò turns to Adriano.

"That's fine by me," he nods.

Antonio raises his glass. Niccolò and Adriano follow his lead.

"To Rome," states Antonio emphatically.
"To Ravenna," proposes Adriano.
"To Venice," counters Niccolò with a wink.

14 THE POPE LOOKS TO THE STARS

    The date of the annual pilgrimage to the Mojave Desert arrives. Lucy and Niccolò stop at the church to pick up two passengers: Sam, the homeless storyteller, and Eva, the nude bimbo. Neither of them have a car. Sam can't afford one. As for Eva, she rarely does any kind of traveling that requires an automobile. But when the need does arise (as with the annual pilgrimage to the desert), she counts on God to provide. In this case, God has provided Lucy's van. Eva's life is at the beach, where partial nudity is pretty much the norm, "almost there" nudity is popular among the younger generation, and full nudity is a thrilling–but not all that terribly uncommon–occurrence that shocks only those tourists with children in tow. Eva lives in a small apartment a couple of streets from the beach, and she usually rides her bicycle there wearing nothing but her thong and a fishnet handbag, both of which usually end up dangling from the handlebars at the bike stand. Sun block in hand, Eva roams the beach looking for the perfect spot in the sand. Needless to say, she has no interest in shopping the oceanfront boutiques. She is shopping for Adam….

    Eva always wears a thong in the company of fellow church members. This morning, she wears a black thong featuring the iconic green alien head with big black eyes. She has left her boa at home, and instead has sprinkled her ample breasts with clear glitter, though she has added a pinch of green sparkles around the nipples... Eva hopes to meet an alien tonight. Perhaps an alien named Adam. After all, tonight their eyes will turn to the stars!

As the van leaves the outskirts of L.A., Niccolò, whose green eyes captivate Eva, turns his attention to Sam. "So, where exactly are we going?"

Eva intervenes. "Have you ever been to Landers?"

"Landers?" Niccolò shrugs.

"The Giant Rock! That's where George Van Tassel–"

"Eva!" interrupts Sam. "We're not going to Landers."

Eva dismisses the remark as she leans closer to Niccolò so she can look deeper into his green eyes. Niccolò avoids her interrogating stare.

"Were you born with green eyes?"

Niccolò realizes that only a simple answer will do. "Yes."

"Aliens have black eyes. But they have green bodies. And they are *totally* naked."

"Well, that is the popular conception," agrees Niccolò.

"Our destination is a place called Oja," says Lucy, glancing over her shoulder. "It's not on the map. But there's a hot spring there. That's where Carly was taken."

"It isn't anywhere near Landers," adds Sam.

"It's *somewhere* in the Mojave Desert," explains Eva. She squints, as if trying to figure out exactly where.

Niccolò nods. "Carly is Jeffrey's sister?"

"Uh-huh," confirms Sam.

"Did you know that God is an alien?" asks Eva.

"Don't let Jeffrey jerk you around, Eva." Sam redirects his attention to Niccolò. "All we know is that Carly will be returned to us on the anniversary of her abduction."

"And she'll be naked," adds Eva.

Niccolò frowns. Eva is really beginning to annoy him.

Eva notices this, and turns to Sam for support.

"That's right, Eva." Sam turns to Niccolò. "She's right about that, Poppy. You see, Carly was bathing in the hot spring when the aliens came down and nabbed her. So, it's very likely she will reappear in the spring. Bathing. As if nothing ever happened. Jeffrey has a fresh change of clothes for her."

Eva shakes her head, and rolls her eyes. She silently mouths, "Clothes!"

"And what was she doing out here in the first place?" asks Niccolò.

"Camping. Hiking. Exploring."

"Alone?"

"No. With her brother, Jeffrey."

"And Jeffrey witnessed the abduction?"

"Not the abduction *per se*. Carly was having a late night soak in Oja, and Jeffrey was fast asleep in his bag. The incident happened just after midnight. The desert suddenly lit up. Jeffrey opened his eyes and turned around towards his sister's sleeping bag. He was immediately blinded by a beam of light coming from a black disc hidden among the stars. The beam of light tore through the darkness and shone directly on the spring just a short distance away. Jeffrey heard his sister scream, 'Oh, my God!' and ran to the spring."

"You see? God *is* an alien!" Eva makes a sweeping gesture of triumph.

Sam chooses to ignore it. "By that time, Carly had vanished! Transported by the beam of light directly to the alien spacecraft. Once the beam was extinguished, Jeffrey could make out the spacecraft's chromatic light array."

"And what makes Jeffrey think the aliens will return his sister to the same spot. On the anniversary of her abduction?"

"Alien telepathy. They told him before they left."

Eva is tapping her head.

"This is our sixth pilgrimage," adds Lucy. "Jeffrey is very optimistic about this one."

The van is a few decades old, and therefore does not have auto-drive, so Lucy has to keep her eye on the road and her hands on the wheel.

After a drive of several hours, some of which is on rough desert roads, the van arrives at the rendezvous point. It is late afternoon. A few other cars and motorcycles have already shown up; other pilgrims will come later. To reach the hot spring, they must hike a vague desert trail up a narrow canyon, following the occasional cairn. Thanks to the cairns, they can largely avoid the boulders and rock shelves that would otherwise involve rock scrambling.

By sunset, everyone has arrived at Oja. Some church members had to take off early from their job in order to make the pilgrimage. The group holds communion around a campfire, which is confined by a ring of rocks. Sleeping bags and blankets are scattered about. The hot spring is only a few steps away, around some rocks, and at the base of an abrupt rock formation.

Jeffrey has taken the clothes out of a small suitcase and placed them in a neat pile on a rock next to the spring.

At eleven o'clock, the stars are shining bright. Jeffrey stands up, his shadow dancing in the desert, and scans the skies for the first sign of an approaching alien spacecraft. "Come back, Carly!" he says under his breath. "Come back tonight!" The group echoes his words softly.

"Someone tell Eva she has to get out now. Story time in 15 minutes."

Charlotte walks to the spring, accompanied by her dog, Ramon. "Jeffrey says you have to get out now. There's not enough room in that spring for the two of you." Before she can continue, or Eva can answer, she shouts, "Ramon!"

The Pope Looks to the Stars

Ramon has just fetched Eva's thong, which was lying on the same rock as Carly's clothes. Charlotte grabs the thong strap, but, of course, Ramon decides to engage in a tug-of-war. This results in a considerable amount of shouting.

Kimberly shows up. "What's going on?"

Back at the campfire, Burt is praising Franklin for his excellent weather forecast.

"When I was a boy, I wanted to change my last name to Merriweather," admits Franklin.

"As in Virgin Mary Weather," laughs Barry.

"Steinkamp would have been more appropriate," chimes in Edgar, noting that Franklin always drinks his beer out of a frosted glass mug.

Litzy, an attractive Hispanic teenager who is obviously pregnant, waves her hand. "And so, Franklin, what is your last name exactly?"

"Yeah, Franklin. Tell her!" teases Barry.

Franklin takes a drink, and wipes the beer off his lips with the back of his hand. "My last name is Woolsey. My father, who had a wicked sense of humor, wanted to name me Lynn C. Woolsey. But my mother was Jewish, and she said the kids would call me "The Shatnez" for short, and that I would spend my childhood under the weather. Since I reminded her a bit of Benjamin Franklin, she proposed a compromise, and my father accepted. For obvious reasons, I never use my middle initial."

Litzy shrugs. She doesn't get it.

"Linsey-woolsey is a sturdy fabric made of wool and linen. Wearing it is strictly prohibited by the Torah," explains "Father Grimwold," who is a self-proclaimed expert on names.

Back at the hot spring, Eva is still holding her ground, so to speak.

"Eva, it's time to get out!" insists Charlotte, who now has Eva's thong in hand. Ramon is dipping his paws in the water.

"Why don't you jump in and pull her out?" jokes Kimberly.

Eva is defiant. "I am *not* coming out." She sends a splash of water in Charlotte's direction. "Maybe the aliens want to trade!"

For a moment, Charlotte and Kimberly consider the advantage of a trade.

"Hey, I'm all for the trade," admits Charlotte.

Kimberly adds, "I'll even give them three hundred dollars! Make a fair deal!"

Back at the campfire, Niccolò has just had a word with Litzy, who is rubbing her tummy with a smile on her face. Niccolò returns to Lucy's side.

"I would like to name my baby tonight," announces Litzy. "My last name is Muñoz-Cruz. Does anyone have a suggestion? Poppy suggested Rafaela."

"I have two," says Brad. "Mother says to call her Alma. But that's a pretty common name. Maybe you'd like something a little more exotic, like Zeyla."

Litzy looks around at the other church members.

"What about Yesenia?" suggests Tiffani.

"Or Sunny?" offers Franklin.

There is a long moment of disbelief before Edgar speaks in behalf of the group. "The verdict is in.... We think not!"

"How about Carlita?" suggests Jeffrey. "You know, after my sister."

"No way," says Barry. "You should call her María."

Edgar raises his hand. "I like Ramona."

"Woof! Woof!" barks Lucy mockingly.

"So? Lucy?" Edgar is wide-eyed, clearly wounded.

"I don't know.... Astrid, maybe."

"Father?" asks Litzy.

"Why not Yolanda?" shrugs Father Priestley.

Charlotte, Kimberly, and Eva rejoin the church group. Eva is wearing her thong, which looks a bit chewed upon. Charlotte has a smug look on her face. Kimberly is dripping wet.

"We're suggesting baby girl names. Would you like to join in?" asks Lucy.

Eva plops down near Sam. Charlotte sits next to Edgar, who giggles when her dog Ramon crawls into her expansive lap. Kimberly sits next to Litzy. She holds up her finger, flashes her ring, and says, "Five thousand dollars! Plus tax!"

"You're all wet," cracks Franklin. Several people burst into laughter.

Kimberly snaps back, "Charlotte pushed me in!"

Edgar winks at Charlotte approvingly.

"What about a *name*?" insists Franklin.

"Hmm…. Esmeralda!" says Kimberly, looking at the emerald ring.

"Not bad," admits Franklin.

"You've got to be kidding," grumbles Edgar.

"Just name her Eva!" proposes Eva.

Charlotte shakes her head. "That's your name!"

"So?" protests Eva. There is *another* long, silent moment of disbelief.

This time, it's Niccolò who breaks the silence. "We haven't heard from our resident soothsayer. Which name will it be, Burt?"

Burt ponders for a moment. "The name that is on the tip of Sam's tongue."

Everyone turns their attention to the resident storyteller. "Sam?"

To this chorus of voices, Sam replies, "I don't know. I can't get it off my tongue." Sam clears his throat. "But since we're on the subject of names, and since Litzy is new to the group—¡Bienvenida!—let me enlighten her as to the significance of names. My father and Franklin's father were apparently birds of a feather. They both had a sense of humor. My father named me Sam X. Rayburn. I used to hate it when the dentist flashed a bitewing in my face and jokingly said he would file it under 'X-ray burn.' But the truth is, I've always liked my name because if you spell Sam X. backwards, you get Xmas. I was not born on Christmas Day, but I am in charge of the Christmas program. My favorite story will always be the Christmas Story."

"The Star of Bethlehem," says Burt, pondering the sky.

"The Three Wise Men," adds Tiffani.

"Joseph and *Mary*," sighs Barry.

"Oh, Christ!" complains Edgar.

Niccolò makes a sign of the cross.

Father Priestley frowns.

"Oh! Sorry, Padre!" Edgar grips his heart again.

"Not here, Edgar," insists Father Priestley, who turns to the group after checking the time. "Speaking of stories, we only have about twenty minutes before we prepare for the midnight ritual. Sam?"

Niccolò turns to Lucy, who explains, "First we get in a circular formation. Then Father Grimwold passes out the green light sticks. After a brief prayer, we all break the light sticks on cue. Finally, we begin walking around in a circle. It creates a welcome home vortex. And we sing."

Sam claps his hand. "Well, then. I'd better get to it. Tonight's story is called *The Cuckoo Clock*."

There is a general murmur of curiosity among the church members.

"I can see where you're going with that," gloats Burt.

"Veronica!" shouts Sam. "That's...the *name*...on the tip of my tongue."

Litzy smiles. "I love it!"

Burt sits back, arms folded. Nobody is particularly surprised, but everyone is disappointed their own name suggestion was not chosen.

"Congratulations, Burt!" Niccolò's voice does not ring sincere, perhaps because he feels that his own suggestion, Rafaela, was truly inspired.

"Veronica," repeats Sam quietly, proud of himself. He proceeds with his story.

There was once a man named Greg. He was not a Christian, but, to be honest, he was a pretty good man. He was already getting up there in years, and began to turn his thoughts towards death. As a nonbeliever, he didn't believe in heaven or hell, but neither did he savor the atheistic prospect of eternal nothingness. One day, to cheer himself up, he went to the circus to relive some of his fond memories of youth. While at the circus, he met two lively performers, Clarence the Clumsy Clown and Cathy Cupcake. Clarence wore a wacky wig and tangerine trousers. Cathy wore granny glasses and pedal pushers. Greg applauded their mission at the circus, but added all the humor in the world didn't detract from the sobering realization that death awaits us all. Clarence and Cathy gave each other a wink.

"Cathy once learned how to make a very special cupcake, Greg. If you dip it in malted milk, you will be transported to Cloud-Cuckoo-Land where you will be given twelve chances to be granted immortality. We are still young, and so we haven't made the journey ourselves. The fact is, if you fail in your quest, you will die prematurely. But you are getting old already, so perhaps you are willing to take that chance."

Greg laughed. Cloud-Cuckoo-Land? Really? But he nodded. "Make the cupcake!"

"You have to pass a test first," said Cathy. "A sort of open sesame."

Greg shrugged. "Okay."

"You have to alliterate. In twelve seconds, name a towering tree."

Greg began to think.

"Five, four, three..." counted Clarence, his eyes on his wristwatch.

"I don't know," grumbled Greg.

"One second left. Goodbye!"

But then Greg's face lit up. "Ponderosa Pine!"

"Very good!" complimented Cathy.

"Now, here's what you need to know," said Clarence. "In Cloud-Cuckoo-Land, you will find a dark forest, but tiny shafts of light will allow you to find your way. You won't be able to see the treetops. They are lost in the clouds. One of the trees is for you. You will know which one it is. And on that tree is hung a cuckoo clock. Like any clock, it has the numbers one to twelve, and two hands that keep time. The key to immortality is an alliteration. The cuckoo will give you twelve chances to find the right one. There are no clues. If you find the right alliteration, the cuckoo will close its door forever, and you will return immortal. If you don't, the cuckoo will make its thirteenth appearance, the so-called Cuckoo-de-Grâce, but he will give his voice to another bird. And that bird will announce your fate. Salvation or damnation. You'll understand when the time comes."

"What are my chances of success?" asked Greg.

"That's what the test was all about. Your chances are quite good," reassures Cathy. "But there is something you must know about the journey. Cloud-Cuckoo-Land is an island surrounded by two rings. The outermost region, and the first one you will cross, is called Leaping-Lizard-Land. The Leaping Lizards will devour you if given the slightest opportunity."

"How do I avoid them?" asked Greg.

"You can't avoid them. You must frighten them. Can you do jumping jacks?"

Greg shook his head.

"You know, like this." Clarence performed a few jumping jacks, but being the clumsy clown, he accidentally stepped on Cathy's foot, and slapped her cheek. Cathy reacted by leaping aside and covering her face.

"Okay, he's got it!" shouted Cathy.

"If you're good at jumping jacks, the Leaping Lizards will leave you alone," assured Clarence.

"Might as well be Lounge Lizards," joked Cathy, returning clown-side. "Once you get past them, you'll have one more region to cross. Zippy-Zombie-Land."

"Zippy?" Greg was incredulous.

"Oh, yes. They're quite fast. And they're out for blood. Your blood! But don't worry."

"Jumping jacks?"

"Are you kidding? You have to fight them!" laughed Clarence.

"Can you do kangaroo kicks?" asked Cathy.

Greg shook his head.

"Here, let me show you." Cathy performed a cascade of kangaroo kicks, each one targeting Clarence, as if they were payback for the jumping jacks.

"Okay, he's got it!" shouted Clarence.

"If you're good at kangaroo kicks, the Zippy Zombies will be defeated," assured Cathy.

"Might as well be Zombie Zits," joked Clarence, inching a bit closer to the cupcake maker.

"One last thing," added Cathy. "When addressing the cuckoo, you must say, 'Good Gracious!' Because the cuckoo's name isn't Tick-Tock. It's Gracious."

"So, Greg, is it still a go?"

An hour later, Greg was given a cupcake and a glass of malted milk. He dipped the cupcake into the glass, and immediately was transported to a waterless wasteland beneath a blinding blue sky. Beyond the desert, he could glimpse the wispy wetlands. And beyond that, rising high into the clouds, was the wooded wilderness.

"Leaping lizards!" Greg was surrounded by them. And they leapt. Right at him. Greg was so jarred by the size of them, he *almost* forgot to do his jumping jacks. But he did them. And it worked. He jumping jacked all the way to Zippy-Zombie-Land. When he got there, he first tested his footing. The *terra* was more *molla* than *firma*, but it was passable, and so he forged on. Of course, the zoned-out zombies caught wind of him, and before long they waded out of the malodorous marsh, shook their fetid feet, and rushed towards Greg, but in a zigzagging fashion.

"Zounds!" cried Greg. "The Zippy Zombies!" Greg didn't have time to think. He immediately put his kangaroo kicks to the test. And he kangaroo kicked himself all the way to Cloud-Cuckoo-Land. He had to cross an arm of the malodorous marsh on stepping stones. He proceeded on a narrow path that led straight into the foreboding forest towards a distant tick-tock. As he approached the tree, he heard the rustling of feathers.

And then he saw the cuckoo clock–an old-fashioned, weight-driven cuckoo clock with a small trap door and pine cone weights. The clock was nailed to a tall tree that smelled strongly of butterscotch. Yes, it was a ponderosa pine!

The clock's hands were white crosses, slowly creeping from one cardinal number to the next. The weights hung from thin chains whose links were hidden within a black coil.

"Good day, Greg!"

On a pine branch perched the raven that had spoken. There was a whole raft of ravens. All of them were perched on the same side of the tree. On the other side of the tree perched a dove. One lonesome dove.

"My name is Mortimer. Over there? That's Vivian. Pretty little powder puff, isn't she? But she rarely speaks. Ready for the guessing game? Remember, if you lose, Gracious goes all tongue-tied on the thirteenth hour. In that case, we croak. And you croak, too."

"Okay. That's damnation. What about salvation?" Greg pointed to the dove.

Mortimer ruffled his feathers. "Gracious is still hush-hush. But Vivian coos. And that's kudos to you, kid!"

"But if I lose, how do you decide which one of you voices my fate?"

"We don't make that decision, dimwit! Gracious does—with a *glance* or a *glare*. A glance? Vivian coos, and you're good! A glare? We all croak, and your goose is cooked!"

"Okay, that's if I lose. But if I win? I'll be rewarded with immortality, right?"

"Good guess! Now, I have to ask you a qualifying question. What was the name of the cuckoo clock in the Garden of Eden?"

"It wasn't a cuckoo clock. It was a clepsydra."

"Clever!"

"So can I play?"

"Please do. But first, are you familiar with alliterations?"

"A little bit. I'm sure I can come up with a few."

"Well, alright. But remember. Only one is correct. You are probably doomed to drop dead." The other ravens fanned their feathers. "But if you were a living legend, you wouldn't be here. So…"

"Let's get on with it, Mortimer!"

"Your first try."

Inspired by the Garden of Eden reference, which may have been a clue, Greg cleared his throat. "Adam's Apple!"

The clock's chains made a clankety-clank, the little trap door flipped open, and Gracious, the cuckoo, popped out. "Cuc-koo!" Gregg, who hadn't really noticed the time, now saw that the hour hand pointed directly to the number 1.

"Good Gracious!" cried Greg, but it was too late. Gracious had already disappeared.

"Do you need me to walk you through it?" asked Mortimer.

"No."

"Then try again."

"Bible Belt!"

"Cuc-koo! Cuc-koo!"

"Christmas Card!"

"Cuc-koo! Cuc-koo! Cuc-koo!"

"Easter Egg!"

"Cuc-koo! Cuc-koo! Cuc-koo!" And one more.

"That wasn't exactly an alliteration, Greg. Keep going!"

"Passion Play!"

"Cuc-koo! Cuc-koo! Cuc-koo!" And two more.

"Song of Solomon!"

"Cuc-koo! Cuc-koo! Cuc-koo!" And three more.

"Lord of the Lyre!"

"Cuc-koo! Cuc-koo! Cuc-koo!" And four more.

"You're wasting time, Greg."

Greg began to stress out. "Dust Devil?"

"Cuc-koo! Cuc-koo! Cuc-koo!" And five more.

"Water Witch?"

"Cuc-koo! Cuc-koo! Cuc-koo!" And six more.

"You must be crazy," croaked the raven.

"Well, I'm not overly optimistic. But I'm not a penny pessimist either."

"In other words, you don't expect much whipped cream on your pumpkin pie, correct?"

Greg didn't answer.

"Please continue!"

Greg considered the word 'crazy.' Perhaps it was a hint? "Funny Farm!"

"Cuc-koo! Cuc-koo! Cuc-koo!" And seven more.

But while the bird cuckooed, Greg implored: "Good Gracious! Good Gracious! Give me a clue, won't you?"

But Gracious had already found refuge behind the trap door. Greg's heart was beating a bit faster now. He was beginning to fear the dictum of Fate.

"Come on, you lily-livered lunatic." nagged Mortimer insultingly.

"I don't know any more! Let me see. ... Frolicking fruitcake?"

"Cuc-koo! Cuc-koo! Cuc-koo!" And eight more.

"That was bad, Greg. Dumb and desperate! Come on, yo-yo! One last try!"

"I can't think anymore! I feel like Simple Simon!"

"Cuc-koo! Cuc-koo! Cuc-koo!" And nine more.

Greg's jaws dropped. "That wasn't my guess!"

"Yes, it was."

"No, no! It wasn't!"

"Well, what was it then?"

"Bird Brain!"

"Good grief!" sighed Mortimer.

The trap door opened. Out popped Gracious. But Gracious did not cuc-koo. Instead, she glared at Greg. And right on cue, Mortimer and his choir of rapturous ravens all croaked!

But then a soft voice spoke. It was Vivian. "Good Gracious, Greg! The answer was right there on the cuckoo clock.... Number nine!"

Greg went mad. In the horror of the moment, he began to pull his hair out by the roots.

"Spare us the temper tantrum. You can't escape my fine-feathered friends!"

And with that, the ravens all descended upon Greg. The last thing he saw was Vivian, disappearing into a shaft of light.

"Dead as a doornail," announced Clarence the Clumsy Clown.

"I'll get the body bag," replied Cathy Cupcake.

Sam concludes his story. "And so, you see. It's absolutely crazy to seek immortality. I therefore recommend that you get your head out of the clouds. Life is short. Live it while you can. And let God determine your final hour. He will reward you with everlasting life in heaven." Eva gives Sam a big hug. A really big hug!

It is midnight now, and all eyes turn to Father Priestley. He stands up and begins passing out the green light sticks.

"Father who art in heaven..." begins the priest. After the prayer, the church members stand up, form a circle, break their light sticks, and begin walking around the campfire, singing "My Carly flies over the desert . . . So bring back my Carly to me" rather than a church song. As they sing, they ponder the vastness of the cosmos. After a few minutes, the ceremony is interrupted by Jeffrey, who shouts, "Look!" He excitedly points to the sky above the canyon wall. Everyone strains their eyes. They see a pinpoint of light, at first undistinguishable from a star. But then it takes on mass. Suddenly, a black disc, with an array of brightly colored lights, sweeps across the sky overhead. It hovers for just a moment above the silent spring, then zips off beyond the jagged crest of the canyon on an upward swing.

The group exhales heavily with disappointment.

"God be with you, Carly," sobs Jeffrey.

The Pope Looks to the Stars

"Amen to that," says Father Priestley.

Charlotte's dog, Ramon, barks.

"I'll get the clothes for you." Father Priestley attempts to console Jeffrey with an affectionate pat on the back.

Litzy approaches Niccolò.

"Thank you for blessing Veronica."

"It was a real privilege," replies Niccolò.

"Can you write down those Latin words for me?"

"Of course."

"I'm going to sleep now." She passes in front of Franklin, who is having one last beer for the night.

The next morning, after coffee and hot chocolate, the church group gathers up all the sleeping bags, and heads back to the parking area. Litzy asks to ride back with Poppy, and trades places with Eva, who accepts Brad's offer to accompany him, an offer he made in behalf of his mother.

"So, Poppy," begins Sam. "What did you think of our annual pilgrimage?"

"First of all, your story was quite interesting. It shed light on the lunacy of wishing terrestrial immortality. Secondly, I was very interested in the revelation that your name is both a blessing and a curse, but more of a blessing now."

Sam flashes his teeth. "He was a good dentist. But I'm glad you liked my story."

Litzy is rubbing her tummy. "Poppy, is that your real name?"

"That's a popular question, Litzy. No, actually my real name is Niccolò di Montachiesa." He notices Lucy's smile in the rearview mirror.

"He claims to be the Pope. So I call him Poppy."

Litzy frowns deeply.

"Litzy, look into my eyes."

"Yes?"

"I am Pope Ignatius I. And I've come to the States to revive the Catholic Church. The only one that remains is Father Priestley's."

Lucy can see that Litzy is confused. "That's Father Grimwold. Our priest always uses an alias. His real name is Sherman Priestley."

Having been distracted by Lucy's explanation, Litzy looks back into Niccolò's green eyes. "I believe you."

"Then that's a beginning," says Niccolò softly, putting his hand gently on Litzy's tummy.

"Hey, Sam," says Lucy. "Where did you get that cuckoo clock story from?"

"From a vision. A vision from God. As with all my stories."

Niccolò raises an eyebrow. "Do you believe that, Litzy?"

"Not for a minute," laughs Litzy, much to Sam's dismay.

Niccolò, though, is quite amused. And perhaps somehow reassured.

"What about UFOs? Are you convinced now?" asks Sam.

Litzy shrugs. "I don't know what I saw. And, really, Sam, I don't care. But I hope Jeffrey finds his sister someday."

Sam nods. "He will. Burt says he will."

"And do you believe Burt?" asks Niccolò.

"Come on Poppy. Have some faith!"

"I do have faith, Sam. I have faith in Litzy. Faith in Veronica. Faith in the positive impact of your stories, which are truly inspirational. And, above all, Sam, I have faith in the future of the Catholic Church."

15 THE POPE PERFORMS MIRACLES

The following Sunday, Niccolò and Lucy attend church. They are among the last to arrive. Edgar spots them, but since most of the seats in the hotel's small conference room have been taken, he is unable to move any closer. As a result, his heart begins to flutter....

"Good morning. I'm Father Breitz. Some of you are disappointed that our alien friends did not return Carly to the Christian community this week as we had hoped. Carly was in our prayers, but, of course, we pray to God, not to the aliens. But, we can truly say that aliens, like God, work in very mysterious ways. We have no doubt that our friends had a legitimate reason to call Carly to the heavens, but we also are quite confident that they will return her in due time. We must not lose faith. Today's sermon is called *The Lighthouse in the Desert*. And it is a story built upon a foundation of faith."

There are whispers of anticipation in the congregation.

"First, though, we have some church business. Franklin?"

Franklin steps up to the podium. "Thank you, Father Breitz. I have today's weather forecast."

Niccolò turns to Lucy. "And what about the two weeks ahead?"

Lucy shrugs. "It's a ritual. But you're right. It doesn't make a lot of sense."

"Skies are currently overcast, but will clear by early this afternoon. Today's high will be 77 degrees Fahrenheit. That's 25 degrees Celsius. Dew point is 59 degrees Fahrenheit, or 15 degrees Celsius. Heat index is 81 degrees Fahrenheit. That's 27 degrees Celsius. UV Index stands at 11, so sunscreen is advised. Winds will be from the west southwest at 5 to 15 miles per hour. That's 8 to 24 kilometers per hour. Humidity is at 60%, and visibility is 10 miles, or 16 kilometers. We have a low-medium pollen count of 3.9, primarily due to grass and Elm. The air quality index is 45, which is good, borderline moderate, with ozone levels remaining stable but with slightly increasing levels of carbon monoxide and nitrogen dioxide late this afternoon. In short, God has blessed the good citizens of Venice, and this Sunday congregation in particular, with heavenly weather. We live under subtropical conditions, but at God's mercy. And so we must continue to praise God for his meteorological love. Thank you, Lord. Thank you for a beautiful day on this day of worship. In God's name, amen."

Ramon barks. Father Priestley shakes Franklin's hand, then proceeds.

"Tiffani? Are you in the company of men today?"

"Yes, I am." Tiffani stands up, and walks to the podium, accompanied by two Whites and one Black. Generally, this is the way it goes, though sometimes she brings along an Hispanic, Asian, or Pacific Islander.

"Father Breitz. Fellow members of the church. Let me introduce the Three Wise Men. They are: Neville Grainger, Carl Stearns, and Jackson Holmes. May I please have the pie?"

Father Priestley hands the pie to one of the Hispanic choirboys, who then presents the pie to the congregation before handing it to Tiffani.

"And now a word to the wise," continues Tiffani. "This pie has been cut into three slices of equal size. However, one of the slices contains the magic bean."

"Amen!" acknowledges the congregation.

Ramon barks.

"Pray to God that you choose the slice with the magic bean. For, if you choose wisely, you will be rewarded with three nights of heavenly bliss in my loving arms. All three of you have been selected as new members of our church, so you may count your blessings regardless of your choice. Now, you will choose your slice of pie, but don't bite into it until I give you the sign. Neville, the first choice is yours. Then Carl and Jackson."

The Three Wise Men each select a slice of pie. Tiffani, who is wearing a provocative outfit, but in good taste, holds out her hands, palms up. "You may begin."

Each of the Three Wise Men glances at his competitors, then takes the first bite. After a moment of suspense, Carl spits the bean out into his hand and shows it to Tiffani.

"Congratulations, Carl. Now, you must swallow the bean. Believe me, you will thank me later."

A muted laugh comes from the congregation.

"Neville. Jackson. Thank you for participating. You may join me later for a cappuccino. I'll go over some details pertaining to church membership. Let us give the Three Wise Men a warm Christian welcome!"

After a general applause, Tiffani, putting Carl's arm around her waist, conducts the Three Wise Men back to their seats. Neville and Jackson smile politely, but they are visibly disappointed. Father Priestley returns to the podium. He is radiant.

"Neville Grainger. Jackson Holmes. We are delighted to have you here today. And, of course, we look forward to seeing you again next meeting Sunday. But now I must have a word with God." Father Priestley looks up towards the ceiling. "Our Heavenly Father, we ask that you bless this holy union between Carl Stearns and Tiffani Putnam. Carl is a lost sheep, but through Tiffani's love, he will be brought into the fold. For three days, Tiffani will cleanse his soul of past sins, and on the fourth day, Carl will find purity in his soul. We ask that you give Tiffani the strength she needs to fulfill this sacred mission."

A thunderous voice replies, "Carl Stearns. You have the Lord's blessing! And bless you, also, Tiffani Putnam, for spreading the gospel!"

The congregation responds, "Amen to that!"

Ramon barks.

"And now, let us turn to today's lesson. *The Lighthouse in the Desert*. We are all familiar with the story of Noah and the Ark. There is a key element of that story, however, that is widely known among Biblical scholars but which rarely finds its place in the popular narrative of the Great Flood. This is a tragic oversight, for the story of Pharisus and the lighthouse he built in the desert is one that must be told. The undertaking of this humble man, and the faith required of him, was no less magnificent than Noah's. And, in fact, without the guiding beacon of the lighthouse, which shone down upon the rising seas from the highest peak, the ark would not have come to rest where God intended. So let us look in on Pharisus. Like Noah, he was a devoted husband and father, and a tireless servant of God. Pharisus was a sheepherder. He made a living selling wool, which was an important commodity in the colder climes where he and his countrymen lived."

Niccolò enjoys the sermon, which is not, strictly speaking, biblically correct. But his attention turns to Brad, who is having an argument with his mother. He keeps his voice to a whisper, but it is a strong whisper.

"But you heard me, Mother! I told Eva my middle name was Adam. Brad Adam Ganske. You were right there in the car with me.–You heard Eva laugh!–And, you know what? I don't blame her. It's a convenient lie! My middle name is Lee. And I can't change that!–Okay, so I could change it. But I'm not going to go to the trouble of doing it.–What do you mean?–Mother. It was Adam and Eve. Not Brad and Eva.–Oh, I see what you mean.–Yes, I know. Cain, Abel, Seth.–No, they were not the Three Little Figs.–Okay, so that was a joke.–'And the days of Adam after he had begotten Seth were eight hundred years; and he begat sons and daughters.' That's fine, Mother. But none of their sons were named Brad or Lee, or even Bradley. Those are not biblical names!–Yes, Mother. You have a point. She probably wouldn't notice the absurdity of it. But, Mother….–Yes, of course I'm attracted to her. So is everyone else. Men *and* women, Mother.–Yeah, there was this one lady named Chelsea McAdam. She hit on Eva big time.–I don't know. You ask her!–Mother, I mean really!–Okay. I'll try again.–But she'll notice the inconsistency.–Okay, so she *won't* notice the inconsistency. Maybe she doesn't find *me* attractive. Did you ever think of that?–No, Mother. I refuse to take off my shirt and pants. Especially not in church!–I'm not exactly well endowed, Mother.–How would I know?–The Bible doesn't talk about things like that!"

Niccolò looks the other way. Edgar Cosgrove is taking his pulse, his lips mouthing the count, and his eyes on his wristwatch. He looks concerned with the results, and leans over to Burt, whispering something in his ear.

"I'm trying to follow the sermon, Edgar. Try to focus on Father Breitz."

Niccolò glances at Lucy. She is totally absorbed in the story of Pharisus, which has obviously been fabricated by Father Priestley. But does the congregation realize this? If not, should he endeavor to set the record straight, one member at a time? Should he discuss it with Father Priestley? Niccolò decides that it's best to leave it alone. His mind begins to wander.

"Poppy?"

Lucy nudges Niccolò. "Father Breitz is calling on you."

"Yes, Father—"

"Breitz," whispers Lucy.

"Father *Breitz*."

"Poppy, you have been giving today's lesson much consideration. I could see you were deep in thought. I've never seen your eyes turn such a dark green. Would you like to share some of your more intellectually accessible reflections with the church?"

Niccolò hesitates, but he grants Father Priestley his wish, and offers the congregation a brief perspective on the Great Flood, which he claims was somewhat exaggerated in scope despite the fact that ancient mythologies from around the world tend to corroborate it. Niccolò dismisses the lighthouse story outright, but praises the story's message, which is that great personal achievements may come to those who strive to maintain their faith in a world of professed nonbelievers and religious hypocrites. Despite his efforts to cushion the blow of his remarks, Niccolò's comments are not well received. It is clear that neither Father Priestley nor the congregation is willing to share his turf. On several occasions, he is interrupted by someone with a countering view. When, finally, Edgar begins to heckle him, saying that he would be excommunicated by the Pope, if the Pope hadn't flushed the Vatican down the shithole and made a mad dash to nowhere, Niccolò decides that it is futile to come to his own defense. Instead, he apologizes and sits down, aware that Lucy has wiggled aside a few inches.

"Father Breitz," says Charlotte. "I think Poppy must be confessed."

"But not in his own van!" laughs Barry.

"There's a rumor going around that he's an undercover agent from the ACLU," adds Kimberly, who is obviously unaware that she owes Niccolò a big debt of gratitude for his intervention in behalf of Adriano.

"I think he's just seriously uninformed. I don't know where he gets his information, but–"

"From Vatican archives," whispers Niccolò to Lucy, who gives him something of a cold shoulder. After all, she is the one who brought him into the congregation.

Litzy stands up. "Father Breitz. Am I the only one here who believes that our membership is blessed by the presence of His Holiness, Pope Ignatius I?"

Some church members laugh. Others simply groan.

Litzy is undeterred. "Pharisus never existed. The lighthouse never existed. The whole story is bogus."

The thunderous voice of God resounds in the church. "Silence! You, Litzy Muñoz-Cruz, are one of my children. Do not believe the heresy of this man. Or your child will be cursed!"

"You don't fool me, Father Breitz!" Litzy seats herself. Despite her bravado, she shivers in fear.

Sam stands up. "Father Breitz. Fellow Christians. I believe that Poppy is of sound mind and charitable of heart. That is not to say that I agree with him. We all have trust in the Word of God. And if God says that Pharisus built a lighthouse on a desert mountaintop in order to guide the ark to safe haven, then surely we must believe this story is true. However, we should not be quick to judge Poppy in a bad light. He only knows what he's been told. Let us be patient and understanding with him. Father Breitz, you will show him the light. And we will all help you lead the way. Thank you."

Niccolò and Lucy decide to take a walk on Venice Beach after mass.

"Look, Poppy. I'm not saying you're wrong. But you can't challenge Father Breitz like that. He has God on his side."

"Father Priestley has good intentions. I don't deny that. But there is such a thing as religious integrity."

"Yes, but Father Breitz is all we've got," Lucy reminds him. "Maybe someday, we'll find a better shepherd. But for now, we must be good little sheep. The church is small. And fragile. We can't afford to entertain reformists. You don't want the church to fall to bits. You know, like the Vatican?"

Niccolò smiles bitterly. "I need time to think, Lucy. Do you mind?"

Lucy heads for the confession van. Niccolò, head hung low, turns about and walks in the opposite direction along the oceanfront.

"Hey, you're going the wrong way!" shouts a voice from behind.

Niccolò looks over his shoulder.

"You're Poppy, right? The guy that does confessions?"

Niccolò barely acknowledges the fact.

"My name is Merle. I have a magic shop down the way there. Merle isn't my real name, of course."

Niccolò fails to see the humor. He hastens his pace, hoping to be left in peace.

"Hey, Poppy. Just one question. You don't really believe all that religious crap do you? I mean, all that miracle stuff that Jesus did was fake, right? He was a trickster. Like me. But if you'll excuse my lack of modesty, Jesus was not as good as me. Magic tricks get better. We pass down our secrets from one generation to the next."

"And God?" asks Niccolò.

The Pope Performs Miracles 173

"You want my opinion? God is nothing but pure fiction. He's no more real than Zeus, Odin, or any of a hundred or more of those other ancient deities. They were all made up by ignorant people. Why do you think the world has gone secular? Science explains everything. Hey, I was just reading up on the Higgs boson. They discovered it a good while back, you know. But it's back in the news. According to the article, a handful of idiots out there still refer to it as the 'God particle.' I mean, get real, man! We're talking about modern science here. God has absolutely nothing to do with it! Because he doesn't exist! It's that simple! Let me tell you something. Our society has got to stop pandering to the religious minority. And we've got to stop holy mackerels like *you* that seek to profit from the moral conscience of fools. Shame on you, Poppy! You are nothing but a charlatan."

Niccolò has listened patiently. "Would you say such things to the Pope?"

"The Pope? He's gone, man! Nobody knows where the hell he is. And, you know what? Nobody really cares!"

Niccolò is feeling very much alone. The church has ostracized him. This magic shop owner is ridiculing him. Ridiculing religion. Ridiculing God.

"Perhaps I can open your eyes," says Niccolò finally.

Merle scoffs, "Oh, give me a break!"

"Are you willing to give me a shot at converting you? I will pray that God grants me the privilege of performing a small miracle for you. What do you say?"

"I would prefer something magnificent. But go ahead. Show me your stuff."

Niccolò kneels and prays silently while Merle watches, somewhat embarrassed. He shrugs as passersby turn their heads to look.

"Will you buy me a cup of coffee?" asks Niccolò.

"What? Are you kidding me? Just snap your fingers or something. But then, I guess making money is no small miracle!"

Niccolò stares at Merle with only a hint of mercy.

"Okay, here." Merle takes something from behind Niccolò's ear, unfolds it, and hands Niccolò a five dollar bill. "That should buy you a cup!"

Niccolò and Merle enter a coffee shop. In the corner, Tiffani is chatting with Neville and Jackson over cappuccino. Carl is nowhere to be seen. He obviously has an evening appointment. Tiffani glances at Niccolò, but does not interrupt her conversation.

Moments later, Niccolò and Merle are on the beach.

"Okay, Poppy. Let's do it."

"I've already done it. Look." Niccolò guides Merle's eyes towards the cup.

"What?"

"You saw them pour me a cup of coffee. And you've watched my every move. Will you concede that I haven't taken the slightest sip out of this cup? And that I haven't spilled a single drop?"

Merle shakes his head. "That's it? You turned coffee into water, and I'm supposed to be all 'Wow!' about that? Here, let me show you some real magic!"

Merle takes the cup, passes it around his back, and presents it to Niccolò. "Take a look!"

The cup, which moments earlier was full to the brim with clear sparkling water, is now filled with dry sand.

Niccolò is somewhat puzzled by this. "That was just a starter," he explains. "I anticipated your move. Now, *you* take a look!"

The sand has hardened into sandstone. Niccolò peels away the Styrofoam cup. "Bottoms up!"

The Pope Performs Miracles

"Oh!" puffs Merle. "That's child's play!" He takes the sandstone block, which is in the shape of a truncated cone, and carves a happy face into it, as if it were made of soft clay.

Niccolò is impressed. But he is not one to be easily outdone. He takes the sandstone block and squeezes it like a sponge, creating a stream of red wine. "I assume you like Merlot?"

"Oh, my God. How pathetic!" exclaims Merle.

"You're half right," admits Niccolò.

Merle snatches what looks like a cork stopper away from Niccolò. He attempts to squeeze more wine out of it, but it is solid, gritty sandstone.

"That's a really cheap trick!" snorts Merle. He takes the sandstone block, rounds it into an egg shape, then taps it with two fingers, and breaks it into two halves. Some loose yellow sand–the yoke, if you will–pours out, some of it onto Niccolò's shoes. "Yoke's on you...." Merle then joins the two halves together behind his back and hands the sandstone egg to Niccolò. "There. Let's see if you can top that!"

Niccolò is totally exasperated. He takes the sandstone egg, and, perhaps thinking of his experience at Oja, flattens it into a flying disc. He flings it into the air. It soars above the waves, catches the ocean breeze, and returns. Niccolò catches it with his eyes closed.

Merle is unimpressed. "Let me have it," he insists.

Niccolò hands the sandstone disc to Merle. But as it passes into Merle's hands, it becomes incredibly heavy, and Merle drops it on his foot.

"Aïe! Aïe! Aïe! Aïe! Aïe!" cries Merle. "That really hurt!"

"The truth always hurts," points out Niccolò.

Merle picks up the sandstone disc. The happy face he carved into the truncated cone has somehow survived all the shape-shifting. But the smiley is now on top of the disc, and has undergone stretching without any change in proportions. Niccolò has an idea. Before Merle can conduct his next operation, the happy face broadens its smile and speaks. "Cheer up, loser!"

"Do you wish to repent?" adds Niccolò.

Merle shakes his head. "Only if you can make it sing the 'Ave Maria'–in Latin."

Niccolò wipes his forehead. He is getting really upset, but is able to maintain his calm. "As you wish, Merle!" he says flatly. The happy face begins to sing the Catholic prayer version of the "Ave Maria."

"You really do think I'm gullible, don't you?" chuckles Merle. "You're not only an amateur miracle worker, but a pretty lousy ventriloquist, too."

Niccolò is on the verge of losing his temper.

Merle raises his hand in the spirit of peace, but does not offer an apology.

"Tell you what. If you can turn this thing into the Moses tablet, you know, the, uh, Ten Commandments, whatever, *then* I'll believe in your God. Is that a fair deal?"

Niccolò takes a deep breath. He is about to comply. But he looks into Merle's eyes and realizes that Merle is just prolonging the game. Merle is an atheist, through and through. And he will always be an atheist, no matter how many miracles he witnesses. Small miracles. Big miracles. It doesn't matter. There is no winning the battle. Niccolò shakes his head no.

"Don't take it so badly, Poppy. Look, if you'd like to learn a few more tricks–better, more sophisticated tricks–come by the magic shop sometime. You're a bit old and rusty, but... Hey, enjoy your singing Frisbee!"

"Thank you, but you may recall that I ordered a cup of coffee." Niccolò bends up the edges of the sandstone saucer, recreates the truncated cone of a Styrofoam cup, hollows it out,

The Pope Performs Miracles

and then raises it to his lips. He takes a good long sip of steaming hot coffee. "But do me a favor. Put some cream in my coffee, will you?"

Merle digs into his pocket, takes out a small sealed cup of nondairy creamer, and says, "Here."

16 THE POPE AT THE AUBERGE GINETTE

In Venice one summer day, a card is left on the van's windshield. It reads: "Auberge Ginette. French suites. Famous eggplant beignets."

As a child, Niccolò thought eggs grew on plants because his mother used to hide Easter eggs in the vegetable garden. He's intrigued.

The Auberge Ginette belongs to Francine Friboulet. She often drives around the valley in her old Fiat 500Pi, tagging windshield wipers with her business card in an effort to drum up business at the inn. More than once, she has been mistaken for a meter maid.

Niccolò pays a visit to the Auberge Ginette. He follows a loud whiny-crunchy noise coming from the dining area, and finds who he believes to be the proprietor, leaning against a lavender kitchen counter, which goes nicely with the eggplant-painted walls. The noise is coming from a blender, which is set on pulse. The lady, who is in her late 50s, but aging very gracefully, is totally absorbed in thought, staring at the blender, but not actually watching it. Although she is not facing him directly, the lady seems vaguely familiar, with her peculiar hairstyle and somewhat eccentric clothing. Sitting precariously near the edge of one of the small tables near the counter is a large bowl filled with hard boiled eggs. Their shells have been removed. After a moment or two, the lady turns off the blender,

The Pope at the Auberge Ginette

satisfied. When she turns around, she is somewhat startled by the presence of her visitor, who appears to be quite puzzled.

"Eggshell powder. Fertilizer for the plants," she explains. "Oh, I apologize. I didn't hear you come in. Are you looking for a room?"

Niccolò has a brief flashback to the Easter egg hunt fiasco, but shakes it off. "No. Actually, I'm looking for you. I just wanted to ask you a question about the name of your inn. You are . . . Ginette, I presume?"

"Everyone calls me that because of the business, although they usually pronounce it Jeanette. Anyway, Ginette is actually my middle name. You can call me Francine."

Suddenly, Niccolò knows why she seemed familiar to him. He totally abandons his question. Instead, he studies Francine's face. Take away 40 some odd years, and...

His thoughts turn back to his biker days, when he was known simply as Nic. One day, not long after Olivier had returned to Nice, young Niccolò met a French girl from Paris named Francine, and they spent an unforgettable week together. Niccolò had to start an argument with Giulia, who was on her best behavior at the time, in order to devote his time to Francine, who had responded enthusiastically to his invitation to ride with him on his bike. Niccolò made the arrangements quickly, because Francine was about to return to France to see to her ailing parents. She agreed to postpone the trip home by a few days. During their week together, Niccolò and Francine engaged in frequent sex. He proclaimed his love for her, and promised to come see her in Paris right away. But God had other plans. He triggered the Civitavecchia earthquake, and shone His light on Niccolò, who abandoned his past life that day and devoted his life to God.

Niccolò smiles. "Nice to meet you, Francine. Everyone calls me Poppy."

Francine laughs, but then gasps. She has finally noticed the sparkling emerald eyes of her visitor. She immediately dismisses the ridiculous notion that this man could be Pope Ignatius I, and yet the resemblance is remarkable.

"Are you okay?" asks Niccolò.

Francine shakes her head with disbelief. "I apologize, but you bear a striking resemblance to the Pope."

"But I *am* the Pope," replies Niccolò, stroking his goatee.

Francine remains frozen for a good long moment. "I believe you are!" She studies Niccolò as if to find something to confirm her belief.

"Oh, my God! You really are the Pope!"

"You can call me Poppy."

Francine shakes her head. "Oh, no! That's very disrespectful. I could never call you that!"

"I have a friend named Lucy. She gave me the nickname because she doesn't actually believe I'm the Pope. It caught on, so everyone calls me Poppy."

"But I can't. May I call you…Ignatius I?"

"I prefer not. I was born Niccolò di Montachiesa," he says proudly. "So why not just call me Nic?"

Francine is floored. Not only does this name jump out of the shadows of the past, but she is suddenly very aware of the fact that ever since she looked into those green eyes, she has fancied this man. Perhaps now she knows why. And yet, she is not totally convinced that this man could be Nic, the Italian lover who vanished from her life forty years earlier. To think that a biker could one day become the Pope is just too extraordinary a jump of fate to be true.

"That is such an amazing coincidence!" admits Francine nevertheless. "When I was young, I had my mind set on becoming a nun. I kept up on all the issues facing the Church, and went to church every Sunday. I was a good little Catholic. Still am! Anyway, I even vacationed in Rome once. And that's where I met a handsome young Italian biker named Nic. He was the love of my life!" Francine bites her trembling lip, and fans her long natural lashes. She does not want to show any tears.

"So you've been to Rome," confirms Niccolò. "Et ce jeune Italien, Nic, avait-il une particularité?"

Francine smiles. Of course, the Pope speaks French! She responds in kind. "Oui. Il avait un tatouage sur sa poitrine. *Hells Angels*." Realizing how ridiculous this conversation is, she puts her hand to her mouth.

"I'm sorry…Nic?"

"Nic."

"Nic…. It's just that–"

It's true. Niccolò had "Hells Angels" tattooed on his chest one day when he and Olivier had drunk a bit too much. Olivier's tattoo had held up well. Niccolò's chest was not as firm as it once was, so his tattoo had lost some of its luster. The tattoo was something of an embarrassment to him once he enrolled in the seminary, and it remained a secret during his later papal tenure.

"No, that's very interesting, actually. And what happened?"

Francine assumes a very serious face. "Nic and I spent a few days together. The timing of my vacation was not very good. My parents were suffering. They needed me back home. I couldn't stay long. But I wanted to stay in Rome. With Nic. He had this shiny green Moto Guzzi. The most beautiful green, like Nic's eyes." Francine looks deeply into Niccolò's eyes, sees her own reflection, becomes self-conscious, clears her throat, and continues her story. "We spent most of our time riding the streets of Rome. And when I wasn't riding Nic's bike, I was riding the biker. And what a ride it was! Nic was one of those

Italian lovers you always hear about. Making love with Nic was like going to heaven!" Francine realizes her gaffe. "Oh!"

"It's quite alright," says Niccolò, encouragingly.

"Those days in Rome, I'll never forget them." Francine points to her head. "It's all sharp and clear. I can still feel him." Francine looks down, a bit embarrassed. Niccolò imagines she is looking down towards the deep recess in her lap.

"So you returned to France. Then what happened?"

"Nic promised he would come see me right away. He said he loved me. And I believed him. But he never came. And then I discovered I was pregnant. What rotten luck! My parents were furious. They demanded an abortion. After all, the father was a biker, a real 'loser,' who had vanished into thin air. Not a word from him in nearly two months. So I had the abortion. My parents lived a few more years. They died within a week of each other. Father first, then mother. She loved him so much." Tears well up in Francine's eyes, and, this time, she does not fight them.

Niccolò takes Francine's hands into his own in order to comfort her.

Francine looks into Niccolò's eyes again, as if searching for something. "I gave up the baby, Nic. That was the day…I fell from grace. I lost more than Nic's baby. I lost my soul. I no longer felt worthy of becoming a nun."

"So what became of you?" Niccolò ponders the picture of Saint Bernadette on the wall.

Francine smiles. It's a silly question, but she understands what Niccolò means. How did she get from there to here…? She rubs her eyes; takes a breath.

"Well, as you might imagine, it all began with Ginette. My grandmother, Ginette. Ginette Pelletier. She opened the original Auberge Ginette." Francine briefly describes how Ginettte married Raymond Pelletier, and how, after opening the inn, they had three children: Maurice, Clarisse, and Antoinette. Antoinette married Georges Friboulet, and they had two children, Francine Ginette and Fabrice Maurice.

"Fabrice learned to play the guitar, and he picked so well that he decided to form a rockabilly band. He met an American girl, Christina. A charming little cornhusker from Omaha. Anyway, they married in Vegas, and rented an apartment in L.A. But it didn't work out. They couldn't make ends meet. The rockabilly band never quite happened. After the divorce, Fabrice began singing rockabilly tunes at the beach. It wasn't much, but it paid his way through school. Today, Fabrice is a chef at L.A. Bonne Table, a French restaurant near the beach. He still likes the beach, but he doesn't sing there anymore. Not since he broke up with a young lady who sells religious stuff out of a van. You mentioned a girl named Lucy. I think that was her name, too. Another coincidence!"

Niccolò forms an inquiry in his mind.

"When my mother died, rather than sell the Auberge Ginette and split up the money, Fabrice proposed that I move to L.A. So, here I am. We opened up a new Auberge Ginette. We have a financial partnership in the business. He stops by now and then to say hello, and, sometimes, I'll go for a bite at L.A. Bonne Table."

That night, Niccolò sleeps in the van as usual. The van jiggles now and then. Inside, Niccolò tosses and turns, but also responds physically to the conflicting advice handed to him in his disturbing dream. First to appear in his dream is the Devil, who tells him that he should reveal his tattoo to Francine, and that they should become lovers once again. God is love, after all. And so shouldn't the Pope, who is now just plain old Nic, a wacko on the public dole, feel free to express his feelings of love? The Devil even promises to buy Niccolò a Nissan Altima. Niccolò raises a wavering eyebrow, as this has always been his dream car.

But then, he clinches his fist in defiance. He is ashamed that Francine had to abort his only begotten child. Now, God himself appears to him in the dream. He advises Niccolò to beg forgiveness for his past transgressions and to maintain his papal dignity. The Pope must keep his identity a secret. It is a blessing that Francine has not made the final connection between Biker Nic and Niccolò di Montachiesa. Niccolò folds his hands in prayers: he does not want to fall prey to sexual urges, but he does wish to confess to Francine that he is the wayward father. Niccolò wants forgiveness.

In the end, Niccolò promises to abide by God's wishes. He will reveal nothing.

Meanwhile, Francine cannot sleep. She lies in bed, clutching an old photo of Biker Nic. She is tormented by doubts. She refuses to believe. And yet she knows. By mentally adding 40 years to Biker Nic's face, and adding a mustache and goatee, only one conclusion can be drawn. Nic is the Pope! But she must have proof. The tattoo! But how...?

The next day, Niccolò returns to the Auberge Ginette. He wants to sample some of her eggplant beignets.

"You know, I can't believe my good fortune," admits Francine. "Don't you see the irony? I turned my back on the convent, murdered my own flesh and blood, and gave up my soul forever. And now? Now, I'm on a first-name basis with the Pope!"

"We all bear sins, Francine. The collapse of Catholicism weighs heavily on my shoulders."

Francine nods. "How could God allow such a thing to happen?"

"I have asked Him that very question. Many times, I can assure you.... And so far, He has not provided an answer."

"You know what they say. Misery loves company."

"We do not have to be miserable. We have to strive for happiness. It is within reach."

"Nic, I'm glad you came back. Your company brings me happiness. It brings me joy. This may sound pretentious, but I hope we can become close friends."

"Another 'Nic' stepping into your life. Can you handle that?"

"Yes, but… Don't ever leave me, Nic."

"As long as Saint Bernadette hangs on your wall, you will find me at your table. Besides, I think I'm hooked on your eggplant beignets."

"There's no sin in that!"

Over the course of the next two weeks or so, Niccolò joins Francine for breakfast. It becomes a pleasant routine. Niccolò usually sleeps in the van, and since the trip to the Auberge Ginette requires about forty-five minutes by bus, and even more time to walk, he wakes up much earlier than Lucy. He dresses, leaves a note in the van, and leaves before sunrise.

As she serves breakfast, Francine engages Niccolò in conversations about the past, hoping to find out more about what she calls his Pre-Papal Period, or PPP. Niccolò remains vague about his biker days, preferring to focus on his childhood. However, when Francine prods him to talk about the life he led prior to his entry into the seminary, Niccolò substitutes a white Karmann Ghia for his green Moto Guzzi, and is very careful to avoid mentioning Francine's name or any activity in which she played a part. Moreover, as a precaution, he always assigns a pseudonym to "Giulia" whenever telling a story that involves her.

After breakfast, Niccolò departs. Francine tends to business affairs at the inn, or else goes tagging, and Niccolò hurries to the beach where the confession van awaits.

Francine grows impatient with this routine. She decides it's time for a date. It's time to introduce Niccolò to family. One morning, Niccolò arrives a bit earlier than usual. After a brief childhood story in which her brother, Fabrice, fell into a pond full of carp while trying to fly a kite, Francine cuts to the chase.

"Nic, would you like to come to the restaurant with me? To meet my brother?"

"I would be delighted."

Francine nods. "Do you have a nice shirt to wear? I mean, I like your t-shirt. The crucifix makes perfect sense. But the rhinestones would probably be seen as a bit tacky at the restaurant. L.A. Bonne Table is a bit snobbish, strictly upper class. The décor is French. But very understated."

Niccolò smiles. "You needn't say more. I will see if Lucy can loan me a few bucks."

Francine leans forward. "Nic! I have an idea. I make all my own clothes."

"Yes, I know. I mean, it's obvious. I've never seen such a creative style of clothing in the shops here. And they suit you perfectly. They reflect your personality. Your originality. So what do you have in mind?"

"I think you know already. I'm going to make you a shirt."

"That would be splendid!"

Francine rises quickly to her feet. "First, I have to get some measurements…."

"I know my measurements. I used to have a tailor."

"I think you've lost some weight since then. I'll be right back." She disappears for a moment, and then returns with a tape measure.

Niccolò stands up, and stretches out his arms.

"Well, if you had a tailor, you must know that I have to ask you to remove your shirt."

Niccolò suddenly realizes the mess he's gotten himself into. He puts his hand on his chest. "Oh, this t-shirt is quite tight on me—"

"It has to come off," insists Francine, eyebrows raised imploringly.

"Francine. I'm afraid there is still a bit of Pope in me. I apologize, but I—"

"No, no. You're right. You're absolutely right. I'm the one who must apologize." Francine turns away.

"It's okay, Francine. I want to be measured. But a loose fit will do. You know how Italian men are. We wear tight shirts that strain the buttons so that our bushy chest hairs can poke through here and there and perform a public display. We particularly like to perform for the female public. It's how we advertise our virility. But those chest hairs eventually turn gray and scraggly. We are ashamed of them, and keep them under wraps. Even at the beach."

"I certainly don't want to embarrass you," reassures Francine, unrolling her tape measure. She begins to measure Niccolò: chest, waist, neck, arm length. "You know. That's funny. Nic. My lover Nic. He had a smooth chest. A few hairs around the nipples. That's all. Nic used to tell me that he thought wearing shirts that burst with chest hairs was vulgar. He got away with that point of view because he had this natural aura of virility that spoke softly to women. And—well, I suppose I should stop there!"

"How long will it take you to make the shirt?" asks Niccolò. If he keeps his promise to God, he will never reveal his hairless chest—and bald lie—to Francine.

"A few days. I have to buy the fabric, the buttons. Oh, I have drawers full of buttons. But they're not for a man's shirt."

Several days later, Niccolò returns. The shirt is ready.

"That's a nice color. Pink?"

"Salmon. It's a good color for you. Try it on. I hope it fits."

Niccolò looks about for a place to change.

"You'll have to remove your t-shirt, of course. But I promise not to look." She closes her eyes, and shields them with her right hand. But she is peering through the fingers.

Niccolò turns his back to Francine and quickly sheds his t-shirt. He slips on the new shirt. "A perfect fit!"

Francine, who is frustrated once again in her efforts to see the tattoo, nods cheerfully. "So, what do you say? This Friday night?"

"It's a date."

17 THE POPE GOES TO HOLLYWOOD

Six months have gone by since Niccolò arrived in Venice. He is becoming somewhat well known amongst the Venice Beach hustlers and tourists. He has long overstayed his visa, but since L.A. is a sanctuary city, no one ever asks him to confirm his immigration status.

"Wake up, Poppy. There's someone here to see you."

Niccolò realizes that he has overslept. He changes his t-shirt, puts on some fresh socks, and pokes his head out of the van, which is already parked on the oceanfront. The visitor is browsing the various chains and crucifixes on display.

"I'll take all of these," he says.

Lucy gulps in disbelief. "Sure. Just give me a second on the calculator."

While Lucy adds up the prices, the visitor notices Niccolò peering out of the van.

"Hey, look. I'm sorry," yawns Niccolò. "Can you come back in about an hour? Say, around ten thirty? I'll give you two sessions for the price of one. No date restrictions."

"I'm not here to confess, Poppy. But I can see you're not ready to discuss my proposal. Have yourself some breakfast. I'll be back. Ten thirty." He makes the finger-gun gesture, accompanied by a sly wink and a tongue smack.

"One hundred seventy-four dollars and ninety-five cents. You can have that bag over there. Complementary."

The visitor fetches the denim bag, which is embroidered with a multi-colored peace sign, and hands it to Lucy, who carefully wraps the chains and crucifixes and places them inside.

Lucy drops her voice. "Poppy isn't having breakfast. He's a bit short on confession funds this week, if you know what I mean."

"That's great!"

"What?" Lucy freezes.

"What I mean is…Poppy needs money. And I have money to offer. He can earn a few hundred bucks."

"Really? I'm sure he'd be interested." Lucy resumes her work. Once she has the final crucifix in the bag, she says, "There, you're all set. Do you want a receipt?"

"No thanks. But here." The visitor hands Lucy a twenty-dollar bill. "That should buy Poppy a decent breakfast. I can't discuss business with a man whose mind is on an empty stomach."

"That's very kind of you. I'll see that he gets it. See you at ten thirty!"

Some young ladies stop by. They are looking for incense, and Lucy has a good selection.

Niccolò pops out of the van. "What was that all about?"

"I don't know exactly. He has some kind of *job* for you, I think. And here. This is for you." Lucy hands Niccolò the twenty-dollar bill. "He said to go buy yourself a good breakfast."

Lucy's customers buy some Indian incense–primarily, clove and patchouli.

"Oh, Poppy. I forgot to tell you last night. Father Kruegel has invited you back to church. You can thank Litzy and Sam for that, I think. Kimberly checked with the ACLU. You're not an agent. Just a religious crackpot like the rest of us."

"And Edgar?"

"Don't worry about Edgar. His heart is like an old pocket watch with a broken mainspring. A few more ticks, and he's history. Do you want me to join you for breakfast?"

Niccolò shakes his head.

"No, really. Hey, Travis! Can you cover for me? You owe me one."

Travis is a street performer who bills himself as "The Gerbil." He does amazing stunts with velocipedes, unicycles, and monowheels. He typically sets up his performance venue "next door" to Lucy's "shop" and Poppy's confession van due to the public bicycle rack there.

"How long?"

"We'll be back at ten thirty."

"Sure." Travis verifies that his monowheel is securely chained to the bicycle rack. Then he walks over.

"We're going for breakfast," says Lucy. "I'll bring you some doughnuts."

"None of those powdered sugar ones, okay?"

Lucy and Poppy leave Travis in charge, and walk to the nearest outdoor café, just a few hundred feet down the way.

"How's it going with Francine?" inquires Lucy over a bowl of hot oatmeal. "I'm just asking because you normally pop in over there for breakfast. Getting tired of eggplant beignets?"

"No. It's just that… It's a long walk. And I'm short on bus fare. Plus, I have to get up really early if I want to be back in time to confess the masses."

Lucy is not convinced. She knows that the confession business is spotty at best.

"Anyway, I think Francine is busy passing out business cards this week. Did I tell you she made me a shirt over the weekend?"

"A shirt? You mean a real shirt? I've never seen you in a shirt, Poppy. Can I see it?"

"It's on a plastic hanger at the Auberge Ginette. She's keeping it there until Friday. We have a date."

Niccolò finishes off a heap of pancakes, and dips his sausage in the maple syrup.

"Well, that's good news, Poppy. When do I get to meet her?"

"Whenever you like, I suppose."

"So what are your plans? If she's made you a shirt, then you're obviously going out. Probably for dinner. A nice restaurant somewhere near the beach. After that, a nice evening stroll by the sea. A chance to take your shoes off. Let the surf tickle your toes. Then you relax. Watch the sunset. Share an ice cream cone. Laugh and tell stories. Then go back to Francine's. And–"

"You can stop there, Lucy."

Lucy smiles, somewhat embarrassed.

"But you're right. We're going out for dinner. It's a French restaurant called L.A. Bonne Table."

"Hmm…. I think I've been by that place. Very classy."

"That's what Francine says. Perhaps you know her brother. He's one of the chefs there."

"And how would I know a chef that works in a restaurant I can't afford?"

"Oh, he used to sing rockabilly on the beach."

Lucy frowns. She pushes her empty bowl aside, then takes a sip of cranberry juice.

"I hope it's not who I think it is," stammers Lucy.

"Fabrice Friboulet."

Lucy looks Niccolò in the eye. "Are you frickin' kidding me?"

"Francine mentioned that her brother had once dated a girl named Lucy. A vendor of religious accessories."

"Well. Obviously, I would be that Lucy! …I can't believe it. He used to play guitar here every single day. Then one day, he made a play for me. And I'm telling you, I simply melted. I mean, who could resist that French accent of his? Not to mention his good looks! And that body!" Lucy finishes off the cranberry juice, but continues to clutch the glass in her hand. "Oh, my God! …We rocked and rolled the van till the damn springs were shot! And then…" She sighs heavily. "And then he vanished!" She shrugs. "It's been a few years now. But it doesn't really matter. I'm sure he got what he deserved. He's probably married to some bimbo like Eva. Only a really fat one! And he cheats on her every chance he gets. Geez! What a jerk!"

"Well, I can't say much. I haven't actually met him yet. But I do know that he is still out there charming the ladies. And he's doing well financially. He's an excellent chef. And he performs at the restaurant. But not rockabilly. Classy low-key songs. In French, probably."

"I should come with you. I'd love to see the look on his face!"

"Well. We can't dwell on the past, Lucy. We must learn to forgive and forget. It's almost ten thirty." He digs the twenty-dollar bill out of his jeans pocket.

"Look, Poppy. Keep the twenty. That guy bought a ton of stuff. This one's on me."

When they return to Lucy's Crossroad Accessories, where Travis is busy making sales, they see that the visitor is waiting patiently by the van.

"SOS Confessions. I like that," he says, shaking Poppy's hand.

Lucy hands Travis a bag of glazed doughnuts, and sends him on his way.

"My name is Koepfer. You can call me Jim. I work for an independent movie company. We don't have talent scouts, *per se*, and we can't afford big name actors, let alone second tier. But we do make movies that people go see. And we're looking to fill a few holes in our cast of players. We don't normally approach beach hustlers, but you're perfect for the role."

"Are you asking me to be in a movie?"

"Yes, exactly. It's not a speaking part. But it's high profile. And it pays three hundred fifty dollars a day plus free meals. It's only for three or four days. But you could probably use the cash, right?"

Niccolò glances at Lucy, who is eavesdropping. "I must confess that business is a bit slow these days. Can I ask you the name of the film?"

"Oh, sure. The working title is *G.O.D.*"

Niccolò's green eyes light up.

"Look, Poppy. I'm really late for an appointment." Jim hands him a card. "If you're interested–and I mean, really, this is too good to pass up, right?–just show up at this address tomorrow morning at six o'clock. Don't be late. And don't worry. It's fun! Believe me. Lucy, it was nice to meet you."

Jim Koepfer leaves in somewhat of a hurry.

"Thanks for breakfast," shouts Lucy.

"Why do you suppose he had to spell it?" wonders Niccolò aloud.

"You mean, God? Well, you can't be too careful these days," replies Lucy. "Hey, I'll drive you in the morning. Give me the card."

The next morning, Lucy drops Niccolò off at an old warehouse. A sign out front reads: "G.O.D. All employees and visitors please report to the gate." Niccolò follows the arrow. There is nobody at the gate. But he is early. So he enters the warehouse through the closest door. He can hardly contain his excitement.

The warehouse is a veritable maze of individual movie sets. Niccolò walks casually through the maze, then stops to inspect a small chapel. It is somewhat foreboding. He wonders what the cobwebs are all about.

"Here it is, Mr. Brock. We had to send the other one to dry cleaning."

Niccolò turns around. A man from the wardrobe department is presenting a priest's robe to the director, who inspects it carefully.

"Okay, that's fine. Where's Percy?"

Niccolò approaches. "Not bad! Where can I try it on?"

"Who the fuck are you?" asks the wardrobe person.

The director smiles. "It's okay, Creason. He's an extra. Report to makeup."

Niccolò is confused.

"That way!" says Creason, tilting his head slightly and pointing down the hallway with his eyes.

On his way to makeup, Niccolò stops in front of a movie poster.

"*Garlic Overdose*," reads Niccolò aloud. Humph!

An actor walks by. It's as if he has stepped out of the poster. "Hey, what do you think? Pretty cool zombie vampire, eh? You're on your way to makeup, right?"

"I'm not in that movie. I'm doing a religious film called G.O.D."

The actor laughs. "And what do you think *G.O.D.* stands for, anyway?" The actor points to the movie poster.

Niccolò's face turns deathly pale.

"You didn't know?" asks the actor. "You must be one of Jim's extras. I can tell you're not from casting."

Niccolò shakes his head. "I play the priest. It's a small role, but an important one."

"Yeah, right. Good luck, chump!" The actor gives Niccolò a slap on the back and leaves in great haste.

Niccolò is confused. After a moment's hesitation, he decides to go the distance. He walks into makeup with an artificial smile on his face.

There are several actors undergoing the transformation from human being to zombie vampire. Attending each one are several makeup artists.

One of them rushes over to meet Niccolò. "Ah, there you are. Poppy, right? You're the one who gets toasted by the flame thrower. Have a seat over there."

Niccolò turns to stone. He grasps his cheap trinket cross, backs up, and escapes.

"Hey, wait!"

Moments later, Niccolò is on the street.

"I should have known," he grumbles. "But I got the message." Niccolò looks skyward. "Thank you, G.O.D. You have shown me the importance of maintaining one's dignity when in the service of the Lord. With your blessing, I will continue to help those who wish to repent for their sins. I firmly believe that 'SOS Confessions' is an honorable endeavor. And I assure you Jim Koepfer, I am not a 'beach hustler.' I am a disciple of God. Do you know what G.O.D. stands for? The Gift of Dignity! God has given me this gift, and I must show myself worthy of it. So, yes, it is without hesitation that I make this promise. I will be a good boy on Friday. I hate to disappoint you, Lucy. But, I am the Pope. And I must act like the Pope."

"Poppycock!" exclaims an old lady passing by.

18 THE POPE'S FOLLY

On Thursday, the wind kicks up, black clouds roll in from the sea, the mercury drops, and it begins to sprinkle. A storm threatens. Most of the vendors resist the temptation to call it a day, and there is no significant decrease in the number of potential customers on the Ocean Front Walk. There is something romantic about troubled waters, troubled skies. And, besides, storms are a rare treat in this part of the world.

Franklin stops by Lucy's Crossroad Accessories to deliver the weather forecast. "I don't want to alarm you, but–"

"Just get to the point, Franklin. Do I close up shop or not?"

"When the storm hits, all these people are going to scatter." Franklin's attention turns to the sliding door of the confession van. A middle-aged man, with a peaceful expression on his face, steps out and glances skyward, as if expecting to be blinded by the radiance of God. Instead, he takes a heavy raindrop in the eye. He wipes away the splatter with two passes of a forefinger, shakes Niccolò's hand, and thanks his confessor with a smile.

"Come back and see me, Mr. Harcroft," urges Niccolò, his hand resting gently on his client's shoulder. "And may God be with you."

"Hey, Poppy!" calls Franklin–his voice full of cheer–after Mr. Harcroft has left. "How's business in there?"

Niccolò is a bit annoyed by the word "business."

"Business is always good, Franklin. Because I'm in the business of mending souls. And that can only be a good thing."

"Of course! But you do have a price structure there." Franklin points to a magnetic sign on the van. "'Five dollars. Minimum fee.' A man has to make a living, right?"

"It's not a fee, Franklin. It's a charitable donation."

"It's an investment in one's soul, right Poppy?" interjects Lucy.

"Exactly."

"Franklin tells me we're in for a big storm, Poppy. I think we'd better pack up and leave."

Lucy turns to Franklin, but he interrupts her even before she speaks.

"Sorry, Lucy! I would love to donate my time and energy. But I can't. Not really. I need to make people aware of the storm alert. Maybe you can help?"

"I'll spread the word," offers Niccolò as Franklin departs.

"See you on Sunday," shouts Franklin over his shoulder.

"There goes Paul Revere," giggles Lucy. "Bad weather is coming! Bad weather is coming!"

Niccolò quietly laughs as he dismantles one of the crucifix displays.

That night, Venice and its neighboring communities batten down the hatches and weather the storm.

Lucy lives in a small one-bedroom apartment. Niccolò usually sleeps in the van. For one thing, Lucy's tufted couch has

The Pope's Folly

too many dangling buttons that poke the flesh. For another, the couch is too short, and not firm in the least. Moreover, it's difficult to access because the floor is always cluttered despite the occasional valiant attempt to organize the place. This night, however, Lucy decides to sleep on the couch. She offers Niccolò her bedroom.

"I'll make the bed," she says, swinging open the linen closet door and breaking out some clean white sheets.

"It's too much trouble," objects Niccolò.

A sharp clap of thunder rips menacingly through the air, which is so heavy that it mutes the voice and belabors the lungs. Lucy twitches nervously.

"The van leaks," she explains. Niccolò doubts the veracity of this excuse. He suspects that Lucy simply needs the comfort of companionship on a stormy night.

Once he has fallen asleep, Niccolò dreams of zombie vampires—and, of course, he's one of them! Who says a zombie vampire cannot have once been a priest? Or the Pope? As Niccolò looks about nervously for the flame thrower he suspects will toast him, his eyes fall upon Francine, standing barefoot in a white transparent taffeta gown. When Niccolò begins slowly teetering towards her, she recognizes him, and raises her hand to stifle the inevitable gasp of horror. For a moment, Francine is utterly petrified, but as Niccolò draws near, she recovers the use of mind and limb, and is able to narrowly escape her pursuer's grasp by breaking into a small (and shrinking) chapel that has somehow materialized in the dream. She dashes through the pews to a cross sitting on a table by some flaming candles and a pile of dusty church programs. As Niccolò advances sluggishly towards his prey, hissing and flashing his brilliant fangs, Francine seizes the cross and brandishes it in his face, but this does not deter him in the least. Niccolò's piercing *red* eyes remain fixated on her neck, and Francine is forced to retreat to the wall, where she becomes momentarily entangled in the chapel's cobweb drapery.... Refusing to believe in the total ineffectiveness of the holy cross, Francine grips it even more tightly—so tightly, in fact, that her knuckles turn white, and her palms begin to bleed. But despite her faith in the role of the cross in traditional vampire lore, she cannot persuade the cross to perform its duty. Clearly, the cross alone will not save her.... Francine successfully evades her undead assailant, and dashes back to the table, where she grasps a candle with her free hand. Waving it frantically in her aggressor's face, she screams, "Go to hell!" Niccolò, however, mocks the flame, which, in any event, is soon extinguished by a sudden rush of chill air, and pushes his victim back to the table's edge. Francine drops the dead candle, and begins jabbing Niccolò in the chest with her cross—but to no avail.... Niccolò cannot be stopped, and Francine can no longer escape. The chapel has so shrunk in size that it will soon become a coffin. With calm resignation, Francine leans back over the table, closes her eyes, and turns her head aside, revealing the tender flesh of her neck. Niccolò drools with anticipation. But before he can sink his fangs into Francine's neck, Niccolò—despite being a zombie *vampire*—is violently assaulted by a swarm of angry bats that has surged up from the chapel's secret hell pit. In short order, the bats shred Niccolò to bits. And then they consume his soul.

  Lucy is startled awake by a harrowing shriek. She jumps off the couch, fights her way through the clutter, and nearly rips the knob off the bedroom door. She finds poor Niccolò sitting up straight, pale as a ghost.

  "Nightmare?" she asks, taking a deep breath.

  Niccolò nods. "God has sent me a message. I need to face my demons."

The next morning, the streets are wet, and it is overcast. The rain is light, and spotty. Niccolò turns over in bed, and finds Lucy sleeping on the floor beside it. Her nose is hanging off the edge of a couch pillow, and her body is all twisted inside a cheap blanket.

Niccolò climbs slowly out of bed. He kneels down on the side of the bed opposite Lucy and quietly prays.

Later, on the oceanfront, Lucy and Niccolò are hailed by another familiar face. This time, it's Litzy.

"Lucy! Niccolò!"

"Litzy. How are you?" Lucy glances at Niccolò, who is obviously pleased to be called by his real name.

"Veronica and I are doing just fine, thank you!"

Lucy checks out Litzy's baby bump. "What brings you to the beach today?"

"Well, I can't say it's the sun. How is it going?"

Lucy shakes her head. "Not much business today. And Poppy is leaving early. He has—"

"A dinner engagement. With an old acquaintance," interjects Niccolò, glancing at Lucy, who was on the verge of calling it a date, something perhaps not altogether befitting of the Pope.

"That's wonderful," says Litzy. "I just came by to let you know that I had another chat with Father Priestley. He showed me his Ouija board."

"Oh? Was he looking for an alias?"

"Uh-huh. But it's a secret! Anyway, he began asking questions about you, Niccolò. And guess what?"

"I'm in the clear?"

"Well, let's put it this way. You got a clean bill of health. But you're definitely not the Pope."

Niccolò shrugs. "Well, I certainly feel better."

Lucy rolls her eyes.

"So are you coming to church on Sunday?" asks Litzy.

"Yes, of course. Lucy told me you and Sam already put in a good word for me. What made you see Father Priestley again?"

"Oh. I had some questions about Veronica's baptism."

Lucy laughs. "So the curse is off?"

"Well, the Ouija board confirmed that Niccolò is *not* a heretic. Just a bit off in the head, that's all. So God had a change of heart, I guess. But Father Priestley did caution me to take whatever Poppy says with a grain of salt. But I'm with you all the way, Niccolò. You can count on that!"

Niccolò smiles.

"Oh, I have something for you." Litzy digs an envelope out of her bag, and hands it to Niccolò.

Niccolò opens the envelope.

"It's a postcard my mother sent me from Santa Fe a few years ago. That's a picture of San Miguel Mission on the front. It's yours to keep."

Niccolò flips the postcard over to read the description, and glances at the handwritten note from Litzy's mother. It's in Spanish.

"I don't even read Spanish," admits Litzy. "I had to have it translated!"

"¡Bienvenida!" laughs Niccolò, remembering Sam's aside at their annual pilgrimage in the desert.

"Oh, it's okay. Rosita talks to me in Spanish all the time. And Carlos forgets. But they should know better. Their children don't speak a word."

"But they can *sing* it," jokes Lucy, putting a bit of screech in the word "sing."

"Well, Litzy. This is really very touching, Litzy. Thank you." Niccolò gives her a warm hug.

That evening, Niccolò arrives at the Auberge Ginette. He is a bit nervous.

"I promise to be a good boy," he reminds himself as he steps into the eggplant-colored lobby.

A voice rings out from the bedroom.

"Have a seat, Nic! I'm just putting the ironing board away. Is it still wet out there?"

"Streets are dry," replies Niccolò.

"I washed the car yesterday afternoon, and now it's got rain spots all over it."

Niccolò notices a fish tank that wasn't there before. "You bought an aquarium?" He walks over to have a look.

Francine exits the bedroom with Niccolò's salmon-colored shirt on a hanger. In her other hand, she is carrying a white undershirt, freshly ironed.

"They're all tetras. Isn't that crazy? That one is a cardinal tetra. You'll also find some green neon tetras, a couple of blue tetras, and a bleeding heart tetra in there somewhere. They swam in from the street last night. So I made a home for them."

Niccolò laughs. "You forgot to remove the 'Fish-N-Moor' tag on the tank."

"Oh, yes. You're right." She tosses the undershirt to Niccolò, who catches it with great reluctance.

"I bought it for you this afternoon."

Niccolò's eyes plead for an explanation.

Francine lifts the salmon shirt slightly. "You can't wear this over a printed t-shirt, now can you?"

Niccolò balks at the idea.

"Oh, come on now! Stop your puffing. You can change in the bedroom. But watch out. There's a picture of the Pope on the wall."

"A picture of me?"

"Your predecessor. Pope What's-His-Name."

Francine and Niccolò both laugh.

"Oh, we used to shower together. Back when I was just a cardinal."

Francine laughs even harder. She shakes her head, walks to the aquarium, and grabs the fish food. "And here's your dinner. It's not French cuisine, but I'm sure you won't mind."

Moments later, Niccolò comes out of the bedroom. His eyes are sparkling.

"Oh là là!"

Francine parks her Fiat 500Pi behind the restaurant. The car is a metallic purple, but it has a gray sunroof cover.

Niccolò and Francine are greeted at the restaurant door. "Welcome to L.A. Bonne Table. I'll let Fabrice know you have arrived."

"Thank you, Roberto."

"Roberto?" whispers Niccolò incredulously, as they are seated by a server and given menus to ponder.

"My name is Reuben. I'll be your server tonight."

Niccolò maintains a straight face. But just barely.

Francine hands the menus back to Reuben. "I'm sorry, Reuben. We've already ordered. But we'll keep the wine list."

"Very well. But I am still your server," insists Reuben with a wink of the eye.

"You are quite amused," states Francine after Reuben has departed.

"Thoroughly amused," confirms Niccolò.

"You can order online," explains Francine.

"And what did you order?" inquires Niccolò.

"The *Chef's surprise*! But don't worry. You can't go wrong with Fabrice."

"Well, then." Niccolò taps his cotton napkin with an air of anticipation.

During the meal, Niccolò tells Francine about his misadventure in the movie industry. Francine laughs till her eyes weep. Niccolò also confirms that his friend, Lucy Ferguson, is *the* Lucy with whom her brother had a romantic fling.

"He had to ditch the funky beach party scene, Nic. Things got serious for him. You were talking about dignity a moment ago. That's what it's all about. Fabrice has an image now. He represents L.A. Bonne Table. He's been on television."

"I understand. But Lucy is not a volleyball bimbo. She's a vendor of religious accessories. At the very least, she deserved a dignified goodbye."

"I'm sorry, Nic. You're right. Hey! Maybe I could meet her. She's on the Ocean Front Walk, right?"

"Lucy's Crossroad Accessories. But it's easier to just ask for 'The Gerbil.'"

Francine laughs. "Okay! Whatever! Look. I'll stop by. We can go shopping. I'll buy you some more underwear!"

Niccolò laughs, then clears his throat, somewhat embarrassed. "You'll like Lucy. She's a kind of love child. Very spiritual. In her own way. But she'll probably put you on the spot. She's very upset with your brother. And I must confess. I brought her up to speed."

"Don't worry. I can handle the girl talk. Whatever she says about Fabrice, I'll just let it slide off my back. I really can't defend what he did, not from a female perspective. Besides, he did to Lucy what the Old Nic did to me. But I hope she understands why Fabrice pulled the rug out from under their relationship. You said it yourself. She's a free spirit. She wouldn't fit in here. Not with this crowd."

Francine glances about the restaurant, as if to prove her point. Niccolò nods, but Francine suspects that he is not truly convinced.

"Fabrice makes a great sauce Soubise, don't you agree?"

As dinner progresses, Niccolò and Francine lose themselves in the conversation. Although they polish off their plates, the wine continues to pour. Reuben, their server, is only too happy to bring another bottle.

Niccolò approves. "My compliments to the sommelier."

With a wink, Reuben replies, "Your brother wishes me to inform you that he will be taking the stage in five minutes. He said he would stop by your table."

A few minutes later, a man in his early fifties approaches Francine's table at a brisk pace. "Francine!"

"Fabrice. I would like you to meet Niccolò di Montachiesa."

"I am truly honored, Your Holiness," says Fabrice. "Francine has told me so many wonderful things about you."

"There is no protocol here," advises Niccolò. He thrusts his hand out to meet Fabrice's, and engages him in a firm handshake. "Oh! And you may call me…Niccolò, I guess. I look forward to hearing you sing."

Fabrice puffs his displeasure. "These songs? They are all so stale! You won't hear them anywhere else. Except maybe on old vinyl records."

Niccolò chuckles. "But I'm sure you sing them well," he adds politely.

"Hein! We shall see!"

Niccolò pours himself another glass of wine. Fabrice takes the stage and begins a lengthy repertoire of rotten oldies that are nevertheless met with enthusiastic applause. After a half dozen songs, Francine and Niccolò resume their conversation. Francine notices that Niccolò is having a few glasses too many, but perhaps she is secretly considering the advantages this may present to her later at the Auberge Ginette. She figures that Niccolò needs to loosen up, so let the wine do its job. She begins to fantasize.

Meanwhile, Niccolò is spilling Vatican secrets left and right in a mix of English and Italian.

Finally, Niccolò rises to his feet, stumbles to the stage, grabs the microphone from Fabrice's hands, and begins to sing…in Latin! Dreadful liturgical music sung by a wine-slurred voice! Forks, knives, and spoons freeze in midair. When Fabrice tries to regain the microphone, Niccolò slaps Fabrice in the face. "Ça, c'est pour Lucy!" Fabrice is stunned. Niccolò falls off the stage and lands flat on his face. He looks up and is blinded by the spotlight, which has shifted from the stage to the drunk on the floor.

Francine jumps up from the table and runs to his aid. Roberto, Reuben, and four restaurant patrons help him out to the car.

"Well, I guess he had it coming to him," concludes Francine, speaking to Niccolò, and referring to her brother.

Francine's helpers misinterpret her statement, however. They assume she is talking to them, and that her reference is to the drunk.

"Jesus, Francine. You've got a boozer and a bozo all wrapped up in one here!"

"I'd give this soda popper the boot, if I were you."

"If that slaphappy prick of yours had punched *me*, I would've crushed him like a can of split pea soup!"

"You've got that right! I still can't believe the Fab just stood there and took it like that!"

"He'll be calling his lawyer in the morning. You can bet on that!"

"Cast your stones, if you will. But we all have sinned."

Francine chooses to ignore all but the last comment. "Just help me get him in the car," she grunts. As they struggle to do so, Francine quietly thanks the man who last spoke.

Once Niccolò is buckled into his seat, Francine pats him reassuringly on the thigh. "I'm taking you home, Nic." Then, once the car is in motion, she closes her eyes firmly and shakes her head in disbelief. "My God, my God, my God.... What a mess! What a total disaster that was!"

By the time Francine parks her Fiat 500Pi on the sidewalk at the Auberge Ginette, she is so sick of invoking God's name, and so weary of uttering one complaint after another, that she decides to put the evening's train wreck behind her. As Niccolò staggers up the steps to the front door of the inn, Francine draws him close. She helps him maintain his balance, and steadies his bobbing head by cradling it in the palm of her hand. These charitable actions have an effect upon her. They allow her to throw out the last scraps of resentment, and to untarnish the pity she has for this man. Once inside, she guides Niccolò to her bedroom and lets him tumble into the sheets. She looks up at Pope What's-His-Name and heaves a big heavy sigh. "This is your legacy," she laments.

After she arranges Niccolò in bed, she kisses him goodnight, walks to the door, and turns off the light. "Sweet dreams, Nic."

Francine collapses in a kitchen chair. She looks up at Saint Bernadette. "I'll find a way–but an honest way."

19 THE POPE AND THE FISHING HOLE

The next morning, Francine serves her famous eggplant beignets as usual. She pours Niccolò a cup of freshly brewed coffee. The coffee scorches Niccolò's tongue, but he appreciates the strong flavor. He sets the cup down, and rubs the lump on his forehead.

"How do you feel–?" begins Francine.

"I'm a bit sore. And my head is buzzing."

"That's to be expected. How do you feel about what *happened?*"

Niccolò heaves a sigh, and then takes another sip of coffee.

"I think God was looking out for me. I could have broken something."

Francine is clearly dissatisfied with his response. He apparently is not ready to face himself.

"Well," she shrugs, "let's not dwell on it. Listen, Nic. You're in no shape to *confess* anyone today. So I'm taking the reins for the day. The first thing we're going to do is pay a visit to Lucy. She probably wonders what happened to you. Do you have a change of clothes in the van?"

"I think so," replies Niccolò between sips of coffee. "You didn't undress me last night?"

"I took off your *shoes.*"

After breakfast, Francine drives Niccolò to Venice Beach in her Fiat 500Pi. After refreshing Niccolò's conveniently cloudy memory of what transpired at the restaurant, Francine insists on telling the story in all its embarrassing details to Lucy. After all, Niccolò avenged Lucy by slapping Fabrice in the face. Niccolò reluctantly agrees to corroborate the story. After parking the car, they walk to Lucy's Crossroad Accessories. Lucy sees them coming.

"Good morning, Lucy. I'd like you to meet Francine."

"Francine." Lucy's voice is strained, and there is a glint of hostility in her eye. "I had a feeling you'd bring Poppy home this morning. Did you two have a good time at the, uh, *restaurant?*"

The implication is lost on Francine and Niccolò. Instead, they exchange a look, as if to say, "Here goes!"

"I'm going to change," proposes Niccolò once all has been told. Francine, who got little more from Niccolò than the occasional nod, takes a deep breath of ocean breeze. Niccolò heads for the van.

"So what are your plans for the day?" asks Lucy, who by now has warmed up to Francine.

"And pray for my sins," adds Niccolò from afar, but apparently addressing himself, as he closes the van door.

"First, we're going shopping. I'm going to buy Nic a few things. After that, I have to do some tagging–"

"Tagging?" interrupts Lucy.

Francine produces her business card. "I put these on windshields."

"Oh! I have one of those," admits Lucy. "I used to throw them away."

"Most people do. But the name sticks, and I get enough business to make the effort worthwhile."

"So Poppy is going to help you with the cards?"

"No. Actually, he's going to preach from the sunroof of my car."

"A Poppymobile," jokes Lucy.

Francine cracks a smile, but turns dead serious. "Lucy. I know you don't believe Nic. But I can assure you. He *is* the Pope."

"Why? Because he kept his clothes on last night?"

Francine shakes off the urge to offer a nasty riposte. Instead, she chooses to ignore the comment. "Look up Pope Ignatius I on the internet."

"I have. 'Poppy's a doppelgänger.' That's what Father Vögelhau–I mean *Priestley*–always says. But I think it's shameful that Poppy capitalizes on his resemblance to the Pope. I mean, he really plays it up. Sometimes, I think he actually believes it. Delusions of grandeur, I guess. Anyway, it's not very respectful. Especially not in a House of God."

"I understand your skepticism." Francine's eyes drop a bit. "I'm having doubts myself. Not about his being the Pope–that is undeniable–but about who he was before that. I can't really discuss it. But I think I knew Nic as a young man. I've been trying to pin him down on it, but he's a slippery devil!"

Lucy raises an eyebrow.

"So I have no choice but to force it out of him. And to do that, I need proof. And I know exactly where that proof lies. Under his shirt! All I have to do is–"

Niccolò opens the van door.

"Please don't say a word!" whispers Francine.

Lucy shrugs. "Sure."

"We're off to Santa Monica," announces Francine.

"Oh, Goode," quips Lucy, citing a popular expression.

"We'll be back soon." Niccolò blows her a kiss of appreciation.

Francine and Niccolò take the Fiat 500Pi. After an hour and a half of shopping at the Third Street Promenade, they return to Lucy's Crossroad Accessories with a dozen shopping bags.

"What all did you buy?" prompts Lucy when they return.

"Sunday best," replies Francine. "And some street clothes, too."

"But only one shirt," remarks Niccolò. Again, he heads for the van.

"He insisted on it. But I also bought him a nice jacket. Winter stuff on sale," confides Francine.

"What about unmentionables?"

Francine gives Lucy a thumb's up.

By eleven o'clock, Lucy is busy tagging cars, slipping business cards beneath their windshield wipers. The town of Santa Monica retains its Catholic name, despite a nationwide movement to secularize place names. But wherever Mayor Goode goes, he leaves an eponymous gumdrop behind, the most infamous of which is his renaming of Santa Monica Boulevard. It is now called Goode Boulevard, and is part of the proposed Goode-Monrovia Freeway.

While Lucy tags cars at a motel on Mongolian Avenue, Niccolò, looking sharp in his new white linen shirt, pokes himself through the Fiat 500Pi's sunroof. Having prepared his sermon, he now begins to preach to anyone who will stop and listen. The first passersby shake their head or smile with amusement without breaking stride. But soon a handful of people gather round. Niccolò, who is quoting from Mark, Chapter 9, is soon interrupted by a well-dressed man in his late thirties.

The Pope and The Fishing Hole

> Now after six days Jesus took Peter, James, and John, and led them up on a high mountain apart by themselves; and He was transfigured before them. His clothes became shining, exceedingly white, like snow, such as no launderer on earth can whiten them. And Elijah appeared to them–

"Rabbi, it is good for us to be here!" shouts the man.

"And what is your name?" begs Niccolò, both annoyed and intrigued. "Surely, it is not Peter?"

"No, no! My name is Herman. You quote the Bible well," he acknowledges with faint praise.

"I am the Pope," confirms Niccolò. "It is my business to know the Bible. Now, if I may continue?"

Herman juts his head forward and squints. Those who stand near him whisper amongst themselves.

"You're some kind of religious lunatic," dismisses one man, waving him off. He turns on his heel, and walks away. A young couple does the same.

"I half expect a cloud to come and overshadow us," utters Herman.

Niccolò quotes a verse in response.

> And a voice came out of the cloud, saying, "This is My beloved Son. Hear Him!"

Herman looks around. Everyone has disappeared. He is alone with the "Pope."

"I'm listening," assures Herman. "But I prefer to hear you sing. Your Latin is quite good!"

Niccolò ducks back into the car, and a moment later steps out onto the street.

"You're not going to slap me are you?" Herman backs up slightly, but in jest.

"I must confess," admits Niccolò. "I made a complete ass of myself last night."

"Yes, and it took six of us to haul your holy ass out to the car." Herman glances at the Fiat 500Pi.

Niccolò doesn't quite know what to say. But he is puzzled by the smirk on Herman's face.

"I'm Father Grabenstock. Well, I used to be. I work for various charity organizations now."

"Catholic Charities?"

"Not anymore. The charities I work for have dropped their religious banner in order to survive. We have to appeal to community pockets. And most pockets don't have an angel in them anymore."

"It's an honest living," observes Niccolò.

"Yes, but I'm not always an honest man. In fact, I, too, have a confession to make. A really small one, though. I'm not one to make a 'complete ass of myself.'"

Niccolò takes the jab with a bitter smile. "I'm listening."

"My name is not Herman. You asked if I were Peter, which I took as a joke. So I played off the name of the 'high mountain' in the passage from Mark you were citing. You know, Mount Hermon."

Niccolò is visibly embarrassed.

"But I guess it slipped by you. Anyway, my first name is Ervin."

"You are still Father Grabenstock in God's eyes," replies Niccolò. "And in mine."

"That strikes me as a wee bit pretentious. Do you really expect people to believe that you're the Pope?"

"I do, at the very least, expect a Catholic priest to believe me," retorts Niccolò, satisfied to get in a jab of his own.

"Absent the facial hair, you do bear an uncanny likeness to the Pope. And you've done your religious homework. I must admit, you impress me. But people aren't nearly as ignorant or as gullible as you think. They know you're not the Pope. And you certainly can't fool a priest!"

Niccolò pulls a business card out of his pocket and hands it to Father Grabenstock, who accepts it, but barely deems it worthy of a glance.

"If you change your mind, come see me. I'm located on the Ocean Front Walk in Venice. Just look for Lucy's Crossroad Accessories, or my van, 'SOS Confessions.' If you don't find me right away, ask for Poppy. Everyone knows me. Now, if you'll excuse me. I would like to continue my sermon."

"Why are you doing this?" asks Father Grabenstock bluntly.

"I'm drumming up business for God. And, more specifically, I'm advocating a return to Catholicism. Perhaps you would like to have your old job back?"

Niccolò returns to the Fiat 500Pi. By the time he pokes his head through the sunroof, Father Grabenstock is gone. But there are other people in the street, and he clears his throat.

"Back to Mark," he mumbles to himself before he raises his voice and repeats the first words of the sermon he has prepared.

By the time Francine returns, about half an hour later, Niccolò is entertaining a small crowd of some fifteen adults, four of which grip the hands of children, who are fascinated by the sight of a creature that is half man, half car. Francine waits until Niccolò finishes. When he does so, Niccolò reaches down and hands his business card to those who wish to have one. Most of them do. Once the crowd disperses, Francine taps her watch.

"Time for lunch."

"Anywhere but L.A. Bonne Table," jokes Niccolò, who then reveals the details of his coincidental encounter with Father Grabenstock.

"That's going to haunt you till the end of days," says Francine, a bit tongue in cheek.

"There were quite a few people at the restaurant last night. Maybe I should pack up and move to Montachusetts."

Francine recalls the anecdote. "We'll see about that. But first, let's have lunch. I was just noticing that sushi bar across the street." Francine digs a coin purse out of her handbag and slaps some bills into the palm of Niccolò's hand. "Go order us some sushi. Find us a table by the window. I'll join you in about ten minutes. I have to do some inventory." She looks over her shoulder at the box of business cards on the floorboard.

The sushi bar is called The Fishing Hole. Its exterior is immaculate. The beautifully painted faux wood carving above the door features a country boy wearing a straw hat and cutoff jeans dropping a fishing line in a roundish pool of water. His fishing pole has been fashioned from the tree under which he sits. There are concentric rings in the water where the hook has just plopped in. A cut-away view of the pool reveals several catfish swimming in circles just a foot or two below the surface.

Niccolò studies the sign for just a second or two. "Catfish sushi?" he ponders aloud.

"Order a platter," suggests Francine. "Or just pick out a variety."

"Okay," answers Niccolò, somewhat amused.

Niccolò quickly glances left and right, crosses the street and enters The Fishing Hole. There are only a handful of people inside at this hour. Niccolò correctly assumes that this sushi bar caters primarily to the night crowd. He crosses paths with a young man who has just picked up his order. He sashays to an empty table in the corner. Niccolò's attention turns to the Sushi Queue menu posted on the wall, which is decorated with larger-than-life-size fish hooks and a colorful assortment of flies against a blue background. He then examines the sushi case, where the sushi, constantly renewed, is nestled in waves of crushed ice. An attendant awaits his order.

"Do you have a platter?"

"Mostly rounders here," wisecracks the attendant. "Would you like to order?"

"An assortment, I guess."

"Half a dozen?"

"A full dozen. There are two of us."

The attendant glances about the sushi bar. There are several lone patrons, but all of them are already eating.

"Sake?"

"No, no. My head is still swimming from last night."

"That's not an excuse," counters the attendant.

"Do you serve tea?"

The attendant points at the separately posted Swishy menu.

Niccolò quickly scans the tea selection. "Green tea, please."

"Hotbox or Icebreaker?"

Niccolò hesitates. "Hot, please."

The attendant raises an eyebrow, and once again glances around the sushi bar looking for a partner.

"Pay the cashier. We'll bring it to you."

"I'll be sitting by the window," indicates Niccolò.

"Be discreet," warns the attendant with a bit of tease in his voice. "Ever been to the Cutthroat Café?"

Niccolò shakes his head.

"No windows. But we're more open. Oh! One more thing…" The attendant looks Niccolò in the eye. "Keep it clean."

"Don't worry. We'll clean up after ourselves."

The attendant winks.

After paying the cashier, who calls up the order on her computer screen, Niccolò walks to the table which offers the best view of the Fiat 500Pi. He sits down. The table and seats are wooden, but the seats have thick cushions that make them quite comfortable.

Within seconds, a man sporting attire that reminds Niccolò of his biker days approaches.

"I prefer Pi."

"I'm sorry?"

"That's how Fiat used to advertise it." He points to the car with his chin. "My name is Roger. May I join you?"

Niccolò offers a welcoming gesture. Roger's eyes sparkle, and he displays a devilish grin. To Niccolò's surprise, Roger takes the seat beside him rather than one of the two seats directly in front of him. He introduces himself as Roger Shields, prompting Niccolo to reveal his name.

"Niccolò di Montachiesa. But you can call me Nic."

"We're very open here," reassures Roger, availing himself of an oft repeated line. "We don't hide behind an alias, club moniker, or username. You're a new face, Nic. New to the neighborhood?"

"I live in Venice." Niccolò hands him a business card.

"SOS Confessions," reads Roger.

"You can keep the card," urges Niccolò.

"SOS," repeats Roger. He cautiously slips his left hand behind Niccolò's buttocks. "I like that. I like that a lot."

Niccolò shifts uneasily in his seat.

Roger immediately withdraws his hand.

"I do confessions. And the occasional absolution. It depends on the donation."

"Do you want me to come?" Roger's fingers, having alit on the inner thigh of Niccolò's right leg, slowly inch their way towards Niccolò's crotch.

Niccolò squirms, politely fending off what is obviously a sexual advance. He then casts a furtive glance about the sushi bar. The tables are either occupied by single male patrons or by male couples. At first, he is oblivious to the significance of this. But now his eyes abandon Roger completely and take in the full panorama offered by The Fishing Hole. They settle for a moment on a mutually affectionate male couple standing at the sushi case. Both men are young, attractive, and well dressed. One of them gently massages the other between the legs, while at the same time whispering something in his partner's ear. His partner smiles, but continues to place his order. The attendant, who responds to the name Pat, seems unaware of, or uninterested in, the intimate behavior playing out before him. Instead, he takes the order as routinely as if the couple were grandpa and grandma. Niccolò is so fascinated by what he sees that it only slowly dawns on him that he is in a *gay* sushi bar.

All the while, Roger, his voice soft and soothing, has been talking about himself. Mostly about his past relationships, none of which have ended satisfactorily. All of this in the span of two or three minutes. Niccolò's mind has registered the words, but has only barely grasped their meaning.

"May I suggest a prayer?" murmurs Niccolò uneasily, turning his eyes towards the window. Francine, who has just battened down the sunroof, steps out of the Fiat 500Pi. She flattens out the wrinkles of her dress, and, looking both ways, crosses the street to The Fishing Hole.

Roger, who realizes that Niccolò is avoiding eye contact, and that he has allowed himself to be distracted by the activities of a middle-aged woman, gently lifts Niccolò's right hand and moves it from one lap to the other. He then slips Niccolò's hand down into his pants, which are tight but partially unzipped. Niccolò's fingers are then squeezed firmly upon Roger's erect penis.

Niccolò snaps his head around. He immediately withdraws his hand from Roger's pants, as quickly as if he had inadvertently laid it upon a hot stove. He then grips his errant hand with the other, as if to massage the pain of burnt flesh, and offers Roger an icy look of reproach.

Roger is offended and jumps to his feet. He bumps into the sushi bar runner who is delivering the order to Niccolò's table. The runner is able to maintain the integrity of the tray, even though the teapot slides dangerously close to the edge.

"What the fuck is your game?" snaps Roger angrily as he pushes his way past the runner. He storms past Francine, whose smile he greets with a flash of contempt.

"Roger can't take rejection," explains the runner. "That's the second tantrum this week."

"Just in time," remarks Francine, as the runner sets the order down on the table. She gives the sushi assortment a quick look of approval. "Who was that?"

"That was Roger Shields," responds Niccolò dryly as he rises to his feet. He slips around the end of the table, pulls out a chair on the opposite side, and seats Francine.

Francine bats her eyelashes with gratitude. "Thank you, Nic." She peers out the window as Niccolò returns to his side of the table. Roger hops on his electric motorcycle, already humming, and revs it up a few times before violently retracting the kickstand. "He seems to be in a hurry," observes Francine, as Roger punches the motorcycle's engine. He leaps into the street, and veers around an oncoming car, which he narrowly misses. "Reminds me of Biker Nic," says Francine wistfully, tapping the bottom of her chin.

Niccolò frowns. He doesn't appreciate the comparison.

"You look upset. Are you okay?" inquires Francine, feigning compassion.

"Yes. I mean, look around. It's a nice place."

"It's okay," admits Francine.

"*It's so gay*," echoes Niccolò, "because it's a *gay* sushi bar."

Francine notes that practically every patron in the sushi bar is staring at her warily, as if she were a creature from another planet. Amused, she leans forward and says, "Roger that."

After lunch, Francine drives Niccolò back to Venice Beach, where they find Lucy coaching some tourists on how to play Christian Triviaticum, a not-too-popular videogame in which players navigate a moral minefield and answer increasingly difficult trivia questions in order to graduate to the next level of play. God and Satan pop up now and then to tally the points, but players encounter helpful angels and mischievous demons throughout every step of the game.

Niccolò and Francine watch for a few minutes, offer a few words of encouragement and congratulations, and then head to Mr. Crane's bicycle shop across the way. En route, they pause to watch "The Gerbil," who is performing a "looping track" stunt on his unicycle.

"That's Travis, Mr. Crane's nephew. He works part-time at the bicycle shop, and has been known to cover a lunch break or two for the vendors. Travis confessed his sins to me one day. I can't disclose the details, of course, but suffice it to say that his past is not very clean. But he redeems himself every day."

"He's on the right track," suggests Francine.

Niccolò smiles. "You could say that."

Upon entering Mr. Crane's bicycle shop, which is known simply as "Mr. Crane's" by the locals, Francine's attention is drawn to the "Rentals" sign. She fails therefore to notice the empty soda can that has rolled out onto the floor. She crunches one end of it with her foot, and loses her balance. To steady her fall, she grabs Niccolò by the arm.

Mr. Crane tosses aside a bicycle seat cover he was pricing, and runs over to assist them, but Francine has already found her footing. However, she does not release her hold on Niccolò's arm. Instead, she leans into him. Mr. Crane bends down and picks up the soda can, and tosses it into the wastepaper basket sitting beside the rental desk.

"Kids," he groans. "First of all, they can't read. The sign says 'No Food or Drink.' And secondly, they're not content to just drop it in the waste basket. They have to make a long shot. Obviously, somebody missed."

Francine blows it off. "It's not important, Mr. Crane. Really, it's no big deal." She is still clutching Niccolò's arm. "We'd like to rent a couple of bikes."

"How long?" Mr. Crane's mood brightens as he slips behind the rental desk.

"Two hours." Francine turns to Niccolò. "Three?" Niccolò doesn't respond. His mind is preoccupied. "No, we'll go for two. Do you have any purple ones?"

Mr. Crane, who is already preparing the paperwork, points to a lady's bike. "Lavender."

"Oh, that's *perfect*. What color do you want, Nic? What about that metallic green one over there? We'll take that one, Mr. Crane. How much do we owe you?"

Mr. Crane's is conveniently located across from the northern stretch of the Bike Path, which runs alongside the Ocean Front Walk. Niccolò and Francine join the parade of outdoor enthusiasts, and then pedal the meandering bikeway south towards Washington Boulevard. Rather than abandon their bicycles for a walk on Venice Pier, they take the boulevard eastward and turn north on Dell Avenue for some "bridge hopping."

The first bridge arches over Sherman Canal. Niccolò and Francine stop at the midpoint of the bridge to observe a young romantic couple in a gondola which is slipping through the placid water towards them. A rented gondolier is singing an obscure Italian operetta, and now and then makes sweeping gestures, as if inviting the owners of the luxurious homes that border the canal to abandon their rigid schedules for a moment and let their imagination float to the music.

Francine squints. "Have you ever done that?"

"I grew up in Burano," replies Niccolò, implying the affirmative.

"I mean, have you ever taken a *romantic* gondola ride?"

Niccolò is caught off guard.

"Romantic, I don't know. But there was this American girl named Hazel. When I met her, she was putting the finishing touches on the bell tower of San Martino di Burano. The church itself is unremarkable, at least for the natives, but its leaning campanile is quite striking, rising as it does above a bouquet of houses painted in bright pastels that reflect nicely in the water. It's a popular canvas for the budding artist. And Hazel was an art student. She'd rented a studio in Venice for the summer. She didn't speak a word of Italian, so when she realized I was fluent in English, she began to talk my ears off, which left me little opportunity to lay on the charm. Anyway, after an hour or so of describing the scenic wonders of Wisconsin, she invited me to accompany her back to the studio, where she gave me a quick tour of her private gallery of water color paintings. They were not very impressive, but, of course, I praised them with great enthusiasm. Afterward, we walked the canals, and, on a whim, I rented a gondola. And there you have it."

"I think there's more to be had. Did you score?"

"That wasn't part of your question," dismisses Niccolò.

Francine heaves a deep sigh of exasperation. "Can you please explain to me, Nic, why you keep such a tight lid on the sexual exploits of your Karmann Ghia days?"

"My sexual exploits aren't worth a hill of beans."

"Well, why don't you spill a few more beans, and let me be the judge of that."

Niccolò fixates on the gondola, which is about to pass under the bridge. "There's nothing more to tell, really. I guess you could say I scored. But she wasn't much of a lay."

"Oh, really! And how did you come to *that* conclusion?" Francine grips Niccolò's shoulder as he leans forward to ponder the disappearing gondola. She pulls him back, then slips her hand behind his jaw, and turns his face towards hers.

"She wasn't a good lay? Then you've had some experience under the sheets. Tell me, Nic!"

Niccolò gropes for an answer. "She wasn't a good lay because, well, I didn't know how to lay her."

"Nic, you have Italian blood flowing through your veins."

Niccolò avoids the issue by wheeling his bicycle to the other side of the bridge. The young couple in the gondola looks up this time, and waves. Niccolò nods politely.

"Why are you so secretive about your history with girls?" The handlebars of Francine's bike hook onto Niccolò's. "Could it be that you prefer boys?"

"Roger didn't think so," answers Niccolò sharply.

"And neither do I." Their bikes clash as Francine leans over, wraps her arms around Niccolò, and tries to embrace him. Niccolò tries to fend off the kiss, but loses his balance, causing the front wheel of his bicycle to turn aside. He and Francine topple along with their bikes. Niccolò suffers the triple impact of the pavement, his biking partner, and her lavender ride.

Francine finds herself on top of Niccolò, who does not appear to be seriously injured, but who is wincing and is therefore in some pain. But Francine doesn't budge. She is on a mission, and she's not going to let this unforeseen opportunity slip her by.

Niccolò is pinned beneath her, and can no longer resist. But just as Francine is about to plant her lips upon Niccolò's, she is startled by the harsh slam of a car door.

"Are you okay?" shouts the driver urgently.

The car's engine is still running. The driver is already running. And Francine realizes that she's running–out of time! She presses her lips against Niccolò's and delivers a powerful kiss before she is ripped away by the driver.

"We're fine. Just a bit bruised," she assures the driver, who is wearing a business suit.

"Sir?" The businessman takes Niccolò by the arm and helps him to his feet.

"Shaken, thank you."

"What happened?"

"We fell in love?" shrugs Francine, painfully aware of her cliché.

20 THE POPE SAYS A PRAYER

That evening, Francine prepares the final coup.

She begins with the all-important aphrodisiac: a kiss gin cocktail. First, she pours bitter, ginger ale, gin, and tiny ice cubes into a shaker, makes a few swirls to chill the drink, and serves it in two cocktail glasses, taking care to hold back the ice. Then, she selects two Maraschino cherries from a small petal-rimmed bowl, stabs them gently with a plastic sword (green for her, red for him), and slips them into the glasses. Finally, she sets them on a silver tray, upon which has already been arranged a selection of tasty canapés, and walks to the sofa, where Niccolò is reading up on the Venice canals.

"Nic, I have a confession to make." Francine sets the tray down on an oval cocktail table. She curls up on the sofa beside him, and reaches gracefully for the glasses.

"Fire away," encourages Niccolò, accepting his drink. But before Francine can put her thoughts into words, he interrupts her.

"The Sherman Canal was built by the Short Line Beach Company. Look, here's a picture of Moses Sherman. He called the development 'New Amsterdam' because it was based on the Dutch model. Look, here's Fred Howland, an officer of the company. Remember the Howland Canal? We walked our bikes over that one, remember? They don't have a picture of Carroll Daly, but they named a canal after him, too. That's where we saw the old lady in the skiff. I think you were right about her. Those binoculars were for spying on the neighbors, not for bird watching. Let's see here. Hmm! No. I don't see a reference to anyone named Linnie. Remember that little park on the canal, though?"

"All I remember is the startled look in those big green eyes of yours when I kissed you."

Niccolò smiles in spite of himself. He is somewhat embarrassed by this smile, and endeavors to hide it by taking his first sip of kiss gin cocktail. Before he accomplishes this, however, Francine plucks the green plastic sword out of her own drink, and, pucking her red glossy lips, clinches the cherry with her pearly whites. Then, she gently slides the blade out of the Maraschino cherry, and flings the sword aside without care. Now, she peers into Niccolò's eyes, raising an eyebrow seductively. Gently, she lowers her lip, and then bites the cherry.

Niccolò takes the hint. He removes the cherry from the red plastic sword with his fingertips. He chews on the cherry a bit, and then chases it with the gin.

"That's not exactly a confession. More of an observation," opines Niccolò, trying to avoid the moment, and put the conversation back on track.

"A canapé, Nic?" offers Francine.

Niccolò passes over the salmon, and considers the cream cheese. But he picks up the pâté.

Francine chooses the salmon. "Okay, I'll confess. I knew The Fishing Hole was a gay sushi bar."

"I suspected as much."

"It was Pat's idea, not mine."

"Pat? The sushi bar attendant?" frowns Niccolò, nibbling on his pâté.

"Don't be silly, Nic! All my friends are straight. *Miss* Patricia Haggis is a boarder here. And she'd like to meet you sometime."

"And what am I to her, exactly?"

"Well. You're not the Pope, if that's what you mean."

"I'm your boyfriend?" suggests Niccolò.

"She certainly hopes so."

Niccolò nods. Again, he is embarrassed. He turns his attention back to the razor-thin laptop, and flexes its screen as if to make a bridge of it.

"You know, all this time I was mistaken about the canals. I thought they were part of Abbot Kinney's 'Venice in America' project. I read up on Venice before I left Paris for the States. But the writer apparently flubbed his research because Kinney's canals were filled in and paved over more than a century ago. What's interesting is that now they are drawing up plans to build the Kinney Canal. Just one canal, but it's a start. I guess you could call it a rebirth of sorts."

"Sometimes we can pick up things that have been lost to the past," agrees Francine. "And we can begin anew."

"The difference is that Kinney Canal won't be residential this time around. It's going to be part of a new shopping district designed with Venetian architecture in mind. They even plan to have gondola rentals."

"Well, it's a long distance call to Wisconsin. I suggest you find another gondola partner. Maybe this time around, if you're lucky, you'll score a good lay."

Before Niccolò can respond, Francine takes Niccolò's hand. "Come to dinner."

They abandon the serving tray on the cocktail table. One or two canapés remain. The gin glasses are empty.

Francine plays with the dimmer switch, and then begins lighting some church candles on the dinner table.

"Candles?" Niccolò's voice is apprehensive.

"My eyes are a bit weary after all that biking in the sun. And I just happen to have some candles on hand. Sheldon's Candle Shop had a summer blow-out sale last week."

"I see," grins Niccolò. "Do I hear music?"

"Cristina Mossi." Francine adjusts the volume on a small wireless speaker sitting on a shelf along with some knick-knacks.

Niccolò listens for a moment, taking in the Italian lyrics, which are sung very softly.

"She has a very soothing voice."

"Definitely not the kind of music Biker Nic would have liked," comments Francine.

Niccolò clears his throat. "Not all Nics are alike."

"True, but time can change one's tastes. Have a seat," motions Francine, seating herself without ceremony.

Niccolò sits across from Francine. Between them, nestled together, but on separate saucers, are the two scooped out halves of a cantaloupe. They serve as bowls, offering melon balls bathed in port wine.

"Have one," suggests Francine. Niccolò reaches for one of the melons, but Francine's hand intervenes.

Niccolò sighs. He licks his lips, anticipating her unspoken request for a kiss to the back of her hand.

"You spoon the balls," commands Francine with more than a hint of insinuation. She withdraws her hand, unkissed.

"You seem to be in a romantic mood." Niccolò slowly picks up the spoon beside his plate, which is empty save for several slices of garnished Parma ham. He retrieves the melon balls, following Francine's example.

"Is that okay with you, Nic?"

Niccolò pops a melon ball into his mouth.

"Yes, of course. I like cantaloupe."

"Splendid. Why don't you try the ham? I think you'll like it, too."

"Shall I use my knife and fork?" Niccolò lingers on the question.

Francine swings up the prong end of her fork. She whispers, "Fork."

Niccolò nods, appreciatively.

After a few minutes of silence, during which Francine studies Niccolò's face and table manners, Francine's cell phone, which she has left by the aquarium, begins to ring. The ring volume is so low that it is nearly drowned out by the soft music of Cristina Mossi.

"Expecting a call?"

"It's the fish," explains Francine.

Niccolò turns around and looks at the tetras.

"And what do the fish want?"

"They want to be taken out of the oven."

Francine gets up and disappears into the kitchen. Moments later, she returns with a serving tray of the same design as the one sitting idly on the cocktail table. She sets down the serving tray, moves the melon halves aside, and places the fish platter and rice bowl in the center of the table. She then untwists the ends of the parchment paper, which, when peeled back, reveals the trout fillets inside. The fillets, baked in olive oil, are garnished with sliced cherry tomatoes and fresh basil.

"May I present the main course: *Truite en papillotte*. May I have your plate?"

"You may." Niccolò hands her a clean plate. He is clearly anxious about the tone that Francine has set for the dinner. But he is also looking forward to the meal.

After serving the fish fillets, Francine removes the lid from the rice bowl, and serves the basmati rice with a bamboo rice paddle. Once Niccolò has been served, Francine disappears once again into the kitchen. She returns with a bottle of vintage champagne, a brass corkscrew, and two sparkling champagne glasses.

"May I?" asks Niccolò.

"You may."

While Niccolò pops the cork and pours the champagne, Francine helps herself to the trout and rice.

"This all seems well orchestrated." There is admiration in Niccolò's eyes, but there is a mysterious intonation in his voice.

"I'm doing my best to keep up the tempo," admits Francine. "I hope it's not too much of a challenge for your digestion."

Niccolò laughs. "I am not so delicate."

"No, you're not." Francine seems to have entertained a sudden flashback in her mind. She smiles, as if to dismiss a cherished memory.

"Well, then. Let's have a bite."

"Fork and knife," encourages Francine. "But let's not forget the champagne. We should toast the night."

"Of course."

Francine and Niccolò raise their champagne glasses.

"We're a long way from New Year's. But I would like to quote Auld Lang Syne, with your permission."

"I'm intrigued." Niccolò perks up his ears.

"Here goes, then." Francine clears her throat.

> Should Old Acquaintance be forgot,
> and never thought upon;
> The flames of Love extinguished,
> and fully past and gone;
> Is thy sweet Heart now grown so cold,
> that loving canst never once reflect
> on Auld Lang Syne?

"My turn," interrupts Niccolò.

> My Heart is ravisht with delight,
> when thee I think upon;
> All Grief and Sorrow takes the flight,
> and speedily is gone;
> The bright resemblance of thy Face,
> so fills this Heart of mine;
> That Force nor Fate can me displease,
> for Auld Lang Syne.

"Tonight, Nic…" begins Francine. She searches for words, but settles upon, "Let's drink to it, shall we?"

"Cin cin," replies Niccolò with an uncertain smile.

They clink their champagne glasses and take a good long sip.

Francine waits for Niccolò to taste the trout.

"Well, then?" she prompts.

"Delizioso!" confirms Niccolò politely. "Assolutamente delizioso!"

Francine smiles broadly. "Hmm!"

"You should try it," encourages Niccolò.

"I will, thank you."

After a moment of culinary appreciation ("Mmm!"), Francine give Niccolò a puzzled look.

"May I ask you a question, Nic?"

"Fire away," accepts Niccolò reluctantly, albeit with a touch of amusement in his voice.

Francine giggles in spite of herself. "It's actually a very serious question. You didn't say grace tonight. Can you explain to me why? It's not the kind of thing the Pope would forget."

Niccolò pops his eyebrows in recognition of the fact.

"Francine, I–" Niccolò takes a quick sip of champagne.

"Are you hiding from God?"

Niccolò stares at his plate, unable to answer.

"You seem troubled, Nic."

"My heart is about to explode."

"May I suggest a little prayer?" Francine reaches across the table and clasps Niccolò's hands in hers.

Niccolò shakes his head. His eyes begin to tear up. "I can't."

"Listen to me, Nic. I know what you must be feeling in your heart. If you cannot pray to God, then listen to your heart. But allow me to send God a little message of my own. Dear Lord, tonight, Niccolò di Montachiesa belongs to me."

Francine draws Niccolò's hands to her mouth, and kisses them tenderly.

Niccolò turns away. Tears are streaming down his cheeks.

"It's okay, Nic. You needn't hide from me. Let the trout swim in your tears."

Niccolò smiles, and turns around to face Francine. "I'm so embarrassed."

Francine observes Niccolò compassionately as he gently wipes away his tears.

"Don't be." Francine takes a deep breath. "You're only human, Nic. And I know it sounds trout —I mean, *trite*!—but life is terribly, terribly short."

Niccolò laughs heartily. Francine's slip of the tongue, intentional or not, is a jolt of humor that somehow defuses, even if only by a small degree, the anguish he is feeling.

"I suppose a dead trout should be eaten," he suggests finally.

"Before it gets cold," agrees Francine, her eyes filled with the spectacle of the man she loves torn between laughter and tears.

The music of Cristina Rossi continues unabated. The candles continue to burn. And the tetras turn in circles, ever swimming.

Francine empties the champagne bottle in Niccolò's glass, then purrs suggestively, "I'm going to change. I'll be serving dessert on the sofa."

Niccolò offers to clear the table, but Francine turns him down with a slight wave of the hand.

"Don't bother."

Niccolò resigns himself to fate. "The sofa, then."

Francine catches a particularly sentimental moment in her favorite Cristina Rossi song, and begins to hum as she spins about and disappears into the bedroom. Moments later, she reappears, wearing black lingerie that is just sheer enough to fire the imagination. She crosses quickly into the kitchen, depriving Niccolò–who is seated on the sofa now–of the opportunity to hazard a comment, should he be able to formulate one whilst in shock.

A refrigerator door opens and closes. And Francine returns.

"May I present dessert: *Crème Chantilly aux fruits rouges*."

Niccolò cannot help but stare at Francine, who responds with a smile as she hands him a saucer and spoon.

"Here, let me help you get started." Francine plucks a strawberry–upon which she has sprinkled powdered sugar–from the crème Chantilly and feeds it to Niccolò, taking care to wipe the crème from his lips afterwards. Then she takes his spoon, and dips it deeply into the crème, picking up a raspberry in the process. She offers the spoon to Niccolò.

"Can you take it from here, darling?"

Niccolò nods slowly.

Francine snuggles up to Niccolò, and together they spoon their dessert.

"Nic, regarde-moi. Tu me reconnais ?"
"Yes."

Francine takes his empty saucer and sets it aside. She hesitates a moment, before looking into Niccolò's green eyes.

"Alors. Ce que je ressens ce soir, ce n'est pas très catholique. Tu comprends ?"

"Yes, I understand. I'm not feeling particularly Catholic myself."

Francine wraps Niccolò's arms around her. She then begins to unbutton Niccolò's shirt, stopping only once to slip her hand inside to caress his chest. She looks up at Niccolò. He does not resist.

"I'm feeling around for those gray and scraggly chest hairs."

"You won't find them," admits Niccolò.

"Perhaps I'll find something else. Let me take a look." With that, she opens wide his shirt. And in the candlelight, she sees the tattoo.

"Hells Angels," confesses Niccolò.

"It's time to rock and roll, Nic."

"Wh-What do you mean?" stutters Niccolò, who knows exactly what she means.

Francine cuts to the chase. "I want to ride your bike." Upon that, she begins to unzip Niccolò's trousers.

Much to his surprise, Niccolò does not protest. Instead, he gently strokes Francine's face. "I see a light in your eyes. You have the eyes of an angel...."

As the zipper continues its course, Niccolò peels away Francine's lingerie, revealing ample breasts. Francine draws Niccolò to her bosom, and presses him to her heart. She then slowly falls back on the sofa. Niccolò follows. And the trousers begin to slip off....

The next morning, Niccolò awakes in Francine's bed. He glances at the portrait of Pope What's-His-Name hanging above his head on the wall. Francine is busy in the dining room, no doubt preparing breakfast. The lingerie she wore the night before is merely a dark puddle on the floor now. Niccolò slips out of bed, and falls to his knees. He digs his elbows into the sheets, and clasps his hand in prayer.

"Dear Lord. I have betrayed you. I confess, I had a devil of a good time.... But–but Lord, I ask for your forgiveness. Please, I beg you. Please have mercy on my soul. Amen."

21 THE POPE GOES UP

As Niccolò sits down to breakfast, Francine hands him her cell phone.

"Lucy called. She left you a message."

Niccolò puts the cell phone on speaker, and delves into breakfast. This morning, exceptionally, it consists of French toast and three slices of bacon, along with a scattered helping of raspberries (those which escaped the crème Chantilly). Francine drops a sugar cube in Niccolò's espresso, and winks.

> "Good morning, Poppy. It's Lucy. I just called to tell you there's no need to gobble down your eggplant beignets. Take your time. Relax. And enjoy your coffee. 'Cause I've got some bad news for you. The, uh, confession van was stolen last night. You could've been kidnapped, can you imagine that? It's a good thing you spent the night with Francine. Anyway, I just got off the phone with the insurance company, and now I'm off to the police station with, uh, Father *Cornisch* to file a report. Maybe I'll run into Officer Bic. Obviously, I won't be at the beach today. So you might as well just stay with Francine. I'll check in with you

tomorrow. Keep in mind, Poppy, that I can't set up shop without the van. So, we're shut down for the time being. But Father Cornisch says, 'Not to worry. God will provide.' He must have something up his sleeve. So, I don't think you're out of the confession business just yet. But you might hold off on passing out your SOS cards while you're out preaching in the Poppymobile. By the way, Father Cornisch calls what you're doing a 'soapbox derby.' Whatever! Anyway, he's waiting outside for me. Oh, one more thing. Speaking of having something up your sleeve, tell Francine that her brother sent me some flowers. The florist must've been fresh out of red roses, because he sent me blue hyacinths instead. I put them in a red vase on the kitchen table. Oh! ...Hey, I'm looking out the window, and it looks like Father Cornisch is praying for me to get off the phone. [Niccolò can hear Lucy tapping on the window pane.] *Coming Father!* Sorry, Poppy. I gotta go. Ciao!"

"She's using a pay phone," explains Niccolò. "She keeps her cell phone in the van."

Francine doesn't care about that. "Well," she chirps. "You seem to have fallen right into my lap."

"*God will provide*," states Niccolò flatly.

Francine rejects the notion. "God has nothing to do with it. But there is one little problem.... You see the 'No Vacancy' sign in the window–?"

"I can't see it from here. But I suppose what you're trying to say is that you don't have any plans to go tagging today. *Not to worry!* There is absolutely no need to roll out the soapbox. A simple plastic crate will do. I'll string it with love beads and hang some cheap crucifixes on it. Then, we'll see what Father Cornisch has to say about that!"

"If you had a driver's license, Nic, I'd let you *borrow* the Fiat. Anytime you want. But that's not what I meant. What I was trying to say is that the only bed available at the Auberge Ginette is the one you slept in last night. In other words, my bed is your bed. It's our bed now."

Niccolò chews on his bacon.

"Face it, Nic. You're not going back to Lucy. You're with me now. And besides, it's all for the best. Think about it. When Fabrice finds out someone has stolen Lucy's van, he'll step in and buy her a new set of wheels. And then he'll have Lucy in his pocket. And she won't need you anymore. Not as a business partner, anyway. You're *my* partner now."

"You have it all backwards. I needed her, not the other way around."

"Well, you don't need her anymore. And as for the likes of Father Chameleon—"

"Cornisch."

"I thought it was *Priestley*."

"You're right. It is. But—"

"Well, he can go to hell for all I care!"

Niccolò nearly chokes on his espresso.

"Francine!"

"I'm sorry, Nic. But that's how I feel. I didn't mean it literally, of course."

"I should hope not," mutters Niccolò.

"Listen, Nic. I'm having lunch with Pat today. And it's not what you think. Well, maybe it is. She is a bit of a gossip."

Niccolò looks her in the eye.

"Or maybe I am. But only with each other. Anyway, I'll be gone for an hour or two. Do you mind?"

"Perhaps I should call Lucy and make arrangements to pick up my things."

"I'll take care of that tomorrow," insists Francine. "How's the French toast?"

"Look, Francine. Lucy is a very dear friend of mine. I can't just—"

"Don't worry, Nic. I'm sure we'll be seeing quite a bit of her. After all, she's practically my sister-in-law already!"

Niccolò sighs heavily. "Well. It's all worked out, then." He surrenders the cell phone to Francine.

"You do love me, don't you Nic?"

A few hours later, Niccolò walks into Schlick as a Whistle, the bar owned and operated by Marlene Schlick. He sits down at the bar. The bartender delivers a drink to another customer, and then approaches Niccolò.

"Hey, guy. What'll ya have?"

"A Zombie, please."

"Thirstin' for a Zombie? How'll ya handle that?"

Niccolò draws a blank.

"Ya don't get it? Thurston Howell the Third. *Gilligan's Island*. Season one, episode three."

Niccolò shakes his head, and shrugs.

"Voodoo Something to Me...."

Niccolò draws a second blank. "This *is* a straight bar, right?"

"Seriously, come on. Ya weren't watchin' TV back in sixty-four?"

Niccolò cracks a feeble smile. "I'm not quite *that* old, um...."

The bartender extends his hand. "Jordan. But everyone around here calls me Schnappy Jo. Ya wanna straw?"

Niccolò nods.

The bartender slaps the bar. "Okay. Comin' up!"

"Is the owner here?" asks Niccolò.

"Schlick? Ya know her? Nah, she's across the street, checkin' in on Daffodil."

"Dafne Cordillera," mumbles Niccolò under his breath.

"Well, now we're gettin' somewhere!" declares Jordan. "D'ya know Jess, too?"

"Yes," confirms Niccolò. "When was the last time *you* saw Jurassic Park?"

"So you're into movies, eh?"

"I nearly OD'd on garlic," admits Niccolò.

"Garlic, huh?" replies Jordan, shooting the breeze.

"Yes, but I wasn't talking about movies…. Can you call Marlene?"

Jordan pokes the Zombie with a straw before placing it on the counter in front of Niccolò. Then, he points to the door. "Here she comes now."

Marlene enters the bar, and she immediately recognizes her visitor.

"Poppy! Is that *you*?"

Jordan leans over the bar. "Poppy, is it?"

"The rest of the world calls me Pope," retorts Niccolò.

"I'll have a Corona," shouts Marlene to her bartender.

Jordan snaps his fingers, as if he just understood a little joke, and then quickly fetches a bottle.

"So…?" inquires Marlene.

"I just happened by," admits Niccolò.

"I didn't see you in church last Sunday."

"You weren't there."

Marlene smiles broadly. "You're right…. So how are you doing, Poppy?"

"Ever been to Corona del Mar?" Jordan glances at Marlene with an air of complicity as he pours the beer into a frosted glass, which he slides across the counter to his boss.

Niccolò's eyes search for a private table. Marlene gets the hint.

"Drop it, Jo." Marlene picks up her beer, and motions for Niccolò to follow her.

Moments later, they are comfortably seated in a back corner of the bar. Jordan decides to clean some glasses, but keeps his eyes focused on Schlick and Poppy.

"You'll have to excuse Schnappy Jo. Every time Daffodil comes in here, Jo asks her if she's ever been to Corona del Mar. She doesn't get it, either. A lot of the streets down there are named after flowers."

"Poppy Street?"

"Avenue…. Anyway, how are you?"

"I'm fine, Marlene. But I'm at a crossroads. And I think I've just made a wrong turn."

"What do you mean?"

"You must understand, Marlene. It's hard for me to confess something like this."

"Because you're the Pope," suggests Marlene.

"Yes. But you don't believe that, do you?"

"A few more drinks, and I will."

"The fact is that I am in love with a woman."

"Lucy?"

"No." Niccolò grins, embarrassingly.

"You said 'crossroads.'"

"Did I?"

"So who is she, this woman of yours?"

"A French lady. She lives here in L.A. But we met many years ago in Rome before I entered the seminary and lost track of her."

"So you found an old flame. I get the picture. What's her name?"

"Francine."

"So what's the problem? She's married?"

"No. But she wants to marry me. I'm sure of it."

"And you've got cold feet?"

"I have a commitment to God."

"Well, Poppy. I don't see the big deal here. You may have once been the Pope. I don't know. But you're not anymore, right? Look, I have a boyfriend. His name is Lars Vinsson. He's a hard-nosed atheist. And I'm a devout Catholic. You see where I'm going? The other day, he popped the question. And we got into this really big argument. I mean, I like the sound of Marlene Vinsson. But we can't resolve our religious differences. I mean, not only does he absolutely refuse to go to church, he even insists on a civil wedding. And I can't accept that. So what am I supposed to do, Poppy? I don't want to break up with him. But I don't want to live in sin, either."

"That's quite a dilemma," admits Niccolò.

"This lady of yours, Francine, is she a Christian?"

"Yes, she is."

"Then what's the problem, for Christ's sake?"

Niccolò finishes his drink.

"Another one?" offers Marlene.

Niccolò shakes his head no.

Marlene turns her head to the side, and shouts, "Another one, Jo!" Then, she turns back to Niccolò, and lowers her voice. "Why don't you buy her a ring, hmm?"

Niccolò sighs heavily.

Marlene peers into Niccolò's evasive green eyes.

"I would have to abandon the papacy."

"It seems to me the papacy has abandoned you."

In another part of town, Francine is having lunch with Patricia Haggis, a woman roughly the same age, but not nearly as refined. In other words, Patricia is a typical American middle-aged woman.

"Speak of the devil," laughs Francine, glancing at her cell phone.

"Are you going to answer it?" asks Patricia.

Francine grabs the phone. "Hello? Lucy?" After a good long minute of listening, she congratulates Lucy. "I'll let him know. But call me tomorrow, okay? No, he's staying with me tonight. I'll explain everything tomorrow…. Say hello to Fabrice for me. Bye!"

Patricia leans forward. "Well?"

"Lucy's back in business. She just found out her van was impounded this morning."

"That was quick. But why would anyone steal a piece of junk like that in the first place?"

"To haul something, I guess. Stolen goods, maybe, who knows? Anyway, they were pulled over in East Hollywood. The police ran a check on the plates, impounded the van, and let the kids go."

Patricia dabs the corner of her mouth with a paper napkin. "Must have been minors…."

"I suppose so," shrugs Francine. "She didn't say. And who cares, anyway? The van isn't important. What matters is that Lucy has a date with Fabrice tonight."

"That was quick," laughs Patricia.

"You can say that again!" agrees Francine.

"I just did," smiles Patricia. "What about Father Priestley?"

Francine finds the question irrelevant. "What about him?"

"Okay. What about Nic? Are you going to call him?"

"He doesn't have a phone."

When Francine returns to the Auberge Ginette, she finds Niccolò curiously absent. It's late afternoon. An hour later, she begins to worry.

Niccolò steps off a city bus. He appears to be somewhat inebriated. As he weaves his way around the shoppers, business people, and tourists that crowd the sidewalks that run along Goode Boulevard, his attention is drawn to a jeweler across the street. He comes to a stop, and begins rubbing his ring finger. After a moment's thought, he shakes his head, as if to dismiss the idea. He turns his eyes away, and resumes walking, but then his eyes fall upon a pedestrian crossing just ahead, and he reconsiders. Without further hesitation, he enters the crosswalk. A flashing yellow light alerts motorists to the presence of pedestrians. It functions perfectly.

However, as Niccolò nears the other side of Goode Boulevard, he stops in his tracks. Bearing down on him is a vehicle that he immediately recognizes. The confession van!

"Praise the Lord!" he cries, slurring his words a bit.

As a sign of acknowledgment, the earth beneath him begins to tremble. At the same time, the sun pierces a cloud above….

Niccolò loses his balance, and drops to his knees.

Lucy is driving her van home. She has to get ready for dinner with Fabrice. Perhaps she is reliving the highlights of their past relationship, and wondering what the renewal of that relationship would mean in the near and far future. Or perhaps her mind is simply walking through her wardrobe in an attempt to settle upon the perfect outfit for that evening. In any event, her mind is so preoccupied that it barely registers the fact that the light in the crosswalk is flashing yellow. An alert mind would not be content to ignore the warning light simply because no one appears to be crossing the street. An alert mind would instinctively instruct the eyes to drop slightly in search of a child or animal. But Lucy's mind is not focused on her driving. She is, in effect, asleep at the wheel.

No doubt, Lucy now feels a sudden vibration in her tires, but she appears to be oblivious to it. Were she clear of mind, and given enough time in which to speculate, she would naturally conclude that this is a temblor, one of many that gently shake the valley, and which merely serve to annoy those who reside there. However, for once there is no time for even an alert mind to speculate, for Lucy finds herself simultaneously confronted with a more serious phenomenon—a blinding shaft of light descending from the heavens. Her mind is instantly jolted awake, but is also paralyzed. She is physically unable to react, and fails to hit the brakes. It's not until she becomes aware of striking something—some kind of invisible mass low in the street that causes the van to rock, shutter, and stall—that she comes to her senses.

Lucy leans forward, touching the windshield with her forehead. She sees nothing. She slips out of the van, rubs her eyes, and stumbles forward. She still sees nothing. But as she circles around the front of the van, she makes a sudden discovery. She has run over a man.

Lucy crouches down. Most of the body is hidden beneath the van. She strains to see whether the man shows any sign of life. He does. And then she recognizes the victim.

"Poppy?" she gasps.

Niccolò is conscious, but spitting blood. His eyes are riveted upon Lucy.

The Pope Goes Up

"What in God's name have I done?" whispers Lucy, horrified.

Hearing the approach of footsteps, Lucy looks around. She jumps to her feet, and runs back to the van. Immediately, she calls 911. However, she is not the first to do so. Witnesses to the accident have already made the call, and within minutes the ambulance arrives. The EMS crew gently puts Niccolò on a stretcher.

When Niccolò invites Lucy to join him with a weak gesture, one of the emergency team members inquires, "Do you know her?"

"She's my dearest friend, Lucy Fer–." Niccolò struggles, but is unable to finish his response. He has lost consciousness. Lucy is allowed to come along for the ride to the hospital. As Niccolò is being loaded into the ambulance, he briefly regains consciousness.

Lucy takes his hands and offers a smile of encouragement, then turns to the paramedic. "Are you taking him to St. John's?"

"Used to be called St. John's. It's Goode Health Services now."

Niccolò's eyeballs roll backwards, and he expires.

Lucy falls upon his chest, and bursts into tears.

But Niccolò's spirit has already fled the ambulance.

Niccolò is met by a pair of androgynous angels who have come to usher him to Heaven. Both angels wear white robes, but one is fringed in black, the other in red. Each one bears a golden torch whose flame serves to light the way.

Heaven's highway consists of an Up lane and a Down lane. The angels, each grasping Niccolò's spirit by the hand, fly Up towards Heaven, while other angels escort the spirits of unborn children Down towards Earth. Somewhere along the way, one of the torches flames out.

"This one's no good. I'll go get another one." The Black angel excuses himself and whisks away.

When Niccolò asks the remaining angel where the other one is going, the Red angel replies, "You don't want to know!"

While they are waiting alongside the road to Heaven, Niccolò and the Red angel begin to chat. The angel explains that the Devil is buying up some of the real estate in Heaven, because he's getting the lion's share of the spirits these days and needs more space.

Niccolò is taken aback. But he decides not to pursue the issue.

"Do you know who I am?"

"You're the Pope," says the angel matter-of-factly.

"Maybe I can turn things around up there," proposes Niccolò.

"Don't bet on it."

Niccolò eventually arrives at Heaven's door, and he is astounded to find a sign hung on it. The sign reads: "Closed Until Further Notice."

The two angels just shrug. "We've been laid off, but we love our job, so…"

Niccolò knocks gently at the wooden door. To his surprise, nobody answers.

"It's not even Sunday," complains Niccolò to the angels. "So I know He's not too busy to open up."

"He knows you're here," affirms the Black angel.

"Try again," urges the Red one.

Niccolò knocks again. After a pause, he resumes, this time a bit harder.

"It's me," shouts Niccolò, "Niccolò di Montachiesa, your best friend. Remember the light? You sent me a sign!"

Still, God does not answer. Niccolò, frustrated, begins knocking harder and harder.

"Come on, God, open up! You can't say no to the *Pope*! Let me in, okay?"

"He's not listening," says the Black angel sympathetically.

"As usual," groans the Red one.

Niccolò becomes furious. He begins to pound on the door with both fists.

"Damn it, God! I know you're in there! Open the goddamn door!!!"

"Tsk! Tsk!" The angels waggle their fingers, and shake their heads disapprovingly.

Niccolò no doubt wonders if perhaps God is punishing him for falling from grace by way of his sexual romps with Francine, for having gotten drunk and slapped her brother, and for wanting to be a movie star.

The Black angel abandons hope. His white feathered wings droop. "I guess the door is closed for good."

"No exceptions," underscores the Red one.

"We thought maybe–" starts the Black angel.

"But he's sworn off imports," interrupts the Red angel. "Not enough business. He's only into exports now." The angel points to the baby spirit factory across the street.

"What about Jesus? Doesn't he have a say in all this?" implores Niccolò.

"Not a word," replies the Black angel.

"Okay. What about Saint Peter?"

The angels laugh.

"So what the hell am I supposed to do?" whines Niccolò.

"Follow us to the recycling center," invites the Red angel.

"Just one question," adds Niccolò, resigned to his fate. He points to the wooden door.

"Whatever happened to the pearly gates?"

"What pearly gates?" snickers the Black angel. "It's always been just a wooden door."

"Go figure," sighs Niccolò.

22 THE POPE IN MEMORIAM

A few years later, Lucy closes her "brick and mortar" shop, The Poppy Seed, which is located on Goode Boulevard, not far from the beach. In the window, images of the Pope are found on a large selection of religious merchandise. She still has the old van, but now it has a photo of the Pope on it, and she doesn't drive it anymore. Instead, a car is waiting for her. It's Fabrice, who now headlines the wildly successful Rockadoo Gooders. Together, they go to church. A church built on the back of a lotto ticket.

Once they arrive at Our Lady of Venice, they enter the atrium, from which three golden spheres are suspended. Here, one can buy a cup of "wake up" at the Café Lotto, whose motto is "We Pour a Lotto Love." One can also browse the religious merchandise at Lucy's own "outreach" shop, Ticket to Heaven. There is a special display for a book entitled, "The Death of Catholicism: Memoirs of Pope Ignatius I" by Niccolò di Montachiesa. Additionally, there is a table run by volunteers (usually, Jessica, Daphne, and Marlene) where churchgoers can contribute to San Niccolò Mission. After a brief exchange of words with other church devotees, and a bit of "shop talk," Lucy and Fabrice slip through the vestibule, where one can check such items as jackets, hats, umbrellas, and handbags, and walk hand in hand down the center aisle to a pew just shy of the crossing. The church pews are made of solid ash, and are equipped with broad, padded flip-down kneelers as well as a slot for the Bible, prayer book, hymnal, and program. Lucy and Fabrice sit down a few steps in, and scoot to the middle, next to Patricia Haggis.

Our Lady of Venice is, in fact, a small cathedral. The nave is bathed in a soft glow of light due to the stained glass windows that depict the Life of Jesus on the one side, and the Stations of the Cross on the other. The transept has short arms. Each is a chapel. One is dedicated to Saint Bernadette, and the other to Saint Nicholas. Tables with votive candles can be found here below the portraits of the saints. There are also inscriptions on the walls. Beyond the pulpit are the choir, the presbytery, and the altar. The church, which boasts an impressive pipe organ, as well as a large retractable media screen, can accommodate up to 700 "charlottos." It was the Hispanics, who make up the majority of the church membership, who coined the term "charlotto" to indicate the width of a heavy person, which then was generalized to mean the overweight worshippers themselves.

Today, the congregation consists of about 280 members and guests, a good many of whom are indeed charlottos. One of them is Charlotte Potts, accompanied by her faithful dog, Ramon. At the pulpit, leaning over an open Bible, is a woman with graying hair. After a minute or two, she looks up and smiles. She acknowledges familiar faces with a gentle nod. Her eyes first encounter Lucy and Fabrice. To him, she blows a kiss. Then she spots "Merle" (Sean Davoitzler, who incorporates magic into his Sunday morning workshop for kids), Ulrich Cholubski (the former Scientologist whose superiors gave him the boot after he tried to pass off cheap counterfeit slippers as the Pope's), Andy DeLuca (the former ACLU investigator who wears a t-shirt with the "God Bless America" slogan printed on it), Roger Shields (the gay man from the sushi bar), and Carly Sayles, the alien abductee, who has finally been returned to Earth, and whose bestseller, which describes her extraterrestrial adventures, has made her a popular guest on talk radio. The woman at the pulpit winks at Brad and Edgar, who have saved a spot between them for either Brad's mother or the spirit of Niccolò di Montachiesa–depending upon whom you ask. And, finally, she salutes Burt Huffman, the church prophet, who is seated next to Joel Marzoff, the former businessman whose life Niccolò saved, and who is currently in charge of organizing summer revival youth camps. Today, his ex-wife has joined him.

"Good morning," says the lady. "We welcome thirty-four new guests today. I hope you will decide to become members of Our Lady of Venice Catholic Church. My name is Francine Friboulet, and I am the appointed leader of the church. Father Priestley is on assignment, but has a special video message for us. He will be on screen very shortly. First, let us rise and sing unto the Lord." Francine cues the choir director, Carlos Piñeda. His wife Rosita and their seven children, along with a dozen others, begin to sing. Thanks mostly to the new inductees, the choir doesn't sound half bad.

In the early evening following Niccolò's death, a pedestrian fatality was reported on local newscasts and entertainment web sites. He was identified only as "Poppy," a religious hustler from Venice. By midnight, the reports were archived.... However, once the body was identified as belonging to Pope Ignatius I, the world's "breaking news" networks rushed to Venice to cover every possible tidbit of information they could dig up on the Pope. Anyone who ever had any connection with "Poppy" was subjected to at least one brief interview. Lucy Ferguson, Sean Davoitzler, Joel Marzoff, and Sam X. Rayburn were invited on talk shows. Fabrice Friboulet refused to discuss the incident at L.A. Bonne Table, and film director Leonard Brock denied he ever met the Pope.

Billy Phillips kept his mouth shut about his encounter with the mountain lion, first of all because he didn't want to betray the existence of a church depository in the Sierra Nevada, and secondly because his friend, Barry Swift, who actually killed the lion, did not carry a gun permit. In any event, it was unclear whether the Pope's prayer had anything to do with the mountain lion's failure to attack, or with Barry's perfect aim.

Niccolò was particularly enthusiastic that a new Catholic church was to be built in Venice, though he often lamented the fact that a winning lotto ticket funded it rather than church tithes. Nevertheless, he supported the church's decision to fast-track the project. Architectural firms were already submitting design proposals at the time of Niccolò's death.

Father Priestley and his followers were devastated by the news, and tremendously disappointed in themselves for not believing Poppy's claim that he was, in fact, the Pope. They had their hands full consoling Lucy, who was given to drink. Everyone agreed that she would have ended up in the gutter (or worse) had Fabrice not stepped in to offer emotional support. Lucy also met with Francine, who insisted upon a meeting with Father Priestley. It was at this meeting that Francine repeated Niccolò's wish that she become the spiritual leader of the new church. His reasoning was that she was best suited to advance the New Catholicism. Niccolò also made clear that Father Priestley should continue in his capacity as priest for now, but that in the long term he should assume the role and title of bishop. After all, the church owed its very existence to Father Priestley.

Father Priestley did not challenge Francine's word. Instead, he honored the Pope's wishes. Soon afterward, he was contacted by a local media executive who proposed that his sermons be made available to cable, satellite, and internet subscribers. His theatrical approach to sermons, which relied heavily upon ventriloquism, received universal accolades. His videos went viral overnight. And soon show business was frantically knocking at his door. Clearly, God was preparing a new mission for him to fulfill, a glorious mission that would allow him the opportunity to work on a far grander scale. He was destined for "mass entertainment," the purpose of which was to repopularize God and the Bible among religious dissidents, and to promote the message of "inclusion" that characterized the New Catholicism in hopes of attracting religious neophytes. To Father Priestley's credit, he did not abandon his small church. He did not renege on his promise to Francine. He did not dishonor the Pope's wishes. He merely went "on assignment." Whenever his contract schedule permits it, Father Priestley returns to his roots. He delivers a powerful sermon that even God and the Devil cannot ignore. And the church rejoices.

"Thank you, Carlos." Francine turns to the congregation. "Please be seated."

"As many of you know, today is the anniversary of the death of Pope Ignatius I. To the world, he was Your Holiness. But to the members of our small church, he was "Poppy," a devoted friend and ardent supporter of what seemed like an unrealistic goal at the time. To raise the Catholic Church from the ashes of defeat, and pursue a new vision of Catholicism that would invigorate it and put it back on the world stage. Sadly, Poppy did not live to help inaugurate Our Lady of Venice. But I'm sure he watches over it. And he watches over those who join us here to celebrate the Glory of God."

Francine cues the organist. He plays "A Mighty Fortress Is Our God" while the congregation bows its head in individual prayer.

"Thank you, Terry." Francine's eyes fall for a moment on Litzy Muñoz-Cruz. She is in tears, and holds her daughter Veronica tightly to her side.

"I have not prepared a sermon. We are here today to honor the memory of Niccolò di Montachiesa. To do so, we call on an old friend of the Pope's who has come all the way from Paris, France to be with us today. This is all the more impressive when you consider the fact that he had to overcome a mortal fear of flying in order to make the trip…. Please give a warm welcome to Olivier Casali."

Olivier rises from a seat near the pulpit, and the congregation applauds. He relieves Francine, unfolds a speech, and begins to read.

"First, I wish to express my gratitude to Francine Friboulet for allowing me this great privilege…."

After relating a number of anecdotes, none of which tarnish the saintly image of Niccolò that he wishes to preserve, the congregation once again offers a round of applause.

"Thank you, Olivier," says Francine. "We sincerely appreciate what you have shared with us today. We knew Poppy as a humble man who once reigned over the Vatican. You knew him as the man who would be Pope. But now, let me remind you that we have a special video message from Father Priestley."

On cue, the giant media screen descends. "Father Priestley would like to commemorate this special occasion with a very special invitation."

The congregation is first served a montage of a Las Vegas show called "Word of Mouth," a religious extravaganza which stars Sherman Priestley. The montage shows various segments of the show, including those that involve ventriloquism. God and the Devil not only speak, but drive home their message through the use of synchronized stage props, pyrotechnics, lasers, and an arsenal of awe-inspiring special effects. The show also features aerial acrobats who fly like angels, and a dance number, called "In Search of Adam," which features a scantily clad performer named "Eve" as well as a number of male and female dance partners.

Following the montage, Father Priestley appears on screen. Standing beside him is Eva Hathaway.

"Hello. My name is Father Priestley. Around here, they just call me Sherman."

Eva restrains a giggle, and simply nods.

"I hope you enjoyed the teaser you've just seen. The audience sees the whole show, and they just love it. Thanks to "word of mouth," as well as great reviews, our showroom is packed to the roof every single night. Eva and I are spreading God's message to all who attend, and they, in turn, pass it along to those who cannot make the pilgrimage to Las Vegas."

"It isn't really that far!" chimes in Eva.

"That's right. But there are travel expenses, accommodations, and the cost of show tickets. It all adds up, Eva. And not everyone in our congregation can afford to experience "Word of Mouth" firsthand. That's why my producer has agreed to make next Saturday's performance–which includes a special tribute to Poppy–part of "Lady's Night Out." That's Lady, as in Our Lady of Venice! You heard me right! We will provide the buses, the accommodations, the meals, and special front row seating for everyone who is watching right now! So pack your bags! You're off to Vegas!"

Eva clinches her fist. "Yes!"

The congregation gives Father Priestley and Eva a standing ovation.

Some church members are so wildly enthusiastic that they begin chanting, "Vegas! Vegas! Vegas!" Others join in, and it all gets a bit out of hand....

23 THE POPE RETURNS

Twenty years later, at the Pitchfork Palace, a young lady–with dark hair, green eyes, and sporting a tattoo on her left breast that features a poppy flower entwined around a cross–is doing a pretty lousy job of pole dancing. Some of the patrons laugh at her total lack of coordination and grace.

The performance venue is surrounded by food vendors, souvenir shops, and intimate apparel boutiques.

One of the food vendors, Vatikan Cakes, specializes in "sinful desserts." Cocktail servers thread their way through the food court tables that are well situated for viewing the stages on which the girls dance. One of the cocktail servers approaches a man eating his slice of cake. He has finished his cocktail, and is watching the dancers. He is particularly intrigued by the green-eyed dancer, who is hopelessly awkward.

"Would you like another drink?" asks the cocktail server.

"Yes, please."

The topless dancer slips while attempting to perform a sensuous maneuver on the pole. She seems oblivious to her mistake.

"That dancer is a complete idiot. Who is she?"

"Hell, if I know!" replies the cocktail serve. "Ask the entertainment director. She's right over there."

The entertainment director, an attractive red-haired lady in her forties, is visiting with various patrons, shaking hands, exchanging pleasantries, smiling.

The man forks up his last bite of cake, stands up, and approaches the director.

"Excuse me, but—"

"Yes?"

"Who's that dope on the pole?"

The director laughs. "That's a good one!"

Made in the USA
Lexington, KY
30 March 2014